Art Dodger Case File #1

· ·○○●●●○○· · ·

The Mystery of the Missing Majorette

ART DODGER CASE FILE #1

• ○ ○●●●●●○○ • ○

The Mystery of the Missing Majorette

by
L.G. Hewitt

ArbeitenZeit Media

ISBN 13 Kindle Edition: 978-1-941168-15-8
ISBN 13 Trade Paperback Edition: 978-1-941168-16-5

An Original Work
Art Dodger Case File #1: The Mystery of the Missing Majorette is an original work by Linda Hewitt (14 09 28)

The echo of a sad song
lngers longest
in the heart.

Contents

·.·••••••···

One.

···•••❦❦••···

The Girl Who Disappeared

She was a beautiful girl. No, better than beautiful, Dodger thought. It wasn't just her regular features and long, curly dark hair but that she glowed. In any setting, in any group, even though she was just fifteen, she'd be the one you noticed first, and it'd be hard to force your eyes away.

He put down the head-and-shoulders shot stamped in one corner with the embossed logo of a regional portrait studio, and picked up an 8x10" black-and-white glossy that still bore the markings of a press photo. She was the one you saw there too even though the photograph showed a dozen girls posed in line, each wearing an identical majorette uniform of military style. A dozen pairs of maidenly bosoms were harnessed in white, long-sleeved jackets with gold braid all across the fronts. A dozen pairs of girlish knees peeked out from under white mid-thigh skirts. A dozen high, white, busby-style hats loomed over faces with smiles of more or less the same degree of determined cheerfulness. The toes of a dozen pairs of white, cowboy-style boots pointed in the same direction. Even so, your eyes went at once to Danielle Standridge, third from left, whose blazing personality could not be disguised by the heavy fabric, clunky footwear and dated pose.

Dodger turned over the 8x10 and saw the label of a well known PR firm and a word-processed tag that read:

*September 20, 1993. Whitman-Brown majorette squad in costume for **Before A Hero**. The movie, set in the early 1940s, brings to life the story of a high-school boy in a North Carolina mill town who volunteers for the Marines and is sent to the South Pacific, where he dies in action. The girls are wearing*

majorette uniforms typical of the era of the film. The film is
based on the award-winning novel of the same name.

The next glossy was another 8x10" press photo of a line of majorettes performing a hop-and-kick routine, wearing the same old-fashioned costumes as the girls in the other photograph. He glanced from one to the other and realized that the girls were the same as well. In the second photograph, however, they were in a mall parking lot with cars, people, and storefronts visible behind them.

Dodger held up the photo so that the deputy sheriff could see it. "Is this the mall where she disappeared?"

Sutton glanced at it and nodded. "The mall and the day. The majorette squad was demonstrating its routine from the movie. It was kind of a going-away thank you party from the movie company to the town."

"Could we go there, to the mall, now?" Dodger replaced the photo in the file and put it, together with the other materials he'd been examining, into the large, paint-speckled case beside his chair. "I'd like to see the place before I go any further."

Sutton looked at his watch. "We've got time if all we do is take a quick look. Mr. Whitman expects you in half an hour, but the mall is on the way. I'll text him that we're leaving."

Dodger stood and stretched, extending his frame to its full 6'3". His eyes felt overused, dry and desiccated, and he knew if he bothered to look that the dark-blue irises would be surrounded by streaks of red. The drive from Savannah to this old North Carolina textile town had taken longer than he'd expected, and he was tired. He was also grungy. Running fingers through short, sandy hair, he could swear he felt grit. He'd been in such a hurry to get on the road that he jumped out of bed at four, did a Keurig hit, tossed on jeans and sweater over a tee and headed out. He'd give a lot for the shower he'd skipped then.

He'd give something, too, for another chance at his closet. In the bright light of the police station, the jeans turned out to be flecked with paint from his studio session the day before, and the sweater suddenly seemed too small, stretched over his broad upper torso like a bandage. It was as if he'd rummaged through a thrift store and come up with clothes that almost fit, but not quite. Next to the slim, sharply uniformed deputy, he looked like a bum, and he felt like the Hulk, thick and with muscles of the wrong sort. Jess said she liked his heft, that it was manly, but Jess was a writer — words were her business and she always knew the right thing to say. Maybe he ought to go back to hitting the gym with the trainer.

Dodger found himself having this kind of interior dialogue on a regular basis these days, ever since he'd turned forty, in fact, several years before. This one caused him to miss the beginning of whatever it was that Sutton was saying.

"Sorry, I didn't catch that." He turned toward the deputy and grinned. "Wool gathering, as my grandmother used to say."

"I just asked if it's okay if I ride with you," Sutton answered. "Police car's in the shop for repairs, and my wife's taking the kids to Charlotte, to the dentist, in her car today. I can grab a ride back from one of Mr. Whitman's people."

"Sure," Dodger said, although it struck him as odd that a policeman wouldn't have a backup vehicle. "You can give me the guided tour."

Sutton grimaced, as if suspicious that the casual remark were intended sarcastically, but then relaxed when Dodger said nothing further.

Dodger's van was a customized Ram ProMaster he drove on road trips, whether the purpose was art, his profession, or — like now — exploring old tragedies for the Mystery Mavens, the cold-case club that, at the suggestion of the therapist who'd treated him after grad school, he'd joined years before.

Just as Dodger opened the driver-side door and tossed in the case, his cell buzzed. He pulled it from his pocket and looked at the screen. The image of a handsome, rather stern-faced woman with fine eyes and long, dark hair looked back. Damn, it was Jess Hannah. His heart began to beat more rapidly, and the palms of his hands began to sweat. The woman always had that effect on him. He closed his eyes and took a deep breath, as if he could smell the faint clove of her perfume, picturing the way in which she sat while she talked on her cell, with her long legs twisted together so that just a little too much skin showed for comfort.

"Ms. Hannah," he said, trying to sound more businesslike than he felt. "Good to hear from you, as usual."

"Dodger," she responded crisply. "Are you already in Whitman?"

"Yup. I drove up this morning. Got an early start."

"I've emailed the information you wanted. Would you like an overview now, or would you rather we touch base later?"

Dodger glanced over at Sutton, who was looking at his watch. It seemed that Travis Whitman expected punctuality. Anyway he wasn't sure he wanted to take this call with a witness who, in effect, worked for Whitman. "Tell you what, Jess, can I get back to you this afternoon? I'm in the middle of something here."

"Certainly," she said with the cool formality that had drawn him to her from their first meeting. "I've got a lunch interview thing — they're putting me on the spot about the new Maxcliff, but I should be able to talk, say, by four."

"Maxcliff, huh?" Dodger teased as he turned the key and pulled away from the curb. Jess's day job was writing novels of a lurid nature about a man who always caught the bad guys even as he played a mean jazz piano, made the knees of strong women weak in boudoir and boardroom, and spoke five languages fluently. She hated the character, but he was too successful to kill off.

"Yes, Maxcliff," she snapped, already in a bad mood. Dodger did not envy the hapless journalist who'd been sent to interview her.

"Four it is," he said. "I'll call you."

He disconnected and turned to Sutton. "Sorry about that."

The deputy shrugged. "Whatever. Up here's where you want to turn. At the V, take the left fork. The right's a little quicker for Mr. Whitman's place, but the left will take us by way of the mall."

Dodger did as instructed and found himself piloting the van along a wide, short street lined with a dozen or so fast-food restaurants, freestanding stores, and service stations, many of which were closed. He slowed down to take a better look. Things must be pretty bad in this place for it not to be able to support a Del Taco.

"I've got a question," Dodger said.

"Fire away," Sutton told him. "I'm here for you. Mr. Whitman's orders. Guide service on call, information on demand."

"Why wasn't there more publicity about Danielle's disappearance? Given the girl's age and the way she looked, I'd expect the newspapers to be all over this."

There was a long pause. Sutton shrugged again. "I'd guess it was because of the distraction caused by the movie people being in town. It was the biggest thing to happen around here in, well, ever. Other than that, I don't know. Remember, twenty years ago I was still in high school. The next year I went off and pretty much didn't come back until eight years ago."

There was silence in the van as Dodger digested that.

Commercial activity had given way to a brief stretch of scraggly countryside, followed by a street of large brick ranch houses. Then, there was a sign for the Whitman Mall that looked as if it hadn't lit up in a long time.

"This is it," the deputy said. "Take a right."

The van hit a pothole, and Dodger bit his tongue.

"Damn," he blurted, sucking on the offended tissue.

The lot was empty save for a cluster of cars around a standalone building to one side whose sign proclaimed with glowing intensity its status as a dollar store. Following Sutton's direction, Dodger went the other way, across rows of faded white striping, the ProMaster bumping over weed-choked asphalt.

"This is it. Stop here."

Dodger did as instructed.

"It was right there," Sutton said, pointing to a spot some distance away. "That's where Danny was the last time she was seen, by anybody around here, anyway. This is where the neighbor lady was stopped."

"The last one to see her?"

Sutton nodded. "This place was busy then. Until Whitman-Brown started cutting back, you could hardly get in here to park."

Dodger tapped his fingertips on the padded steering wheel, the glimmer of an idea beginning to form.

"Well," the deputy said, looking at his watch. "That's all we got time for today. Mr. Whitman's waiting."

Two.

..°°○○⬤⬤⬤○○°°..

Caught in the Past

The trip to the Whitman estate followed rural back roads so obscure that Dodger was glad of Sutton's guidance.

"Turn here." The deputy pointed to a well-kept driveway that ran past a tiny guard's hut and between twin stone piers.

The iron gates that the guard opened at Sutton's wave were more ornate and sophisticated in design than Dodger would have expected in a burg this small and out of the way. An expert hand with a significant budget had been at work here, he realized. The drive, raked decorative pea gravel edged with well-trimmed hedges, curved through a landscape of specimen trees and an overgrown area that had almost certainly once been lawns. Now, it was being allowed to naturalize; and thick undergrowth crowded tree trunks, the colors of its autumnal foliage making a positive virtue of what may have been an economy measure. Up ahead, the glint of brick and stucco peeped through yellowing trees, and the road turned.

'Mr. Whitman's got himself quite a place here," Sutton remarked. "Old Lady Whitman, his mother, was a big-time gardener, and his late wife kept it up."

"Late wife?"

"She died some years ago."

"Too bad," Dodger said.

He slowed the van to get a better look at the three-story house sprawling across the slight rise in a confusing assemblage of half-timbering, steep slate roofs, craftily crooked chimneys, leaded glass and studded doors. Taken aback, he caught his breath. Its shape and detailing were different — this place lacked the picturesque symmetry of the house in which he'd grown up — but in type it was enough like

6

his family's old home to make his heart skip a beat. His eyes went involuntarily to windows on the second-floor that corresponded to the location of his old room, the one in which he'd somehow slept through the whole thing. There was something different about them, but he'd bet he could guess at the room's oak floors and the dark moldings outlining its ceiling, doors and windows. Around the corner on the same floor, past a bathroom and the upstairs study, would be the equivalent of his parents' suite and, past that, down a long corridor, Abby's bedroom and bath. The image of those rooms as he'd last seen them, when he'd been dragged through by the police, he resisted allowing into his mind. There was, as the therapist had so often reminded him, no point in going there.

Dodger braked as a wave of nausea swept over him, and tried to talk himself back to normal. The last time he'd slept in the Connecticut house that was so much like this one he'd been a senior in college, home for Thanksgiving break. That was twenty-six years ago, an era long gone, as was the house itself. It was time, past time, as the therapist had said before dismissing him, to stop using it as a benchmark for everything else.

For a few seconds, he'd forgotten he wasn't alone and was startled when Sutton asked if he were all right.

"I'm fine," he barked, then forced himself to take a deep breath. "Sorry, I was just startled by the house. It reminds me of a place I once knew."

"It's quite a spread," the deputy said, turning away from Dodger to look at it again. "Wonder what it would be like to live there?"

"Very pleasant, I imagine." Dodger forced a smile and removed his foot from the brake, swallowing bile even as he berated himself. Stupid, stupid, stupid. He'd been sure that he wouldn't let it get through to him again, yet here he was, sweating, heart pounding.

It was because he'd been blindsided by the look of the place. That was all, reason insisted. It was just a mechanical reaction. In fact, examining Whitman's house a second time, he realized the appearance wasn't as close as he'd at first thought. This place was much larger and grander, a textbook example of wealthy people creating what they saw as a bit of Tudor England in a Southern backwater, a place with enough acreage to justify the "estate" description and square footage adequate to house the many servants required to run it in the way that people of their sort would have expected at the time it was built.

Taking a deep breath, Dodger pressed harder on the gas pedal, and the ProMaster picked up speed. As he approached the loop that would take him to the entrance, the massive door opened and Travis Whitman — tall, rail-thin, dressed in a cardigan over shirt and slacks — walked onto the paved terrace and waited while he brought the van to a stop.

"Dodger, good to see you." His eyes swept his guest's clothing choices, and Dodger thought he detected the hint of a grin in the pale blue eyes. "Jase texted from the mall, so lunch is laid. Can you join us, Jase? I'm pretty sure Mrs. Tanner has that cheese thing you like."

"If it's all the same, Mr. Whitman, I think I'd better be getting back to the station."

"Joe's on standby to drive you. You know where to find him." Whitman nodded toward a porte-cochere to one side.

Jase took off in relief, as Dodger and Whitman turned to exchange the obligatory handshake.

Whitman gestured to a waiting servant who came forward to pick up the portfolio and small bag that Dodger had removed from the van. "Just give Ryan your keys. He'll park for you."

Dodger complied but then couldn't resist sneaking another look at the house's façade, along which was massed a continuous bed of bronze chrysanthemums. He realized that Whitman saw the house was of more than casual interest to him, and knew he had to say something or risk questions he had no intention of answering.

"Handsome place you've got here."

"Prepare to be surprised," Whitman warned him. "It's only like this on the outside. Inside is a different story."

He led Dodger into a passage whose paneled walls had been painted white, through a reception hall of equal whiteness, mirrored accents, and thick-piled gray carpeting, and on to the sitting room which was decorated in an elegantly sparse style featuring steel furniture with pale-gray leather upholstery, limed oak floors, and light fixtures of chrome. Even the carved fireplace surround was painted white, and Dodger suspected that the fire blazing on its massive hearth was gas. A wood fire required tending, and there was no way that the immaculate chrome fire tools beside the grate survived regular handling. Above the fireplace hung a large painting of a striking, blue-eyed, fair-haired woman reclining on an angular chaise lounge with a book in hand. Dodger took a second look. Its drenched pigments, thick impasto, and bold brushwork were reminiscent of Lucian Freud.

"When I first remember this place as a child, it was all oak paneling and leaded windows, but both my mother and my wife detested dark interiors," Whitman continued, looking around the room. "Between them, at different times, they re-did the place. The result is a house with a split personality. I'm sure it's given more than a few guests nightmares."

"It's spectacular," Dodger said. Aesthetically, he was offended, for he knew how attractive the original decor would have been. Emotionally, on the other hand, he couldn't be happier. This house in its current state was so unlike his childhood home that he could return to the present without further distraction caused by the memory of the gracious, long-gone household run by his mother.

Whitman's cell buzzed, and Dodger walked over to a bank of multi-paned windows and looked out at the autumn-tinged landscape through which he'd driven to get here. It was beautiful, and he saw that the idea he'd formed of disappearing lawns was inaccurate. The strip adjacent to the drive was returning to forest, but the lawns around the house were extensive and maintained in a way that proved, if one had doubts, that any landscaping decisions here reflected personal preference and not lack of funds to keep things as they'd once been. Whitman-Brown Mills might have left Whitman, the town, for more-profitable venues, but the Whitman who owned Mill House had clearly retained his personal financial viability, here, there, or everywhere.

He heard a noise and turned to see his host replacing the minute cell in his cardigan pocket.

Whitman wasted no time getting to what was on his mind. "Now that you've seen the place where it's assumed Danielle Standridge disappeared, what's your initial impression?" He sat on the steel-and-leather armchair next to the fire and stretched out his long legs, as if prepared for a lengthy discussion.

"It's early days," Dodger warned him, taking the armchair on the

9

opposite side of the hearth. "And you've got to remember that I'm not a policeman. Any impression I have is just that, an impression."

"Understood." He shifted gears. "So what do you think of the mall?"

"It's sad. Looks like somebody took a real bath on it."

"That would be me," Whitman laughed. "I became the landlord when my father died fifteen years ago."

Dodger wasn't surprised. The Whitmans seemed to own everything else around here, so why not the mall?

Lunch, laid on a table in one of the big bays, was simple but well prepared, and the fall vista beyond the windows — which from this angle included a small classical temple in the middle of a green, leaf-dappled lawn — gave the occasion the air of a picnic. Conversation was at first confined to the season and the psychological difficulty of winterizing gardens that remained beautiful even as the season approached.

"The grounds are looking good. Do you keep your own crew?"

"Just the one full time, with a landscaping service that comes in as needed. How do you handle grounds maintenance?"

"My grounds consist of a side yard measuring twenty by forty feet, so a garden service twice a month does the trick," Dodger laughed.

"That's right," Whitman remembered. "You live in an old house on one of the downtown squares in Savannah. That must be pleasant."

"It suits me," Dodger said without elaborating. "Nothing like this, of course. This is an exceptionally handsome house and setting."

"My maternal grandparents — Holman and Ellen Brown — built it in the early 1920s. The last architect who worked on the renovation told me it's typical of Tudor-style houses constructed in the U.S. during that decade."

Dodger didn't mention that he was all too familiar with the style.

"I've got other places," Whitman confided, as if somewhat leery of mentioning the fact, "but this is my favorite. Probably because I grew up here."

Whitman noticed that Dodger's eyes had returned to the large painting over the mantel. He shook his head, smiling slightly.

"It's a Lucien Freud," he said, answering the unasked question, "but you'd know that, being an artist yourself. My mother, who shared my late wife's taste for the avant-garde, at least what I consider the avant-garde, commissioned it for her as an engagement gift and flew her to London for the sittings. Charlotte adored it. Sometimes I'd catch her standing in front of it, staring, the most beatific look on her face."

He laughed indulgently, but there was an undercurrent of emotion that made Dodger wonder if he hadn't resented a taste so alien to his own.

"I could never understand why she admired it so much. I think it's hideous. When she died, in fact, I intended to store the portrait," Whitman admitted. "But, given how much she liked it, removal didn't seem fitting somehow and so I left it. Still, I can't say I like it any better."

After lunch, the two men went onto the terrace where Whitman held out a slim gold cigarette case.

"Never got the habit," Dodger said.

"Lucky you. Mother and Charlotte disapproved of smoking," he laughed as he flicked the lighter. "Somehow I can't believe they aren't still watching somewhere, thinking what a weak character I am."

A breeze came up, and Dodger took a deep breath, inhaling the fragrance of woods and clean air.

"So what happens now?" Whitman demanded, stubbing out the unsmoked half of the cigarette in a glass ashtray on an iron table next to the low wall. He led the way inside.

"What next?" he repeated once they were settled.

It was a question Dodger had been asked before, and he didn't need to think before answering.

"I poke around, ask a few questions, get an impression of how likely it is that Mystery Mavens will be able to achieve anything through its involvement, and then I go back and report to the full board."

"So you're like an advance guard."

"More like a scout. What I do is determine if there's a way forward. The board makes the final decision so to whether to respect my call, yea or nay. If it's to continue, we send in the experts. If it's to stop, the case goes into our deep files should you or someone else come to us again with new information."

"How many of these have you dealt with?"

"Me personally, in this role, in the years I've been a member? This is the fifth. You understand that we don't do this a lot, just when some-one learns of us and makes a presentation that puts forth a compelling reason for a fresh look at a crime that the authorities have given up on. Most of the time, we re-hash our own cases, looking for new angles."

"It surprised me a little," Whitman admitted, "when I learned that you don't do much on-the-scene investigation. You seem more like a support group than a cold-case organization."

"We aren't an organization at all," Dodger smiled. "Just a bunch of men and women who've all had our lives turned upside down by crimes that have never been resolved. You're not too far off when you called us a support group. Most of us have lost people in the kinds of nightmare situations you never quite wake up from, and we help one another process the personal issues we all share."

Even as he regretted his melodramatic tone, he was caught by a yawn so enormous that his host grinned.

"You know, it occurs to me that you might like to check out your room. There's nothing on until dinner at 7:30, so if you've got any calls or messages to check…"

"That would be convenient," Dodger agreed.

Whitman touched a button next to the mantel.

Gladys Tanner appeared in the door within a couple of minutes.

"Gladys, tell Billy that Mr. Dodger is ready to go to his room."

Dodger half-expected to be taken to a central hall where they'd climb a large stair to the second floor, but Billy, a short, muscular black man who had to be at least seventy in spite of his youthful name, instead led him in the other direction to a small elevator.

Upstairs, the hall went in a direction different from what Dodger had assumed would be the case, and he realized he didn't have to worry about any part of this place reactivating memories best left dormant. Thanks to the modern tastes of his host's late mother and wife, this house no longer bore any internal resemblance to the long-vanished scene of the best and worst times of his life.

Three.

·₀₀●●◐◑●◑₀₀·

Memento Mori

Billy showed Dodger his accommodations, which went beyond luxurious and were kitted out with toiletries and other amenities in the manner of a top-flight hotel.

"Should be just about anything you need, but if there's something else, here's my cell number." The servant handed Dodger a card with his name and contact information engraved on it.

"I'm sure I'll be fine," Dodger assured him.

"Would you like me to unpack for you?"

"I can manage, but thanks for the offer."

Billy lingered. At first Dodger thought he was hinting for a tip, but surely not, he concluded. In a household like this with many visitors, Billy would know that a gratuity came at the end of the visit not piecemeal throughout. This wasn't, after all, a hotel, but a well-run private home, and Billy had must have been here for years.

Then Billy cleared his throat, and Dodger realized that what he wanted wasn't money, but the chance to say something.

"Yes, Billy?" he prompted.

"Is it true you're here about Danny, that pretty girl who disappeared the year the movie people came here, the year we won the county football championship?"

"I don't know about a football championship, but it's true I'm interested in the disappearance of a girl named Danielle Standridge."

"She was a fine girl, Danny," Billy said, his voice dropping. "She came here a lot. Gladys is her aunt, you know? Not that she came here to see her, no love lost there, I can tell you. It was Miz Charlotte she came to see. Miz Charlotte thought a lot of her. You know?"

Dodger nodded, and Billy looked over his shoulder, as if suspecting an eavesdropper.

"There's something you need to see," he whispered, half covering his mouth with a gnarled hand.

Dodger followed as he led the way out the door and to the far end of the hall, where he went around the corner and stopped at a Lucite-and-chrome bookcase. He upended the blown glass amphora that centered the top shelf, and used the key that fell into his hand to unlock the adjacent door.

After looking over his shoulder again, he led Dodger into a dim room set up as a small museum, with glass cases and shelving. All Dodger saw when Billy flicked on a light switch, however, was the series of mannequins on a platform between cases.

"Damn," he said, lips pursing in a respectful whistle.

Billy nodded as Dodger stopped first in front of one figure and then another, marveling at the care with which each was dressed. There was a schoolgirl outfit of skirt and sweater, and a casual getup with jeans and a souvenir sweatshirt from a Bon Jovi concert. The remaining figures wore what looked like a prom dress complete with pearl necklace and a majorette costume like the ones from the movie. Each of the four ensembles fit its mannequin as if made for it and was accessorized down to the shoes: Cole-Haan flats on the schoolgirl; athletic shoes with the jeans; glittery heels on the prom-goer; and white cowboy boots on the majorette. What made Dodger unable to look away, however, wasn't what the mannequins wore but their appearance. Each figure was of such high quality that he had the illusion it could, if it chose, at any time begin to breathe; and each was a full-size clone of the missing Danielle Standridge.

Four.

••••••••••

Jess

There were to be guests for dinner. Dodger learned this from Billy as he was being hurried along a different route back to his room.

"Not many," Billy confided. "Just the librarian lady who has her cap set for Mr. Travis and that brother of hers, the one who coaches at the new high school. I heard Gladys tell the girl who's serving. And the gents will be wearing jackets. House rule."

"Thanks for the heads up," Dodger told him.

Billy hesitated at the door. "It'd be good," he said, lowering his voice, "if you don't mention what I showed you just now. Everybody around here likes to pretend that room isn't there."

"Understood," Dodger said. "It's our secret."

Billy gave a thumbs up and left, after which Dodger locked the door. In the bathroom of gleaming black-and-white tile, he stripped, adjusted the shower controls, and stood under a hot jet of water until his skin turned red. Then he shampooed his hair and scraped at his fingernails with a brush, after which he turned the water to cold and forced himself to stand under it for a full minute before jumping out onto the heavy bath mat. As he shaved, he thought about what he'd just seen.

Now, that was unexpected, not to mention creepy. Just how creepy he couldn't determine until he had more time in the room, which posed an interesting challenge. What was the etiquette involved in using a hidden key to access a room that, according to Billy, his host and everyone else in the household wanted to keep concealed? It was an issue that hadn't come up because he'd never before stayed in a private home while scoping out one of these cases. Of course, none of the others had involved anyone of great wealth.

He understood how wealthy when he called Jess Hannah at the designated four p.m.

"All right," Dodger told her, stretching out on the silvery four-poster bed. "I'm listening. Did you find anything interesting?"

"He's rich, maybe even richer than you thought. He's still the major shareholder in Whitman-Brown Textiles and sits on a couple of other boards — a big pharma and a rug manufacturer."

"When did he shut down the American operation?" Dodger asked, thinking of the dead town through which he'd driven. Surely that hadn't happened overnight?

"According to my source at Goldman Sachs, it was his father who began it. Whitman Sr. began to move different lines overseas in the late seventies and accelerated the process in the next decade. By the time Whitman Jr. took over in the late 80s, the move was far enough advanced to be irreversible, although nobody seems to have realized it but the Whitmans because they invented some kind of frictionless fabric that everybody wanted and had a growth surge in the late eighties. That let them keep the local operations pretty much as they'd been for years. By the time Whitman Jr. inherited in 2004, when his mother died, the foreign operations were so much more profitable that it would have been difficult to justify the U.S. operations when there wasn't enough business for both."

"The story of American textiles in the last twenty years," Dodger commented. "You can see it written on the face of this town."

"I gather Whitman, the municipality, isn't a hot bed of activity?"

"You could say that," Dodger responded, pleased that his voice now sounded more normal. "Judging by the architecture, its high mark of prosperity was the mid-twenties to the mid-sixties. Now, it's mainly a row of closed stores and shops. Even the hotel is boarded up. There was no traffic to speak of on the roads, and not many people on foot, even in the center of town — and some of them looked either addled or drunk."

"Sleepy, huh?" She laughed from the economic security of her urban apartment.

"Comatose," Dodger replied, a warm feeling working its way through his torso at the sound of that deep gurgle.

She laughed again.

"Anything personal?" Dodger asked, trying to get back on track. "On Travis Whitman, I mean. What about social life?"

"Keeps a low profile. When he shows up in the media, it's usually in something like *Town & Country's* coverage of big charity events. The guy gives to a lot of causes, mostly education, literacy, and health. He's known to be one of the biggest donors to substance-abuse issues."

"Where's his main base of operations, where does he live most of the time?"

"There, in Whitman," Jess told him.

"You're kidding." Dodger's eyes narrowed in disbelief.

"Nope. And it's not as if he doesn't have choices. He's got a pied-à-terre in NYC, a flat in London, a minor *schloss* on the Rhine, and a penthouse in LA that's so over-the-top that Candy Spelling was quoted as saying it's too much. I can't find any evidence that he spends more than a few nights a year in any of them, and then it's often in connection with some function related to business or one of his business or philanthropic interests."

"Amazing," Dodger said. "So he *prefers* Whitman, huh?" That made no sense, he thought. There didn't seem to be anything in the town to interest a wealthy man with choices. "Maybe it was his wife's idea."

"The dead wife? Maybe," Jess said as if the idea hadn't occurred her to her before. "She was a Pratt, another old Southern textile family, except hers got out of Dodge much earlier. They started offshoring in the early seventies and then sold out. Maybe she didn't like what she saw then and decided this time they'd do it differently."

"Stay around and wave goodbye to the jobless streaming out of town?" Dodger murmured.

"It's a little more complicated than that. He still funds a local clinic and the library."

"Here in Whitman? Interesting. When did Charlotte Whitman die by the way?"

"Give me a second."

Dodger could hear the click of keys.

"In 1999, six years after the Standridge girl disappeared. That's a long time. I'm surprised he hasn't remarried."

"I don't think he's let go yet. He has a portrait of Charlotte still in pride of place," Dodger told her.

There was a moment of silence as each contemplated what it meant to yearn for what was lost.

"Are you finding anything yet?" Jess asked at last, and the awkward moment ended.

"The deputy sheriff is in Whitman's pocket. Whether that has anything to do with anything, I don't know. The mall where the girl vanished is *kaput*, nothing left but some defunct storefronts and a lot of cracked paving. There's a dollar store at one end that looks recent, maybe a couple of years old, but it's not part of the old mall. Most of the population seems to have cleared out with the jobs, and what's left doesn't seem to be shopping locally except for the cheapest necessities."

"Business as usual for once-and-former mill towns," Jess said, and Dodger remembered she'd been an economic history minor in college.

"Pretty much," he agreed. "There's a complicating factor that's unusual here. At the time the girl disappeared, a movie was being shot in Whitman, and everybody was focused on the production and not noticing anything else. It's almost as if the girl fell between the cracks. No one seems to have paid much attention at the time."

"Even her family?" Jess asked, and Dodger could imagine the skeptical lift of her eyebrows. "That's hard to believe."

"The family does seem to be strangely MIA," Dodger conceded. "In my experience, even at this stage of our involvement, they're all over whoever comes in to make sure their concerns and opinions are noted. This time, I've yet to see or hear from anybody related to the girl."

"Maybe Whitman didn't let them know you were coming," Jess pointed out.

"He does seem to be a secretive sort," Dodger agreed.

"You haven't asked about my lunch," she said, shifting gears.

"Sorry, how was your lunch? Did you have a scintillating conversation about Maxcliff?"

"I don't want to talk about it," she laughed. "I just wanted you to ask."

It was good he was lying on the bed, for his knees went weak again.

"I'll find out the next time I see you," he promised.

"I'll look forward to it," she teased. "How long will you be in

Whitman by the way?"

"I'm figuring a few days to a week to sniff around, and then it's back to Savannah."

"I thought you might be returning to Boston." For the first time, her voice sounded less sure, almost vulnerable. He closed his eyes and resisted the impulse to say he'd be on the next flight north.

"Nope, my plan is to report by phone. There isn't time to do it in person. I'm in the middle of prepping the last of the collages to ship to the San Francisco gallery that's staging the December show."

"Well, if I can help, let me know."

"With the collages?"

"Or anything else," she laughed.

"I think I'm good," he said, but then hesitated. "Are you sure you don't want to come to Savannah?"

"You never give up, do you?" she laughed.

After they disconnected, Dodger lay back on high-count Egyptian cotton sheets, hands behind his head and thought about what she'd told him. So Whitman was more than rich. That was no surprise, given this house and the art he'd seen so far. When you were super-rich, you could indulge yourself in all kinds of pastimes and even follies, like the mini-museum he'd seen after lunch, the memorial to the missing girl. It was then that he realized he hadn't mentioned the *memento mori* to Jess. That might be just as well, he thought, until he had a chance to examine it again and get a better idea of what it contained.

Five.

Small Talk

D odger heard a quick burst of laughter as he got off the elevator, adjusting jacket sleeves and brushing damp, sandy hair off his forehead. Clearly, dinner guests had arrived and were gathered in the sitting room. As he made his way up the hall, there was more laughter. Why did the jollity surprise him? The Standridge girl had been gone for twenty years and Charlotte Whitman dead for — what was it that Jess had said earlier — oh yeah, fourteen years. There was nothing odd about laughter so long after the fact. Even the most censorious would find it difficult to fault Whitman. Still, it seemed at odds with the heaviness he'd sensed in his host that afternoon and look of persistent unease on the man's face.

A woman spoke in a pleasing, low-pitched voice, something about eBooks and restrictive publisher policies. When Dodger rounded the corner and got a look at her, it occurred to him that, if a man want-ed to dance on a late wife's grave, this would be a good person with whom to do it. Even wearing conservative dinner dress and in relative repose, she gave the impression of a gazelle about to leap across the tundra. As Dodger moved further into the room, she realized he was there and turned large violet-colored eyes toward him. They exchanged a predator-prey assessment, and for the life of him Dodger couldn't decide which he was in this particular scenario.

Neither possibility struck him as objectionable. This woman had a quality that invited closer investigation. The image of Jess flashed through his consciousness, and he was surprised to feel a twinge of guilt. That was dumb, he thought, given that Jess had made it clear she considered him no more than a colleague, albeit one who had, once, enjoyed friends-with-benefits status.

Whitman began to offer introductions while the other man already in the room came forward, hand outstretched.

"Lisa, this is Art Dodger, a damn fine artist. Dodger, this is Lisa North, our town librarian. The gentleman descending on you is her brother Randy Sizemore. He teaches at the consolidated high school in Blevins."

"I coach," Sizemore muttered.

"Lisa," Dodger gave an abbreviated bow even as he began to take her brother's hand. Expecting the usual firm but unexceptional grip, he was startled when Sizemore seized his hand with such force that his fingers were compressed to the point of discomfort. Well, two could play that game, and Dodger gave as good as he got, causing Sizemore to grunt and his eyes to squint in pained surprise.

"Lisa has been telling us about digital-rights management, wasn't it?" Whitman turned to the attractive woman as Dodger resumed the chair in which he'd sat that afternoon.

"Much too dull a topic for anyone not into libraries," Lisa purred, narrowing her startling eyes as she continued to gaze at Dodger. Randy Sizemore moved closer to his sister and glared in the same direction. "So you're an artist, Mr. Dodger. What's your medium?"

"Whatever comes to hand, but my preference is acrylic. And call me Art."

"Acrylic, Art?" She lifted well-shaped brows. (Surely that kind of professional grooming wasn't available around here, Dodger thought even as he admired the result). "You surprise me."

"It requires less patience than oil and is easier to work with than watercolor," he smiled. "My current interest is collage. Do you collect?"

"In a minor way. Not on the order of Travis, of course." She nodded toward the Freud over the mantel. "I keep telling him he should sell it and enlarge his grandmother's library, but he prefers sentiment to bricks and mortar even though he detests the thing."

Whitman reddened, and Dodger suspected her teasing had gone over the line. No matter how long his wife had been dead, the comment was in poor taste, apart from the fact that the portrait seemed to be a sore point with him.

Perhaps sensing their host's displeasure, Lisa shifted gears.

"You must get teased a lot," she drawled to Dodger.

"Teased?"

"Your name, of course. 'Art' for an artist, then with that last name to boot. I can't be the only person who at once thought 'Artful Dodger'."

"The only one who managed to be quite so beautiful while she pointed it out," Dodger said with mock gallantry, making her turn pink at his counter of her rudeness and earning him a wink from Whitman and even a grudging chuckle from Sizemore.

"Dinner is served, sir," said a young voice from behind him.

"Thank you, Courtney," Whitman said, standing up.

The dining room was large and impressive, albeit in an unexpected way. It retained its original paneling, heavy with touches of Elizabethan grandeur, but all of it was painted dull cream flecked with the most delicate of golds. The effect in the candlelight was striking and, like the entrance gates, showed a sophisticated design taste, Dodger thought. Here, as in the sitting room, a gas fire blazed on the large hearth. A pair of handsome silver candelabra dominated the table, which was set with a showroom's worth of white porcelain chargers, Scandinavian crystal, and heavy silver flatware atop a tablecloth of snow-white damask. A large but low bouquet of blood-red chrysanthemums sat between the candelabra. Courtney stood next to the glass-topped sideboard, which supported an impressive assortment of silver dishes.

"We like to keep things informal," Whitman explained, as he waved the others to the sideboard, where the young maid lifted lids and put serving spoons in each dish.

"Travis's world is a little rarified," Lisa said, grinning as she directed the remark toward Dodger, the only guest who presumably did not understand their host's situation.

"It's an elegant presentation," he said impassively. "The candelabra are particularly fine. Georg Jensen, aren't they?"

Lisa looked at him in surprise and bit back whatever she had planned to say.

Whitman nodded. "My grandmother bought them about the time the house was built in 1922. They were always her favorites."

Over dinner, the conversation drifted back and forth between Lisa North's ongoing warfare with several publishers of digital books, Randy Sizemore's desire to get better tickets for the next season of Tar Heels' football, and Travis Whitman's preference for the painting that hung over this mantel to the Freud in the sitting room.

"Bob Burridge, isn't it?" Dodger asked, surveying the large abstract with expert eyes. "It's unusual to see one of his florals in that size."

"I commissioned it after meeting him at a Chamber event in Los Angeles. An interesting man. Very talented. Very businesslike for an artist."

Lisa North made a face.

"Don't you like it?" Dodger asked her point blank.

"Oh, it's all right, I suppose. It's very colorful, of course, but how can you even compare it to the Freud, Travis? His portraits sell in the millions now."

Whitman laughed. "You'll find that Lisa's primary interest in art happens when it shows up in auction catalogs, usually long after the artist is either inactive or dead."

Dodger laughed, and Lisa shot him a nasty look.

"Now, then," Whitman said, turning toward the maid. "We'll have coffee, dessert, and drinks after in the small library."

Like the others, this room no longer had its original quasi-Elizabethan Tudor decoration. It was not, however, doomed to their steel-and-leather aesthetic. Here the sofas might be gray, but the fabric was textured velvet and the surfaces cushioned. The windows were draped with gray wool. The carpet was dense and felt good underfoot. The hearth was smaller, but the fire larger. The shelves were full of books that looked as if they were there for use, not decoration. The painting over the mantel was a realistic but not cloying oil of the exterior of the house in which they sat. On the desk in the far corner, an open file, a ruled pad and a tumbler full of Bics and pencils showed that someone worked here, at least on occasion.

"Nice," Dodger murmured.

"It's better for real conversation," Whitman agreed. "And I think it's time for that."

Dodger looked at the other two guests to see if they understood what he meant, but they seemed puzzled.

The maid rolled in a trolley with an assortment of sweets and cheeses, as well as a coffee urn.

"Here are the afters you requested, Mr. Whitman. The drinks tray is set up on the credenza. Shall I serve?"

"That's fine, Courtney. We'll help ourselves."

He waved everyone toward the trolley. Each got what he or she wanted, and then took a seat and began poking at their respective choices with delicate dessert forks. The atmosphere in the room was one of expectancy: Lisa and Randy wanted to know what was up; and Whitman obliged them with no preliminaries.

"I've asked Art Dodger to come here to help us try to make sense, after all this time, of what happened to Danielle Standridge."

"I don't understand," Sizemore interjected. "Isn't he just an artist?"

"He is indeed an artist, and a good one, so 'just' is inaccurate. He is also, however, someone who's interested in cold cases. I went to Dodger to ask for his help in getting to the bottom of the girl's disappearance, and he agreed to look things over."

"I don't know what happened to the girl," Sizemore objected.

Whitman sighed. "No one is saying you do. I have, however, asked Dodger to talk to people who knew Danny, and it seems to me that it makes sense he start with you, given what you told the police at the time."

Frowning, but no longer protesting, Sizemore took a bite of chocolate torte.

"What is it that you want us to tell Mr. Dodger?" Lisa North asked, now all business. "We need context."

"You told the police that the girl came into the library quite often and used the reference books and other materials in the back room."

"That's right," Lisa confirmed. "She did."

"I want you to tell him what you remember about those times."

"Well," Lisa shrugged, turning to Dodger, "it isn't much. You have to understand the summer of 1993 was the start of my first year here. I'd just gotten my Master's in Library Science, and Mrs. Wheelock — the head librarian then — had hired me on a trial basis. I was little more than a kid myself, so I was trying to act very grown up. I still remember what a shock it was when the Standridge girl referred to me as 'ma'am'." She laughed, but Dodger had an idea she didn't find it particularly funny, probably hadn't even then. "In any event, I got here in late June. She disappeared, let's see, oh yes, in September, so that was how long I knew her. Not that I knew her in any real sense, but every week, she came in, most days during summer and, when school was back in session, on Saturday mornings and the occasional afternoon."

"What was she doing?" Dodger asked.

Lisa shrugged again. "Who knows? No, wait, she was writing some kind of paper. I remember now. She had a stack of index cards that she sorted and re-sorted. It's funny to think that was how everyone used to do it."

"A paper on what?"

"I'm not sure," Lisa drawled. "I remember she was always asking me to do interlibrary loan on books about textile manufacturing."

"Wait a minute," Whitman interrupted. "I know what it was." He turned toward Dodger. "Charlotte was already looking into scholarships for the girl. She had her doing a project in connection with that. It was something to do with the development of the textile industry in North Carolina. I remember Charlotte had me take the girl down to the factory's archives once and let her select some photographs to copy for the paper."

Dodger nodded. "That makes sense. I wonder if the paper she wrote still exists?"

"I don't know," Whitman admitted. "I'm not sure it was ever finished."

Dodger watched as his host went over to the trolley and got another cup of coffee. It was interesting that the man acted as if his knowledge of the girl and her activities were no more than casual, but how did that fit with the mini-museum he'd seen upstairs? He found himself wondering if Lisa North had ever seen the museum and, if so, what conclusions she had drawn.

"If she did finish the paper," Lisa said, "it's possible she filed a copy with Mrs. Wheelock. I'll look around and see what I can find."

"I'd appreciate it," Dodger told her.

"Girl was a damned bookworm," Sizemore muttered. The others turned to stare at him, and he turned red and frowned.

Whitman smiled in a sneering sort of way and sat down.

Dodger turned back to Lisa North. "So you never interacted with her outside of the library, even though you weren't much older?"

"It seemed more of an age difference at that point in my life." Lisa smiled. "As I mentioned earlier, I felt quite grown up with my new M.S. She was just a high-school kid. Maybe smarter than most, better behaved, but still just a kid in my eyes."

"Did you notice anyone speaking to her in the library?" Dodger asked.

"Well, her father followed her through the side door a couple of times and made a scene. Once I had to threaten to call Mrs. Wheelock if he didn't leave."

"He disapproved of Charlotte's efforts to help his daughter better herself," Whitman explained. "He had the nerve to call here once when he was drunk and tell me to warn my wife to keep her 'mitts' off Danny."

"No one else came to the library to see her?" Dodger persisted. Given what he'd heard of the girl, he suspected that the library might be a portal into her life.

"Mrs. Whitman — Charlotte — came with her a couple of times to show her something about the old archives, the ones you had to have special permission to use."

"Nobody else?"

Lisa glanced at her brother and bit her lip. "Well, Randy tried to chat her up. You see, the general public wasn't allowed in the area where Danny was working — it was a kind of sorting room for books returned by borrowers. But Randy would wait there for me sometimes, and I remember he thought she was cute."

"I said maybe two words to her in my whole life, and you think it's worth mentioning to this amateur sleuth?" Sizemore snarled.

"It was more than two words," Lisa objected. "I heard you ask her out."

"What did she say?" Dodger asked the angry man.

"That she was too busy with her studying," Sizemore muttered. "Of course, she had plenty of time for Jason Sutton, the high school's rock star, now our eminent deputy sheriff. All the girls had time for Jase back then, and she was no different, however high and mighty she acted. And I don't appreciate being ambushed this way. Lisa, I think we need to leave."

Sizemore stood up and took a step toward the door. Whitman held up a hand even as Lisa started to caution her brother, and he froze.

Whitman turned to Dodger. "Do you have additional questions for Lisa and Randy at this point?"

"Can either of you remember anything unusual going on at the time, anything at all?"

"You mean apart from the movie?" Lisa asked. "Once the news got out that a motion picture was going to be shot in Whitman, the movie was all everybody talked about that whole summer. You'd think it was the Second Coming."

Six.

······●●●●●●●●······

Reflection

It was late. The dinner party had finished long before, and Lisa North and her brother had left well over two hours ago. Dodger, pajama-clad for once, lay on the bed in the dark, with his hands behind his head, unable to sleep. It wasn't the fault of the bed, which might be the most comfortable to which he'd ever had access. Rather, it was his growing sense that Travis Whitman had a hidden agenda.

The man was going through all the right motions, like offering to take him around the area tomorrow and setting it up that Deputy Sutton would serve as his guide the following day. Also, he'd invited Lisa North and her brother Randy Sizemore for dinner and asked them to talk about the missing girl. But then there was that business with the room perpetuating Danielle's memory. Dodger wondered when he'd get around to mentioning that, if ever. And what about the timing? Why was he pursuing the girl's disappearance now, after so many years?

His cell buzzed.

"Jess," he said.

"Did I wake you?"

"No. It was a late night. I'm just getting in. What's happening?"

"Not a thing. You sounded a little down earlier, and I've been thinking about you. Has anything else come up that needs researching?"

"Not really. No, wait, see what you can dig up about a woman named Lisa Sizemore North and her brother Randy Sizemore. She's the librarian here, and he coaches in a consolidated high school the next town over."

"How much do you need?"

"Just superficial. Whatever you can turn up fast."

"What are their ages?"

Dodger thought about it and did some backward math, based on when Lisa said she got her Master's. "I'd say she's between forty and forty-five, and he's a year or two either side of that."

"I'll have something for you tomorrow."

"Thanks. It's my guess they're not involved in whatever went on here, but I want to get a better handle on them, especially the North woman."

"Is she good-looking?"

"I suppose so, yes; but she's one of those women it doesn't help much."

"What on earth do you mean?" she laughed.

"Just that when you first see her you're blown away. The woman looks like those studio portraits of Liz Taylor in her prime, down to the violet eyes, but then after a few minutes you forget how she looks because you realize how unpleasant she is."

"Oh," Jess lost interest.

"Her brother is the real heartbreaker," Dodger continued, "as fair as she is dark, with the look of someone who could pose for ads in GQ, and knows it. Guy even has a dimple in his chin."

"Is he as unpleasant as she is?"

"In his own inimitable way." Dodger thought about it. "I get the feeling he's a lightweight compared to Lisa, knows it and resents it."

"Nest of vipers?"

"I doubt it. Just your average, everyday sister-and-brother jerks in tandem."

"Are you getting any of your famous hunches yet?" she teased.

"Maybe the glimmer of one, but I'm not sure it relates to Danielle Standridge, just something that seems a little off."

"What's Travis Whitman like?"

"An interesting man," Dodger said. "With a spectacular house worthy of *Architectural Digest*, not to mention some excellent art."

"As in?"

"There are originals, good originals, in every room I've seen, including a Lucien Freud over the mantel in the sitting room and a couple of Georgia O'Keefes in the room they assigned me."

"You're kidding."

"Nope. What I've seen of the place is like a veritable art gallery."

"What's your room like?"

"Apart from the O'Keefe paintings? Very stylish, very handsome. Everything gray and white. Everything retro Deco and custom-made. Lots of mirrored fronts on chests. Upholstered headboards. That kind of thing."

"Doesn't sound like small-town America."

"Not small town anywhere. This is major stuff, but then from what you said, the guy can afford it."

As they talked, Dodger tried not to picture her. He wished they were close enough that he could ask her to do a — what was it they called it? — oh yeah, a selfie. But he didn't think a one-night stand the year before, one that was almost certainly as much a matter of impulse for her as for him, put them on selfie-to-order footing.

"Thought any more about coming to Savannah in a few days?" he asked.

"No," she laughed. "Was the invitation serious?"

"Of course, it's serious," he said in mock indignation.

"We'll see," she promised, and from the smile in her voice he knew she wouldn't come.

"What's on the agenda tomorrow?" she continued.

"The grand tour, as Whitman put it, with him as guide. Then the next day, he's set it up so I'm with Deputy Sutton, who's taking me to talk with some of the locals who knew Danielle."

"Should be informative," she told him.

"I'm beginning to think it might be," Dodger said, contemplating the mini-museum up the hall and around the corner.

"Be sure you look over your shoulder every once in a while," she warned. "You don't want a repeat of the Wilkerson case."

Dodger rubbed at the place on his head that still throbbed a little in cold weather and grimaced. "Won't happen. I keep my eye on the rear-view mirror these days."

They laughed and ended the call.

Dodger lay in the dark, thinking of Jess, unable to turn off his head. Finally, surrendering to the inevitable, he opened the SmartCover on his iPad mini and tapped the Netflix icon.

Seven.

..•°••◍◉◉◍••°•..

Whitman by Whitman

B reakfast was served in a charming room awash in clear light from its eastern exposure. On the glass shelves of sleek white corner cupboards was ranged a large array of what looked like very early English porcelain decorated with flowers and dragons in bright colors.

"My grandmother had a weakness for eighteenth-century Coalport," Whitman explained, noticing Dodger's admiration of the display.

"It's impressive," Dodger said. "Reminds me of something in my grandmother's house. It's interesting how a craze for a certain kind of decorative object tends to spread throughout a generation."

"Like a virus," Whitman laughed. "They say my grandfather hated the stuff."

"It's a taste," Dodger agreed, and they shared a moment of male solidarity at the foibles of the feminine urge toward acquisition of the pretty and the pointless.

Afterwards, Whitman proposed they begin the day's tour with what he called "my command center out back." Any vision of a converted outbuilding vanished when he led Dodger through a back door, past a multi-vehicle garage range, and across a courtyard to a two-story building, with a footprint perhaps seventy-five feet square, surrounded by a businesslike strip of pavement on which no more than half a dozen cars were parked.

"Once I decided I'd make this my home base, I knew staffing was required, and it seemed simpler to house them on the grounds than elsewhere," Whitman explained. "As it turns out, most of the employees work from home these days, but this is useful for those times when we need to have meetings or have visitors from out of town."

"I see there's a back drive."

Whitman nodded. "It comes off the highway between Blevins and Whitman. All employees use it instead of the front drive, which is for family and guests only. What do you think of the building?"

"Nice," Dodger said as they stood, surveying the stone, brick, and timber structure built in a style mimicking that of the big house.

"It's cozy," Whitman said, with no hint of irony. "Come on, and I'll show you around."

A young Hispanic in uniform buzzed them into the entry area, his eager manner betraying both excitement and a certain amount of apprehension.

"Mr. Whitman," he acknowledged, standing at attention. "What can I do for you?"

"Not a thing, Eduardo." Whitman smiled. "I'm giving Mr. Dodger a tour."

Their first stop was a thick glass wall, behind which an attractive older woman in a designer suit was working at a computer. The office was sleek and stylish as the woman herself. Whitman placed his palm over a pad next to the door. There was a slight sound, and he pushed open the heavy glass panel. The woman looked up and smiled.

"Travis, good morning."

"Good morning to you, Miss Enid. I'd like you to meet Art Dodger. Dodger, this is Enid Blythe, who runs things around here. If it weren't for her, the whole show would implode."

Blythe stood up and extended her hand, her smile still friendly but a little less warm than when directed at her boss. Her handshake was firm, brief and cool, and she remained standing as Whitman explained Dodger's presence.

"I've asked Dodger's organization to look into this old business of the Standridge girl who went missing. Will you make sure he gets any assistance he needs from our end?"

"Of course, Travis."

She pulled a business card from the holder next to her computer and handed it to Dodger. "All my contact information is there. Don't hesitate to call any time."

"Did you know Danielle?" Dodger asked, putting the card in his pocket.

"I did not know the girl *per se*. I remember her, of course. Her disappearance was very puzzling."

"Very," Whitman agreed. "It's been twenty years with no word of her. I decided that's long enough. We need answers."

"Yes," Blythe said.

"Don't hesitate to let Enid know if you need anything in the office line," Whiteman reiterated before turning back to Blythe. "Page Joe and tell him to have the Beemer here in half an hour."

"Certainly, Travis."

"Now, Dodger, let me give you the cook's tour of the building."

Blythe remained standing as they left her office. When Dodger glanced back, she was still watching them, an indecipherable expression on her handsome face. He wondered if she'd lied about knowing Danielle, but why? It was logical she might, in a town as small as Whitman, know the girl without any special significance being attached to it.

"We were fortunate in the timing of the building," Whitman was saying. "While the architects were in the planning stages, it was already apparent that serious attention needed to be paid to IT needs in terms of wiring and communications access, and I had an associate in a Silicon Valley venture firm in which I'm interested get us the latest input. Which was good, as my one personal concession to digital is my cell. So far we've managed to stay up to date without any additional work. For example, our security system is tied to wi-fi, as are the video and audio monitors on the perimeter fencing, as is the communication system used by the guards at the sentry gates."

"Nice," Dodger commented, increasingly impressed as his host led him through the building. With the bright lighting, utilitarian furniture and up-to-date electronics, this was a business, a place where people were expected to function, not a rich man's hobby. Maybe that was what made it eerie to pass offices, lights off and doors open, devoid of occupants. In the entire building, they saw just a handful of employees, all of whom, as the two men approached, at once stopped what they were doing and stood, waiting respectfully for Whitman to reach them. Dodger half-expected at least some of them to "touch the forelock," as his father had called it when subordinates were obsequious. There hadn't been any of that, not quite, but it was clear that everyone who worked for Whitman was wary of offending him.

33

Whitman introduced each employee to Dodger, identifying him as a friend. From this, Dodger deduced that, apart from Enid Blythe, the business staff wasn't to be let in on the secret of why Dodger was in town.

Whitman hadn't seemed to be keeping track of the time, but in half an hour he ended an employee's description of managing foreign currency fluctuations and headed Dodger toward the door. Outside, a BMW 6 Series Gran Coupe stood at the curb. Whitman gestured Dodger toward the passenger side, and went around to the driver's seat. With a flick of the key the engine began to purr. Whitman navigated the drive with efficiency, and then tooted and waved to the security guard at the front gate as they passed through.

"You may find a quick visual of the town helpful. It'll at least pro-vide situational background as it were," he explained as he steered the big car over the curving road.

"Can't hurt," Dodger agreed, although he would rather make the initial tour on his own.

"The area was a community early in the state's history," Whitman began. "In colonial times, it was a cluster of farms the edges of which joined in what is now the center of town. By the time of the American Revolution, it was known as Libertyville. Its pre-industrial population peak was around 1830. By the time my maternal great-grandfather Nicodemus Brown built the first textile mill here in the 1890s, it had dwindled to a few houses. The mill brought more people in, of course, but the town exploded population-wise when my paternal grandfather Albert Whitman injected capital into the enterprise in the early 1920s."

He retraced the route taken by Sutton the day before, until, just before the mall was reached, he took a fork that channeled them into town by a side road.

"This was the oldest part of Libertyville," he continued. "The white house there…" he pointed to a large, classical farmhouse, "is known as the Clumber House, after the family that lived there the longest. It was the largest of the old farmhouses. Dates from the early 1830s. It's been designated a Historic Site. My grandmother was the patron of the committee that saved it. The log building in the side yard is the oldest structure remaining from the eighteenth-century set-tlement. The committee had it moved here in 1975 from what's now the site of Whitman Mall. Up here is the back of the library. I see Lisa North's car is there." He slowed. "We could go in, but you'll be seeing her tomorrow — I've asked Jase to take you there to see what she's been able to turn up in her facilities about the Danny's disappearance."

"Where's the mill?"

"The mill itself is pretty much gone. We sold the main building to a salvage company from Maryland. At this point, all you'll see are stacks of bricks and other materials that haven't been picked up. Some of the auxiliary structures remain, as does much of the mill village where the workers lived."

He turned down a road lined with medium-sized white frame houses, plain but pleasant enough. "This is part of the residential section owned by the mill. This street is called Managers Street. We sold the houses and the land they stand on to any occupants who wanted them at a peppercorn price of $500 each."

Dodger whistled. "I'll bet the offer had a lot of takers."

"You'd be surprised. About half the occupants opted in. The remaining houses were put up for sale at general market rates. I suppose if you didn't have a job close enough to commute, owning property here didn't make sense."

"Still, damn generous of you," Dodger said.

"At the end of the street, you can see a couple of the later warehouses. We haven't decided what to do with them yet."

He made the turn and came to a halt before a rectangle of cleared space two hundred feet long that was clearly the footprint of the demolished mill. Every so often sat a pile of bricks. Apart from that, the view to the river was unimpeded.

"The old water tower was there and the main mill building here. This was the lot where employees who drove to work parked their cars. At the library tomorrow, you can get Lisa North to show you some images of the place in its heyday. I gave the library the company archives years ago."

They sat in silence for several minutes, looking across the site toward the river.

"It still seems odd to me to see it like this, that is to say, not to see it here anymore," Whitman confided. "It was almost like part of the family. When I come here, I feel as if I'm visiting a cemetery."

Dodger, unable to think of anything that seemed like an appropriate reply, didn't offer one.

"You're thinking that makes me a hypocrite," Whitman continued, "given that I'm the one who finished it off in a manner of speaking."

Dodger shrugged. "I think we all understand what's happened to the textile industry in the last half century."

"It's impossible to justify keeping production here when you can do it for so much less abroad," Whitman said. "And, of course, regulation is less complex there."

"I can imagine," Dodger said, biting his tongue to keep from uttering the word "nonexistent."

"Anyway, we kept production here for as long as we could. Once everything was abroad, there wasn't a reason to keep the structure any longer. In fact, according to the lawyers, it became an active liability. Plus the insurance cost had become prohibitive."

"You mentioned the mill village. Didn't we drive through it on the way here?"

Whitman shook his head. "What we saw was one street, where some of the managers lived. The main part of the village is at the far edge of the mill compound, about two blocks up that way. Would you like to see it?"

Dodger nodded. "But before we go, could I ask you something? I'm assuming the mill compound was operating at the time Danielle disappeared in 1993?"

"That's right," Whitman confirmed. "We were running full shifts in 1993."

"Were the premises searched?"

"You mean at once? No. Her family seemed to think she'd run away and would be back at any time, so there wasn't much point. At least, that's what seemed to be the case at the time. About three months later, when it became clear that she was gone. I had our security people do a sweep of the entire compound. They even checked around the village. They didn't find anything."

"How about the demolition crew? Did they report finding anything odd or unexpected?"

"Not to me or anyone reporting to me. If you'd like to talk to the man who supervised the demolition, I can have Enid pull up his contact information for you."

"That'd be helpful," Dodger said.

"Ready to go to the village?"

"Sure."

Whitman drove past the mill site and a couple of large outbuildings, then paused in front of a sizable brick building, plain but substantial and the only structure that remained in use to judge from its parking lot and the activity around its door.

"That's the clinic. We've kept it going, but they tell me fewer people use it each year. The population is dropping as people find employment too far away to commute. And next to it is the mill office."

He indicated a handsome little brick building with elegant Palladian detail. "I should let the demolition company take that as well, but I know how fond my father was of it."

"Did he know production was going abroad?" Dodger asked.

Whitman laughed grimly. "He started the process, almost made it inevitable, in fact, with the commitments he made in connection with various long-term financial arrangements."

"Then it's likely he anticipated this would no longer be needed."

"My hope," Whitman confided, "is that the state will take it over. The old high school is just up the way. The school closed in 2005 when a new consolidated school was opened in the next town, and the state has been negotiating with the county to buy the building for a retraining center for workers who've lost jobs in the textile industry. If the deal goes through, their initial plans indicate they'll need a couple of other facilities in the area, and this building would be ideal for an administrative function."

"You mentioned the old high school. Was that where Danielle went?"

"Yes. Whitman-Brown. She had started her last year there, as I recall. Want to drive by?"

"Sure."

The high-school building was three stories, one hundred feet long, and fifty feet deep with a wing at right angles to one side and a large separate brick building in the rear. It looked in excellent condition.

"We keep a caretaker on the premises," Whitman explained.

"Reliable man named Roosevelt Jones. He was the building superintendent when the school was open."

Whitman paused in the semi-circular drive before the school to allow Dodger to examine its exterior.

"If you'd like to see inside, just tell Sutton to add it to the list. Now," he said, pulling out of the drive, "if we go back this way, toward the river, we'll be in the mill town proper. The big vacant lot between the village and the school is where the company store used to be. It was torn down when I was only five or six, so I don't remember it but there are photos in the company archive at the library. Across the street is the Whitman Baptist Church."

He turned right to enter an enclave of small frame houses, each on a generous lot. Up and down half a dozen long, more or less identical streets, he drove slowly, allowing Dodger to see that the majority of the houses appeared lived in although not well cared for. Most retained their original white paint, dingy and peeling in places, but a handful now glowed in jaunty colors — here a pale blue with white trim, there a bright yellow with black, and up the way Dodger glimpsed three houses in a row in assorted rainbow hues.

"It still seems odd to me to see color in here," Whitman said. "As long as the mill owned and maintained the town, white was the only color allowed."

"So the Standridges lived in one of the larger houses on the first street we drove down on our way to the mill compound?" Dodger asked, trying to get his bearings.

Whitman shook his head. "Her father was a mill superintendent. When he came here with his family, he bought one of the brick houses on what we used to call Vendor Row. I'll show you this afternoon."

He rounded another corner that dead-ended in the parking lot of a large brick church.

"Whitman Methodist," he said, turning the Beemer around.

"Did the mill build the churches?" Dodger asked.

Whitman shook his head. "We gave any organized religious group with fifty members or more a perpetual land lease on three acres for a rent of $1 per year. The congregations built the churches. The two built on mill land were those we've seen plus a Pentecostal. You might have noticed the Presbyterian Church when you came into town, but it isn't related to the mill."

"You really know this place, don't you?" Dodger said, impressed.

"It isn't just the family business. It's where I grew up," Whitman reminded him. "I went away to boarding school and university, but apart from that and vacations, this is where I've always lived."

"It must be hard to see it disappearing."

"You could say so," Whitman muttered. "Still, my father was a tough guy, and the one lesson he made sure I learned was that the price of position is you do what has to be done."

His voice was bitter, and Dodger knew he might have learned the lesson but he didn't necessarily like it.

They sat in silence while Whitman drove toward the town's primary business street.

"I'm hungry," Whitman said. "How about you?"

"I could eat."

Dodger assumed he'd point the Beemer back toward Mill House. Instead, he parked in front of what its sign indicated was The Tastee Grill.

"Best burgers in town," he told Dodger.

When they walked through the double doors into a dining area half full of customers, the man behind the counter greeted Whitman with a friendly wave and a question. "You and this gentleman want your usual?"

Whitman looked at Dodger and lifted his eyebrows. "Burger okay?"

"Sure. Burger's fine."

"Make it two, Joe," Whitman called out. "We'll take this booth by the window."

Several people spoke to Whitman, and he returned their greetings with the easy manner of assured familiarity. Once settled, Dodger saw that, thanks to a slight curve in the Main Street and the lack of structures on the far side of the street, they had a good view of a large portion of the primary shopping area.

"Why is just one side of the street built up?" Dodger asked.

"You can't see the tracks for the weeds, but the railroad that served the mill used to run there. They've started taking up the tracks in the mill compound, but they haven't gotten this far yet."

"Busy place back in the day," Dodger commented.

"Which wasn't that long ago," Whitman pointed out. "There are people who started at the mill after high school back in 1993, when Danny Standridge disappeared, who thought they'd retire from there. All those stores you see up the way, the ones that are shut now, were open and prosperous then. Things went south when we had to start cutting shifts in 1996, and the last of the operations shut down in 2005, when those high-school graduates from 1993 were only thirty. The town died by inches and then by feet."

He spoke without emotion, like a narrator stating dry historic facts, but Dodger could tell the situation for him wasn't simple. He almost certainly remained aware that the loss of its living affected everyone in the town. How did you handle that, Dodger wondered? It must be a lot to juggle, behaving in a way that responsible twenty-first century business practice demanded even as you understood the results of your actions on those who depended on you, just as their parents and grandparents had depended on yours for their livelihood. He thought about what Jess had told him the night before, and understood now why Whitman subsidized the library and the clinic.

The coffee was strong, the burgers good, the fries better, and the apple pie that Whitman recommended for dessert better still. Every once in a while, as they ate, Dodger caught a glance in their direction, but for the most part Whitman's presence in the place excited little attention. He must come here a lot.

After lunch, Whitman drove down the Main Street, past a two-story department store with boarded-up windows and blue porcelain signs proclaiming that men and women's work clothes were sold inside and payroll checks cashed. Up the way, a freestanding theater built in a post-World War II modernist style, boasted a papered-over ticket window but retained a marquee showing its name was Gem and the last movie that had played there was *Star Wars III Revenge*.

The once-and-former furniture store named Peebles now hosted three floors of thrift goods, and a shop formerly specializing in work shoes now seemed to deal in refurbished appliances.

"There's the police station," Whitman said, "but you know that since you were there yesterday."

"And that's the front of the library that we saw from behind earlier," Dodger observed.

"That's right," Whitman said. "My great-grandmother had the

idea, and after her death, the family built it in her honor."

"Handsome place," Dodger commented.

It was a no-nonsense, solid edifice, with heavy Doric columns lining its shallow porch.

Dodger realized they had doubled back and were driving along the street Sutton had taken the day before, the street leading toward the mall. Whitman made no comment as they passed fast-food outlets either closed or with few customers in their parking lots. When they reached the row of brick ranch houses Dodger had noticed the day before, Whitman slowed and pulled into the driveway of an empty residence with a for-sale sign in the front yard.

"This is what we called Vendor Row," he told Dodger as he gestured toward the long, low, brick ranch houses on both sides of the broad street. "The name came about because the first couple of houses were built by suppliers to the mill and lived in by their representative who sold to the mill full time. That was the late 1940s. Other houses got built over time. They weren't cheap. Some were bought by lawyers or other professionals who serviced the mill, some by local storeowners — I remember the Peebles family lived across the street, but later several of the mill managers bought here as well, usually men whose wives had good jobs too. Danny's parents bought the second house, there, and that's where she grew up."

Sutton looked at the location indicated and got the impression of a house perhaps larger than others on the street, with old trees in the front yard and an ancient car in the carport.

This had once been a nice neighborhood, Dodger thought, but it had not aged well. He doubted that their original owners would have tolerated for one second the unkempt borders and dying grass that could be seen in front of most of the houses today. As for the elderly vehicles parked in many of the driveways, it would have been the maids of the original householders to whom such unstylish transport belonged back in the day, not the employers themselves, and Dodger doubted that any of these houses had seen a maid in years.

Whitman's phone buzzed. He listened for a moment, disconnected and turned to Dodger with a look of regret on his long, patrician face.

"Sorry, that was Enid. I am summoned back to HQ." He spoke with the air of a man who is a slave to his staff even though Dodger suspected he was anything but.

"I appreciate the time you've taken," Dodger said. "This has given me a better idea of the environment in which the girl grew up, which is always helpful."

"Glad to be of service," Whitman smiled. "Tomorrow you can get down to business. Jase Sutton's been told to give you every cooperation. If there's any access he can't come up with, just let Enid know and she'll take care of it."

Eight.

...•o•o⦿⦿⦿o•o..

Sisterly Affection

They'd just finished breakfast the next morning when Whitman's cell buzzed. He glanced at it.

"Jase is here. I'm sure you're eager to start, so let's head out front."

The police cruiser was old, but well maintained, and the deputy wasted no time before bringing Dodger up to date on the day's schedule.

"Mr. Whitman thought you might like to start with Debbie Jenkins," he said, turning onto the public road. "She lives in one of those brick ranch houses on Vendor Row."

"Who's Debbie Jenkins?"

"She was Debbie Standridge before she married Ray Jenkins. She's Danny's older sister. She's the only one of the immediate family who still lives in Whitman."

"The parents are dead?"

"Their father, Andy, died back in '03. Their mother May is alive, but she's in an assisted living place out past Blevins. Anyway, she's got mental issues, and some days aren't so good. We'll have to call before we go and I thought you'd like to see Debbie first in case she says anything you want to try to bring up with her mother."

"Good thinking," Dodger said approvingly.

"We're not all hicks in the sticks, you know," Sutton said.

Dodger ignored the sarcasm, and moved to clear up something puzzling in relation to what had just been said.

"Doesn't Danielle's aunt work in Travis Whitman's house? I thought someone mentioned she's the housekeeper."

"Oh, you mean Gladys Tanner. Yeah, she's May Standridge's younger sister. I never think of her in connection with May and her family for some reason, maybe because it was common knowledge that

Andy thought it was beneath anyone in his family to be a servant. From what Danny said, the two sisters hardly ever talked."

"It must have seemed odd to Gladys when Charlotte Whitman started inviting Danielle to Mill House."

"I don't know about that," Sutton said, the finality in his voice suggesting it'd be pointless to pursue the conversation.

In a few minutes they were driving past the Whitman Mall sign, this time from the other direction, as they headed toward the double row of long, low red-brick houses.

"It was a nice neighborhood at one time," Sutton told him. "This was the street where the local lawyers, shopkeepers, and mill bosses had houses, when there was a mill to need bosses. The ones who lived on this street thought they were hot stuff. They're long gone now, like everything else."

Dodger looked at him. "So losing the mill did pretty much mean the end for Whitman?"

"Unless there's a miracle," Sutton answered. "There's talk of a training center in the old high school, the one Danny and I went to, but it hasn't come to anything. I also heard the governor is trying to get one of those high-tech outfits to bring a service center to town, but it's just a rumor."

Sutton wheeled the police cruiser into the driveway of the house pointed out by Whitman the day before, and came to an abrupt stop behind a beat-up Buick probably twenty years old. Like the driveway, the yard was one of the largest on the block, at least a couple of hundred feet wide with the remnants of what had once been extensive landscaping. Now, only the presence of several large specimen trees scattered among the native pines suggested that someone had once put care, thought, and money into this place. Everything else about the yard had pretty much gone to seed, literally. The lawn that divided the house from what had once been a busy road (so Sutton assured him several times) was big, at least a hundred feet deep, but it was now more weeds than grass and needed cutting.

As for the house itself, it was an impressive example of its kind. Of dark-red brick and seventy-five feet wide, its façade was broken by a massive chimney, a curved bay window, and a recessed entrance.

"This was a fine house in its time," Sutton said. "Andy Standridge wouldn't be any too happy with what Debbie and Ray have done to it. He was house proud."

"So this is where Danielle lived with her sister and parents?"

Sutton nodded. "Yeah, Andy bought it when he came to work at the mill in 1985. This is where Debbie and Danny grew up."

Dodger looked around with more interest. "But the house belongs to Danielle's sister now?"

Sutton shook his head. "I'm guessing that May's name is still on the deed, but Debbie and her husband Ray and their daughter Ashley came here to live when May first began to have her trouble. When she went into assisted living, they stayed."

"Convenient for them," Dodger pointed out.

Sutton snorted. "You got that right. The only way anyone'll get Debbie out of here now is with a stick of dynamite."

Dodger offered up the expected laugh just as the front door opened and a woman stepped out. She was tall and thin, with thick, dark, curly hair, cut short so that it sat on her head like a tousled cap. Her eyes were a pale hazel, and her nose had the same tip tilt as her sister's. She was attractive in a used sort of way, with faint furrows etched across her brow and a jaw whose strong line was just beginning to sag. She was, in fact, what any of the mannequins back at Mill House would look like if it came to life and was aged twenty-five years by a skilled hand. She wore cutoff jeans and a long tee with a skull and crossbones on it. Her feet were bare, the toenails painted bright purple and each adorned with a silver skull.

"Well, as I live and breathe," she drawled, scratching the back of her right calf with the toes of her other foot, "if it isn't my old buddy Jase. What's happening, Jase?"

"Debbie," he said, "I'd like you to meet Art Dodger. Mr. Dodger, this is Debbie Standridge Jenkins."

"So you're the one who's dragging up that old stuff about Danny again? What's in it for you?"

"I'm not sure what you mean," Dodger told her, trying hard not to stare.

"Everybody who wants to talk about Danny has an angle," she assured him. "They're thinking about doing a TV show or they want to do psychic research in her old room or they're writing a book or some such, so what's your angle?"

"Now, Debbie, you know I told you that Mr. Whitman invited Mr. Dodger to take a look around and see what he thinks happened." Sutton looked worried, and Dodger saw that he got very nervous whenever anything touched by Travis Whitman wasn't going to plan.

"Like I give a rat's ass about Travis Whitman," Debbie said, turning to go back through the door. "Well, whatever you're about, you might as well come inside and get it over with. That police car stays in the driveway much longer and all these busybodies around here will get the idea that Ash is into something, which she isn't. Jase can testify to her innocence, can't you, Jase? Ash is as pure as the driven snow, just like the saintly Danny. Not that Danny was quite as saintly as everybody thought." She giggled as she led them into the living room, propping a hand on the door surround for a second to brace herself. It was then that Dodger realized she wasn't just tipsy but about-ready-to-pass-out drunk.

"Now, Debbie," Jase warned, reaching out a hand to steady her. "Why don't you go over there on the sofa and talk with Mr. Dodger while I go into the kitchen and make a fresh pot of coffee?"

"Sure," Debbie said, slurring the word. "If Mr. Dodger wants to talk with me, I want to talk with him." She aimed herself at the end of the long sofa and curled her bare legs beneath her as Dodger took the chair at right angles. "So, Mister Dodger, what can I do for you?"

"I'm trying to get a feel for what your sister was like," he began.

"What she might *still* be like," Debbie corrected. "I don't buy this theory of little girl lost. I think the bitch just got tired of fighting with Mama and took off."

"So they argued a lot?"

"Argued more than they didn't," Debbie confirmed.

"About what?"

"Everything. The clothes Charlotte Whitman bought Danny, the way she spent all her time wrapped up in some book or other, the way she volunteered for Meals on Wheels when she never even helped set the table around here — anything and everything."

"How about boys?"

"What do you mean?" Debbie tried to reverse the slump that had her sliding half off the sofa and became more alert.

46

"Was there any special boy she liked, maybe one your mother didn't approve of?"

"Except for Jase, you mean?" she joked as he put a tray with coffee pot and cups on the low table in front of the sofa.

"What's that?" Sutton frowned. "You got to be careful saying stuff like that, Debbie. Mr. Dodger won't know you're kidding."

"Who says I'm kidding?" she chortled, but then stopped when she saw that he was serious.

"You could see there were plenty of guys who'd be happy to get so much as a smile from her," she told Dodger, "but she never gave most of them the time of day."

"So there was nobody your mother didn't approve of?" Dodger persisted, "maybe somebody Danielle had a crush on but hadn't necessarily started dating?"

Debbie shook her head. "Not that I knew about. I think Mama's main problem with Danny was that she didn't take advantage of what Mama tried to do for her, which was a hell of a lot more than Mama ever did for me."

"What do you mean? What did your mother try to do for Danny?"

A stubborn look came over Debbie's face. "I don't want to talk about it. Ask Mama, dearest, darling Mama. Get her to tell you, and good fucking luck with that."

Nine.

. . ₀₀₀₀₀₀₀₀ . .

Good Teacher Gone Away

"Debbie back there…" Sutton started to explain, then stopped as he braked for a kid on a bicycle who swerved in front of him.

"Debbie what?"

"Don't take the tough act too seriously. She's had it kind of hard, what with one thing and another. Whatever she did, Danny did it earlier and better. Then she had to deal with all the crap when Danny disappeared. She got a scholarship to State, but had an auto accident and got hooked on painkillers and lost out on school. Then Ray, the guy she married, turned out to be a real loser. As for her daughter Ashley, she almost died from this mystery infection when she was about three or four, and the medical costs just about bankrupted the family."

Dodger shook his head. "That's quite a run of bad luck."

"Some people seem to attract it," Sutton agreed.

"I gather she didn't care for her sister."

"I don't think anybody realized she felt like that, or not so much anyway, until after Danny disappeared. Then, if anybody so much as asked if she'd heard from Danny, she'd take it as an insult to her. 'Don't I count?' she'd say, as if caring what happened to Danny somehow meant you didn't care about her."

"Why do you suppose that was? Why she disliked her sister?"

"I always figured she was just jealous," Sutton admitted. "Debbie was pretty — you can see she's still pretty, even when she's tanked up — but Danny was something else. You've seen the pictures. Danny flat out lit up a room, and you just didn't see anybody else in it when she was around, including Debbie. Debbie was intelligent, but Danny was in a different league according to the teachers. They were always taking her off to Charlotte or Atlanta to be tested, and people would come to

Whitman sometimes to talk to the parents about what a gifted child she was. Then I'm guessing it frosted Debbie when Charlotte Whitman made a project out of making sure that Danny 'bettered' herself."

"How much of an age difference between the two sisters?"

"A little over two years," Sutton said. "Close enough so they automatically competed, leastways that's what their mother always claimed."

"You know a lot about the Standridges," Dodger commented.

"Everybody knew a lot about everybody back then," Sutton explained. "We all grew up together. Some of our parents grew up together."

"But not Andy, the girls' father."

Sutton shook his head. "As I recall, his folks came from over Lincolnton way. Now, May, their mama, grew up here. Her father was one of the mill foremen — his name was Al Tanner. The family lived in the mill village. I can run you by there if it'd help."

"Travis Whitman gave me a quick tour yesterday. Maybe we could go through again later. Today, let's keep to the schedule you've laid out. Who's next?"

"Guy named Dwayne Simmons. He was a teacher at Whitman-Brown. There was talk at the time that he knew more about what happened to her than he let on."

"Any particular reason why?" Dodger asked.

"Well, he did get into trouble over her the year before she disappeared. Got suspended from his teaching job and never went back to it. Don't ask me what for because I never knew. It was just something the grown-ups whispered about. All I know for sure is he left practically overnight. The end of one term he was there and the beginning of the next he wasn't; and people said it had to do with Danny. He didn't even stay in town — got a job in Hotlanta and stayed gone until five or six years after I came back myself."

"So you haven't been here the whole time since 1993?"

"No way," Sutton laughed. After high school, I got a job in Charlotte that summer with my uncle at his garage, then in the fall I started at State in criminal justice, worked security details in the summers, and after graduation in '97 was recruited for the security department at BellSouth, stayed there until '02 when they downsized the group, consulted for ADT for a year, and then heard the old deputy sheriff died and there was an opening here. Mr. Whitman interviewed me himself."

Dodger digested this as Sutton pulled to a stop and parked on the main street in front of a tidy, two-story white-frame house with gingerbread picked out in pale buff. The picket fence around the front yard was in perfect repair, the hedge well trimmed, and all leaves raked from the patch of grass.

As they opened the gate and went up the brick walkway to the porch, Dodger thought he saw a curtain in the hall drop into place. Someone was monitoring their approach.

Just as Sutton put his hand up to the knocker, the door flew open, and a short, rotund man with a bald head and smiling blue eyes motioned them in. He wore slacks and a white shirt, and his shoes — unlike those of almost everyone else in town — weren't of the athletic variety but were, rather, well polished brown leather loafers.

"Deputy Sutton, it's always good to see you, and this must be Mr. Dodger? Gentlemen, welcome to my home. As it's a warm day, I felt you might be ready for something cool and tasty, so there's lemonade and cookies in the parlor. Please join me."

If he were uncomfortable with their visit, he hid it well, Dodger thought. In fact, if anything, he seemed delighted to have their company as he fussed over them, handing out lace-trimmed napkins and arranging coasters to protect the surface of the pretty tables.

"Now," he said, at last settling into a chair with his own glass and cookie, "I understand that Mr. Dodger would like to speak with me about Danny Standridge."

"Yes," Dodger said, awkward at the prospect of bringing up a distasteful topic.

As if sensing what his visitor was thinking, Simmons at once put him at his ease. "Have you heard something about what happened between Danny and me?"

"Not as such," Dodger said, "just that you might know her better than most of her teachers."

Sutton gave him an amused glance, but said nothing.

"That's true," Simmons sighed. "That's what caused the trouble to begin with. If I hadn't known her so well and tried to help her, none of what happened would have happened."

Dodger lifted his eyebrows. "You're losing me, Mr. Simmons."

"Dwayne," Simmons corrected him. "Do call me Dwayne."

"Then call me Art," Dodger said. "Now, about what happened, could you start from the beginning?"

"It's always so hard to know about beginnings, isn't it, Art? It almost seems as if one minute nothing's happening, and the next things have gone on, so you know something's begun just not when."

"Well," Dodger struggled to get the conversation back on track, "let's start at the very beginning. When did you meet Danielle?"

The answer was prompt and businesslike.

"When I first came to Whitman, back in '84, I taught second grade while I waited for a position to open up at the high school, which was what I trained for. The year Danny and her family moved to Whitman, which was a few months later, she was just starting second grade. I met her then. I could tell at once that she was an exceptional child, truly exceptional. Even at that age, she could understand anything you might bring up in class, and she would ask the most unexpected questions. I remember we did math exercises at the start of the term, simple things like one plus one equals two, and when I asked if there were questions, Danny asked me why 'two' is 'two'. I misunderstood at first and re-explained the solution to the problem. She listened, and then said she understood that part but what she wanted to know was why 'two' is 'two'. 'Who made it two?' as she put it. Why wasn't it something else? Who had the right to say?" He stopped and looked at his two visitors. That little girl at the age of seven was asking one of the most basic of questions relating to symbolism and meaning, one debated by philosophers since the Greeks. Amazing, absolutely amazing."

"Amazing," Dodger agreed, impatient to get to what had happened when Danielle was a teenager not when she was seven.

"In any event," Simmons continued, "The child did well in her classwork, although perhaps not quite as well as I expected because she didn't pay attention, I expect because she didn't have to. At the end of the term I advised the principal to make sure the girl was evaluated and tested for advanced placement. Then I'm afraid I lost track of her, as I went to Whitman-Brown High School to teach Junior and Senior English. When she showed up at Whitman-Brown, I'd been teaching there long enough to have set up a special honors track for the students who qualified, which Danny did. The track involved several options for extra coursework. All of them required after-school time a couple of days a week, and each student had to select one option in order to remain in the honors track. Danny came to me and asked if she might do more than one of the options, and of course I agreed, thinking she meant to do one extra course. Instead, she began to take part in all of them, which meant she was at the school from three to 3:45, then from 4:30 to 5:15 most days. I suppose that was the 'beginning' you're referring to, which is to say the start of the trouble."

"How so?" Dodger didn't see how an honors program could be a problem.

"The forty-five minutes between the two after-school sessions I spent in my office, grading papers or getting ready for the next honors group, and I got in the habit of letting the girl come with me. I'd do whatever I had to do and she'd sit on the sofa and study. There was a teacher named Martha Montgary who resented my being allowed to set up the honors track, and she reported me to the administration. She told them it was possible that inappropriate activities were taking place in my office in that forty-five minutes. The principal interviewed Danny, who was fourteen at the time, and asked her questions about what she called our 'relationship'. The way Danny answered them could be misinterpreted to mean that something had gone on between us. They issued a caution, and then allowed me to resign as of the end of the term. I moved to Atlanta and went to work for BellSouth. I didn't move back to Whitman until my mother became ill four years ago and needed help." The reflective mood sat uneasily on the laugh lines of his round face. "I suppose you could say that Danny was why I left teaching."

"And you didn't blame her for that?"

"It was hardly her fault," Simmons pointed out. "She intended me no harm. She cried when I told her I was leaving."

Dodger looked at the man, wondering if he could be as clueless as he seemed. Didn't he realize what most people would think in such a situation — pretty girl, unmarried teacher, unsupervised time together in his office? Which was the true story — the one he'd just told them or the one the principal had inferred? Was it possible something had been going on between this man and the smart, attractive girl? He didn't seem the type, but such men often didn't.

He heard the front door open and close and seconds later a tall, lanky man came into the room and hesitated when he realized they were there.

"Harry, come in and meet Art Dodger. He's been asking about that poor Danielle Standridge. You remember, the girl I told you about who was so remarkable in second grade."

Dodger stood up and extended his hand.

"Art, this is my partner Harry Gray. We met in Atlanta, but now we're certified Whitman-ites."

"Mr. Dodger," Gray said in a deep voice, giving Dodger a firm handshake.

"Call me Art," Dodger said as Sutton caught his eye.

On the way back to the car, each carrying a cookie pressed on them by Dwayne Simmons, Sutton said that Mr. Simmons was a good teacher.

"He made you work, but you felt like you got something from it. It's too bad they forced him to quit, and he just went along with it."

"Things were less open then," Dodger pointed out. "That could be a motive. He and Danielle were close enough that she might have learned something he didn't want shared."

"I don't buy it," Sutton said after thinking about it. "For one thing, unless he flat out told her something dangerous, how would a student like Danielle have learned anything? For another, he'd not the type."

"Because he offered us cookies?"

"Maybe," Sutton conceded, grinning.

Ten.

. . ●●●❂●●● . .

At the Library

They were eating dessert at The Tastee Grill, cherry pie for Dodger and apple pie a la mode for Sutton, when the deputy's phone buzzed. He looked at its screen.

"Mrs. North is ready for you at the library," he announced.

"Then let's go," Dodger said, pulling out his wallet to leave a tip.

He left the window down as Sutton drove through the too-quiet town, and the air of the late-September afternoon had just the right amount of warmth to temper its underlying coolness. They moved past empty storefronts, the boarded-up four-story, circa 1925 red-brick hotel, and a misguided 1980s attempt to turn the center of town into a brick-paved pedestrian street complete with ornate iron-and-wood benches. The library and its grounds occupied all of a short block. It was the only building with cars parked in its lot, also the only one that appeared to have had its trim work recently painted. This was the "Mary Green Whitman Memorial Library," recipient of Travis Whitman's ongoing largesse. He followed Sutton between the Doric-capped columns and through a door with a semi-oval skylight over it.

Inside, in the center of the large front room, sat a girl, fingers flying over a computer keyboard as she looked from the screen to a wooden box of index cards. The library, Dodger guessed, was still in the process of digitizing some of its records. There were two doors at either side of the desk she occupied. Sutton knew where to go, for he did not hesitate as he turned toward the one at the right, which led to a hall off which several doors opened. Lisa North emerged from the end space and motioned them to join her. Today, she wore a conservative gray pant suit with a white silk shirt and, if anything, looked sexier than on the night of the dinner.

"This is the room where we sort the returns," she told Dodger. "The returns can be made any time of day or night, either at the front desk or through the big brass drawer you see over there. The books are put into the rolling shelves and then brought here to the end table for sorting."

"I see," Dodger said. "So this was the room where Danielle worked on her paper. Has it changed much?"

North shook her head. "Not at all. Danny was set up at the table at the other end, because the old textile archives are on the shelves just there, to the side."

"And not just anyone could wander in here?" Dodger confirmed.

"The only people who came in here while Danny was working, as far as I know, apart from the library staff, were Charlotte Whitman, Danny's father and my brother, of course. Most of the time she worked alone unless one of the staff came to sort books."

"It'd be useful to see the paper she was working on. Have you been able to learn whether any copies survived?"

"As to that," she smiled, "I have what I think may be a welcome surprise for you. I found some of it. Not the paper *per se*, but materials related to it in a folder kept by Mrs. Wheelock, the head librarian. In fact, yesterday I located several things I think you'll find interesting. I've set them out."

She led him to the long table that Danielle had used. Arranged in neat stacks on its scarred wood sat a variety of files and loose papers, together with a manila folder and a large scrapbook.

"First, here's the outline and précis. The next file contains the interlibrary-loan requests the girl made throughout the year she disappeared. Next you'll see a letter from Charlotte Whitman to Mrs. Wheelock asking her to give the girl every consideration as she researches and writes her paper. The scrapbook contains newspaper clippings about Whitman-Brown Mills. The manila folder next to it has a collection of postcards showing the mill and the town. And here's what I've been able to turn up, so far, from the files of the old newspaper office. They sent their morgue — their archives — over to us when the paper shut down eight years ago. We've been downsizing ourselves, and no one's had time to catalogue them, but I spotted this file on Danielle Standridge because it was so much thicker than any of the others. There's another file somewhere else, because this one seems to end before the disappearance. They would have started another file then because this one is already full."

"I'll say," Dodger replied, impressed.

"That's all I've come up with so far, but I'll keep looking."

He grinned. Lisa North might be a bitch and a half, albeit gorgeous, but he gave big points for this level of efficiency.

"It'll take a while to go through this," he told her. "Is it okay if I do it here?"

"Of course. Travis said you're to be given every possible courtesy."

"Then, I'm for the salt mines," he grinned.

"You want help?" Sutton asked.

"I wouldn't know what to tell you to look for," Dodger admitted. "Why don't you go back to the station and leave me to it?"

"I'll return in a couple of hours," Sutton said, his expression happy at the prospect of resuming his regular routine. "If you need me before that, call."

Dodger watched the two of them leave, and then he was alone with the archives. He opened the fat scrapbook first, and found a Whitman-Brown Mills Corporate Library stamp on the inside front cover. This was the official newspaper record of various events in the life of the enterprise, everything from the appointment of officers to the introduction of new technology and the announcement of fabric innovation. It ended, he noticed, just as the mills began to slow, the last clipping about the transfer of certain product lines abroad, several years before Danielle disappeared. This wasn't the sort of information he needed, so he turned to the files and began his search for clues about the life of the missing girl.

It was when he got to Danielle's outline and précis for her paper that he understood what Dwayne Simmons had meant when he said the girl's mind was exceptional. In spite of the childish handwriting, it was hard to believe a fifteen-year-old girl had produced what he held in his hands. Not because he thought it had anything to do with what had happened to her but because he thought it would intrigue Jess, he got out his iPad mini, tapped the *CaptureMe* icon and scanned both outline and précis. Next he examined photocopies of the interlibrary-loan requests the girl made in the year she disappeared and scanned them as well. Each slip, printed by someone who took care to form the letters with exactitude, showed author, title, publisher, and date of publication. The requests formed a mixed bag. Andrews's *The Men and the Mills: A History of the Southern Textile Industry* was followed by Cash's *The Mind of the South; Clark's Directory of Southern Textile Mills, 1912-1970*; Conway's *Rise Gonna Rise: A Portrait of Southern Textile Workers*; Houston's *Shakespearean Sentences: A Study in Style and Syntax;* Marlow's *The Loom of Sappho's Sisters;* Sinclair's *Industrial Security: The Good, The Bad and The Ugly;* Thompson's *Social Construct and Personal Identity;* and Warner's *Brown Lung: Causes and Consequences.*

Dodger re-read the list, and guessed it might represent requests for materials relating to other schoolwork in addition to the paper on the textile industry.

The postcards varied in subject matter and quality, but the earlier, hand-tinted cards had a mellow beauty that surprised him. He scanned several, mostly of the mill buildings from across the river.

He turned next to the fat clippings file Lisa North had turned up. He hoped that this was where he might find something to give him an idea as to what Danielle, the girl, had been like.

The typed label on the file tab said "Standridge, Danielle Elizabeth," and the items at the back, the oldest, were dated years before the girl's disappearance. There were press photographs and clippings about dance recitals, essay contests, choir concerts, church outings, prize days at school, and holiday festivals. In the earliest, Danielle was a pretty little girl, always the standout among peers. In the more recent, she was becoming the teenager who turned heads wherever she went. Dodger didn't bother scanning any of those materials unless the photograph included both her and her sister Debbie. Those, he thought, might come in handy should he speak to Debbie again.

When he reached the year 1992, he took out his magnifying glass and studied each photograph with greater care. The very first photograph showed Danielle as one of three students receiving an award from Charlotte Whitman while town dignitaries, among them Travis Whitman, looked on. It was when Dodger looked at the photograph a second time that he realized what was odd about it: everyone else looked at the students, but Travis Whitman had eyes only for his wife. The next item wasn't an original photograph but a page clipped from the

Whitman *Courier Loom* describing the Whitman-Brown High School majorette tryouts the summer of 1992. The photographs showed a dozen girls vying for two vacant positions. Even in grainy, yellowed newsprint, it was Danielle you noticed first. The camera loved the girl.

The next clipping from October 1992 showed the Whitman-Brown majorettes posed in uniform with their batons held aloft in front of the high school. The next 1992 item was an article about Whitman-Brown students who volunteered with Meals on Wheels to deliver Thanksgiving dinner to housebound seniors — the photograph showed an earnest Danielle handing a plate to a man who was looking up at her, a grateful smile on his face, while another student served his wife.

A clipping from December 1992 was headed "Whitman-Brown Students Decorate City Hall" and pictured an enormous Christmas tree with Danielle straightening the star on top, while other students steadied the ladder and looked up at the jeans-clad girl. In January 1993 was an announcement that Danielle Standridge, daughter of Andrew J. and Mae T. Standridge, had received a scholarship to a summer camp for gifted students in a competition sponsored by a national textile foundation for the minor children of textile workers.

The next month offered up a full-page article about the students who'd been inducted into the Whitman-Brown Honors Club, which was — the writer proclaimed — "limited to sophomores, juniors, and seniors who'd exhibited the highest levels of academic achievement and personal integrity." An individual photograph of each of the inductees accompanied the article. This time, the format was so standardized that Danielle, in a dark blouse with a white collar like the other girls, came across as pretty, no more.

Then there was nothing until May, when an 8x10" glossy with crop marks showed Charlotte Whitman presenting a large trophy to Danielle while three men and a woman looked on. Everyone watched the award recipient, save for Travis Whitman, who — as in the earlier photograph of prize giving — was focused on his wife, who was herself smiling at Danielle. The girl was in a sweater and skirt, while the grown-ups wore business suits and dresses. As with the other photographs, hers was the most vivid presence, so defined and crisp that all of the adults, save for the fair-haired Charlotte Whitman, were no more than a pallid supporting cast. Pasted on the back of the photo was a word-processed strip of paper dated 6/1/93, identifying Danielle as the winner of the WB Honors Award and the five adults as the mayor, town clerk, president of the Chamber of Commerce, president of Whitman-Brown Mills, and "the lovely Mrs. Travis Whitman."

Dodger scanned this photograph, front and back, and kept going. Summer seemed slow as far as student coverage was concerned, as the only glossy from those months showed Danielle and several classmates cavorting with inner tubes at a local lake, with a caption that read "Taking a Break."

In August, things picked up. There were a couple of shots of Danielle and the other Whitman-Brown majorettes at practice on the school's football field in shorts and halter-tops. Next came a large article about the movie that was to be shot in and around the town. Several locations were mentioned, among them the Whitman Baptist Church, the high-school football field, Ceil Mountain Gap, Clumber House, and Whitman Memorial Cemetery. Mention was made of the fact that the Whitman-Brown majorettes would appear in the film, and each member of the squad was named, including Danielle. Then there was a duplicate of the press photo he'd already seen of the majorettes in the movie costumes. All this he scanned.

There was nothing discordant in any of the images or information in the file. Even at this remove, it was clear that Danielle had been a girl of great promise who'd used her abilities to the extent that a setting like Whitman afforded. A senior at fifteen, she was embedded in the community, not a girl to remain apart, waiting until her exceptional abilities would take her off to college and, in all likelihood, a life very different from those her fellow students could expect. Or her sister Debbie, Dodger thought, with a sudden appreciation for what childhood was like for the older sister of this paragon.

Turning back to the file, he found one last photograph, very different from the others. Another 8x10", it showed Danielle in the period majorette uniform from the movie, perched on the hood of a blue 1990 Plymouth Sundance. She'd removed the tall white hat, which now lay on its side next to her. In her lap was a book, on which she was focused, her body curved in a studious slump, her long, dark hair obscuring part of her face, one hand propped on the car's hood, the other poised to turn a page.

The intimacy of the image took his breath away. The girl obviously had no idea she was being photographed. What he saw now was the real Danielle, not the one putting on a face for the benefit of cameras or award-givers. He flipped the Kodacolor print over to find taped to its back a glassine envelope containing what appeared to be the original negative and a release form signed by Jason Sutton, together with a receipt for $15.00. The information on the release form showed the photograph was taken at four p.m. 9/24/93 at Whitman Mall, the exact time and place where the girl had last been seen.

He was, he realized, looking at what might be the last photograph ever taken of Danielle Standridge, and Deputy Sutton was the photographer. He felt the hairs rise on the back of his neck.

Eleven.

..·••◕◑◕••·..

Reporting In

Dodger sat on one of the iron-and-wood benches and stared at the brick pavement as he waited for Jess to get back to him. All around, leaves in shades of purple, yellow, gold, and red rustled in a brisk breeze. One other person was making use of the benches in the pedestrian area, a black man of indeterminate age holding a paper bag and dressed with painful respectability although even from here Dodger could see that his shoes were old and worn and the sleeves of his coat rumpled and frayed. He caught Dodger looking at him, got up and moved on with a disappointed air. Dodger felt bad for disrupting whatever comfort he found on the hard, unyielding bench and wondered what his story was. Was he disabled? Was he an alcoholic? Was he one of those who'd been made redundant when the mill closed and had returned when he'd been unable to find another job anywhere else? Or maybe he was one of those lost souls who seemed to turn up wherever you went nowadays.

His cell vibrated. It was Jess.

"Hi, sorry I couldn't talk earlier, but there was a writer in my office about a Maxcliff profile for a *Vanity Fair* article she's writing."

"I know that made your day."

"Hey, it's publicity. Until I get the guts to kill him off, the guy's a good meal ticket. Anyway, I learned something from her that might be interesting."

"As in..."

"A friend of this writer has been trying to sell *VF* on the idea of a major piece on unsolved disappearances of teenaged girls."

"Huh. That's quite a coincidence. How'd it come up?"

"She told me what a coup it is to be featured in *VF,* as if I didn't know that, and gave her friend as an example. So far, they've turned him down. I said that was too bad and asked if he'd already written the piece. She said all he'd done was make a few phone calls and write a proposal. I asked her if these are the same cases you see over and over again on those TV shows about crime, and she said no. It seems he's come up with half a dozen girls whose stories when they disappeared had been treated as simple runaways but who hadn't afterwards turned up."

"So Danielle might be on his list," Dodger said.

"It's possible."

"I wonder how he generated the names, given that runaways wouldn't have gotten much publicity?"

"She said he got the idea from a Facebook page set up by relatives of a girl who's been gone for ten years, so he started trolling social media."

"If he found his subjects online, I doubt Danielle is one of them. Her disappearance predated widespread Internet use, and I'm not sure there's anyone left who cares enough that she never came home to send out so much as a tweet, much less set up a Facebook page."

Even as he made the comment, Dodger was surprised at his disappointment. It would be interesting to see what a writer exploring disappearances of several teenaged girls thought of the way in which Danielle vanished.

"You may be right," Jess conceded. "But I told her I might be able to point him toward a publisher if he wanted to do a book. She said she didn't have permission to give out his contact information, so I gave her mine. I'll let you know if he gets in touch."

"That'd be good."

"So you don't think there's anyone in Whitman still missing Danielle? That's sad."

"I don't understand it," Dodger admitted, "but I can't come across any evidence that anyone's given her much thought since she vanished. With one exception, and that reminds me of something else I need for you to do."

"And what's that?"

"First, I'm sending you a picture."

"Something artistic, I hope."

"Don't get your hopes up. The afternoon I arrived in Whitman, one of the servants slipped me into what looks like a museum in one of the rear rooms on the second floor of Whitman's house, and I sneaked this picture of one of the displays when he was fiddling with the light switch."

"Got it. Whatever it is. This is bizarre. What are they supposed to be?"

"It's four mannequins dressed like Danielle. It seems that Charlotte Whitman — at least I assume it was all down to her — went around after the girl disappeared and gathered up anything she could find to do with her. These mannequins are dead doubles for Danielle as she appears in the photographs taken not long before she vanished."

"Which means they had to be custom made," Jess told him. "So what is it you want me to do?"

"While I was examining them, Billy — the one who took me to the room — pulled up the sleeve on the majorette outfit, and sure enough there was an embedded maker's mark inside the mannequin's wrist. The maker seems to be Display Dollies, and there was a number — M936-2, which I'm guessing relates to the model. Think you can locate the company?"

"Any idea of where they might be or when they were active?"

"Time-wise, let's say 1993-2000. As for where, the name and number were the only pieces of information on the embedded tag. Try New York or LA first. My guess is they're theatrical prop suppliers."

"And what do you want from them?"

"To see if they keep records of custom mannequins ordered. I'd like to confirm who ordered these and when, what was provided for reference, and if the company has any correspondence relating to the order in their files."

"Will do," she said. "What else?"

"I'm sending you a scan of a list of books."

"I'm waiting," she confirmed. "The Internet is acting up."

"What's the weather like there?" he asked, to kill time.

"Autumnal. How about there?"

"Same."

She laughed, and he could swear he felt sexy vibrations in the air.

"Got the list," she said. "What are you after re this?"

"I'm not sure. Those are titles for which Danielle put in interlibrary-loan requests the summer before she disappeared. They may not mean anything except that she was one conscientious student, but see what you can come up with. Don't bother with the ones that are about textiles — they're pretty self-explanatory. Go after the titles that are more general or about another topic entirely."

"All right. Anything else?

"You got any information yet on Lisa North and Randy Sizemore?"

"The brother-and-sister jerks? Haven't had a chance to look. It's at the top of my list for this p.m. I'll let you know what I come up with. How are you making out there?"

"All right, nothing spectacular but not a total waste. I'll tell you more tonight."

"I'll look forward to it."

"Me too," he said, meaning it, wishing that Jess were here, beside him in the bright September sun.

When they disconnected, he looked up the street to see if Sutton were underway, but the cruiser was still parked in front of the police station. He stood up and looked around. This area seemed to have been intended as a pleasant interlude for those cruising the shops of Main Street. There were not only places to sit but also trees to shade the area, not to mention a sculpture in the form of two female shoppers with overloaded bags. Trash receptacles with curved iron containers stood every few yards, and a label on each proclaimed that it was serviced by Municipal Outsourcing, the company to call should there be a problem. Another nicety paid for by Travis Whitman or his foundation? Dodger guessed so and wondered what would become of this place should Whitman tire of treating its transition as a form of expiation for his guilt.

He looked around at the stores, all of which were closed. From where he sat he could see the remnants of half a dozen signs: Colonial Tea Room; The Darling Shop; Flora's Flowers; Whitman Furniture; Greenstock Newsstand; and Talbot's Jewelry. The other stores lacked the dignity of even that degree of commemoration. He got up and made a tour, looking in the windows that were not boarded up or papered over from the inside. Some of the premises were empty, swept bare. Others still had merchandise on the shelves, as if the proprietors had become too discouraged even to call in the clearance services that bought remnant stock at deep discounts.

A horn blared, making him jump in the quiet afternoon. He turned to see Deputy Sutton waiting at the end of the pedestrian area in the cruiser.

"Admiring the town center?" he wisecracked as Dodger got into the passenger seat.

"It's well done. Someone spent real money," Dodger said.

"They did that when I was in grade school, right about the time they realized that the mall might kill the stores in town if the town didn't act fast."

"Oh, yeah, the mall," Dodger said. "That reminds me. Could we go there again?"

Sutton shrugged. "Sure. Any reason?"

"I'd like to take another look. I found a couple of photographs at the library that make me want to check something."

"In the old newspaper file Mrs. North found?"

Dodger nodded, watching Sutton to see if he'd react.

"Not surprised at that," he proclaimed. "The editor, Mrs. Johnston, was a real packrat. She had stuff in those files about everything that ever happened in this town."

"When did the paper shut down?"

"It must have been eight, nine years ago. She moved to Florida to live near her daughter."

"Is Mrs. Johnston still alive?"

"As far as I know. We can try to give her a call if you like."

As they talked, the cruiser had moved through the quiet streets. Now they were almost in front of the house in which Danielle and Debbie Standridge had grown up. The ancient Buick was nowhere in sight, but a small cluster of girls stood in the driveway, talking and laughing. Dodger guessed that one of them would be Ashley Jenkins and the others school friends. He debated asking Sutton to stop. He wanted to check out Danielle's old room, but decided to save it for another time.

If anything, the sign for Whitman Mall looked even more decrepit today and the few cars around the dollar store even lonelier. The cruiser bounced across the ruined pavement, back to where Sutton had stopped the first day.

"So, what now?" the deputy asked as he tapped the steering wheel with restless fingers.

"Who was the last person to see Danielle here at the mall that afternoon?"

"It was Mavis Cutliffe, Mavis Karroll as she was then. I double-checked the file, like you asked."

"What makes you think she was the last one to see Danielle?" Dodger persisted.

"One of the deputies — there used to be more than one — made up a list of where Danny was and when that afternoon. According to his schedule, several people noticed her trying the car doors and then giving up. A couple of others watched her climb up onto the hood. That was about 3:45. Then Mrs. Cutliffe saw Danny slide off the hood and wave to somebody. She knows it was after four because she was waiting for her husband in their car and had just checked her watch."

"Could she see who?"

"The list of times doesn't say. And Mrs. Cutliffe is where the list ends."

Dodger thought about that for a minute.

"Okay, then, let's go at it from a different angle. You were here." He said it as a statement to see what Sutton would say.

"Yeah, I was a member of the Photography Club, and we'd come to shoot the majorettes for the school paper."

"Did you notice anything unusual?"

Sutton thought about it and shook his head. "Not that I remember, except for the big truck and RV belonging to the movie people. They were parked back up there, at the far edge near the highway. And there was a big table next to the RV that had Cokes and cookies for anybody who wanted to go and talk with the crew."

"So the movie crew staged the mall show?"

Sutton nodded. "Like I said, they promoted it as their farewell to the town."

"They didn't do any actual shooting then?"

"Sure, they did. There was a videographer and a guy with this terrific Nikon kit. I remember we were all drooling — I checked on what it cost when I got home, and it was as much as my old car. The official videographer and photographer were set up near the majorettes, taking shots of the whole show. I didn't notice them pay any attention to any one girl, even Danny. They were talking. From what you could hear, they were ready to get away from here and back home. I remember being surprised, and it began to hit me that what looked so glamorous from outside was just a job for them."

"Did you notice anybody or anything out of place?" Dodger asked, trying another tack.

Sutton thought about it, frowning. "Not really. Just the usual cars you'd expect to see, what with people heading for the shops and some who'd come to see the majorettes do their routine or who wanted to jaw with the movie people."

"All right, think about it from a different angle. Who do you remember seeing here?"

"Well, there was that hot red Porsche 911 of Mrs. Whitman's. I remember I was surprised to see it 'cause I thought she was out of town with Mr. Whitman. And the old Olds that Mrs. Hufstutler, the principal always drove. And the blue '93 Toyota of Ms. North, Miss Ryan as she was then. And Mrs. Standridge's '90 Sundance. And the '92 Taurus that Mr. Karroll bought second hand. That's all I remember in particular."

Dodger grinned.

"What?" Sutton asked. "What's funny about that?"

"It's clear you were a teenaged boy at the time. You remember the people because of the cars, not the other way around."

Sutton shrugged, still irritated, but then his face changed.

"Wait up. I do remember somebody I didn't know."

"As in?" Dodger prompted.

"There was a Caddy, '91, I think. Dark, maybe black. Big fat guy at the wheel. I remember we kidded about how often he drove past the majorettes while they got ready to go on."

"And you didn't know him?"

Sutton shook his head. "Never saw him before, never saw him again, at least not to recognize. My guess is he just happened to come to the mall and found all the stuff going on and got a little too interested in the girls."

"Would there be any way to get the Caddy's license number?"

Sutton shook his head. "Not unless somebody got it in a picture. There wouldn't have been any reason to record it at the time, and the mall never ran to security cameras in the parking lot."

"So nobody else?"

"You know," Sutton recalled, "I'd forgotten the Ford Escort, '88 I think, that belonged to the guy in Blevins who was so obsessed with Danny. She told me he'd followed her around for months. As far as I know, she never reported it because he hadn't done anything all that terrible, just followed her and every once in a while made a weird phone call or sent her a note that didn't make sense."

It was the first time anyone had mentioned a stalker, and Dodger jumped on it at once.

"You wouldn't happen to remember his name?"

Sutton shook his head. "Not right off. I have an idea it might be in the police files because several people at the school knew about it. It was kind of joke. The kids called him 'Danny's Dunderhead.' I'll bet somebody at the school mentioned him to the sheriff after she disappeared."

"Can you take a look?"

"Sure. I'll have another go. I flipped through the the files when I knew you were coming, but I won't pretend I did anything else except check about a couple of specific facts you asked for. I'll see what a serious eyeballing can turn up."

Dodger stood on the rough pavement and looked around, trying to picture the mall as it was that day, with the stores open, people hurrying to their cars or into the mall, the majorette squad excited and giggling, men ogling them, the movie people wanting to get the afternoon over with so they could be on their way and locals trying to chat them up to see how to get in the movies. He thought about what Sutton had said about who was here.

"You said the Whitmans were away. How did you know?"

"Mrs. Whitman sponsored a club at school, and she missed a workshop she was supposed to give a couple of days before. They announced it was because she would be out of town with Mr. Whitman that week."

"So they must have come back early. Was Mr. Whitman with his wife at the mall?"

"No. I think she was alone, but it was hard to tell. Anyway, he couldn't have been there. As I recall, he was with some business types up north that day."

"Did you speak to her?"

Sutton shook his head. "I just saw her drive by from a couple of rows away."

"How about Mrs. Hufstutler, the principal. Is she still around here?"

"Not around anywhere," Sutton said. "She died a couple of years back."

"So you can't remember anything else you noticed the day of the disappearance that struck you as odd, then or now?"

Sutton shook his head. "Other than the movie people and the Whitman-Brown majorettes, it was just like any other Friday at the mall. Well, the mall as it was then." He looked at the desolate storefronts and shook his head.

"Where did the Whitman-Brown majorettes perform the routine from the movie?"

Sutton started up the cruiser and drove about two hundred feet to an area midway between the mall stores and the road that ran in front of the parking lot.

"There was a roped-off area just there," he said. "That's where they did the routine from the movie. Danny left right after that. I don't remember the exact time, but I'm guessing about 3:30. I remember they let school out an hour early for the celebration."

Dodger looked around and was surprised. "I didn't realize you couldn't see the main road from this vantage point."

"The mall was built in an area that's lower, which means that the bank dividing the parking lot from the road pretty well blocks being able to see in either direction unless you're on top of it." Sutton nodded toward the long hillock.

"And it was like that when Danielle disappeared?"

"Pretty much, except the trees and shrubs weren't as big."

"That explains how she could be driven away without anyone noticing from here."

Sutton turned around to look. "I guess so."

"Did you see what happened next, after Danielle left the roped-in area to return to her mother's car?"

"One of those guys from the movie crew talked to her for a couple of minutes. I didn't see anybody else go up to her. Lots of people were looking. People always looked at Danny, wherever she went, but I didn't notice anybody else speaking to her."

"Did you talk to her?"

Sutton shook his head. "I was busy with the Photography Club, over there. One of the guys had a new lens and we were all trying it out."

"Did you happen to see what she did when she reached her mother's car?"

"You mean the '90 Sundance? Sure. She walked around, trying the doors, but they were all locked."

"What then?"

"I was messing with Johnny's camera, so I didn't watch her the whole time."

Dodger took out his iPad mini and found the scan he'd made at the library.

"That was when you took this."

Sutton looked at the somewhat fuzzy image, perplexed. Then his face cleared. "We were testing the focal length."

"You'd forgotten that photograph?" Dodger let disbelief creep into his voice.

"It wasn't on my camera," Sutton explained. "It was on Johnny's. It's kind of coming back to me why I didn't remember the picture. I only saw it once. I think it surfaced when Mrs. Johnston appealed for anyone with any photographs of the afternoon to come forward, and Johnny did. A bunch of the kids in the Photography Club had messed with his camera during the afternoon; but, once the film was developed, this was the picture she wanted because it was the only one that showed Danny by herself. Johnny guessed I'd taken it and sicked Mrs. Johnston on me. I remember she came to the high school and gave me a few bucks and I had to sign something."

"A release," Dodger told him, showing him the scan of the form that he'd signed twenty years earlier.

For the first time, the significance of the photograph seemed to hit Sutton.

"Do you think this is the last picture of her?" he whispered.

"It's possible," Dodger said.

A choking sound escaped the deputy, and he turned his face away.

So there was someone who still cared, Dodger thought. He was glad. It'd be a shame if all that promise, all that loveliness had meant so little to those who'd known it best. He found himself feeling friendlier toward the deputy, who up until now had struck him as no more than a tool of Travis Whitman's.

"I'm sorry," Dodger said, meaning it. "I didn't realize you were that close."

"Danny was a couple of years younger, but she got double-promoted along the way and we ended up in the same class. We dated a couple of times," Sutton said, clearing his throat.

"What did you do on the dates?"

"The first time, we went to a school dance. The next time we went over to the movie theater at Blevins and saw *Jurassic Park*."

"What was your impression of Danielle? Was she the kind of girl who would have gone off with someone she didn't know? Could someone have tricked her, for example, claimed she was needed at home or school or anything like that?"

"No way," Sutton declared. "She was smart, and she was careful. A girl that pretty, she'd had guys hanging around with their tongues out since she was a kid, so she knew how to handle herself. A lot of the fellows wanted to go out with her, but I was the first one she said yes to."

Dodger thought about what Randy Sizemore had implied about Sutton being the school stud back in the day.

"Was she just another girl you dated, or was she special to you?"

"Who knows? I liked her a lot. I mean, what wasn't to like? I don't think I've ever seen a prettier girl. She was interesting. She could talk about things and she liked to hear you talk. More than that, she was different, like I said interesting. I've thought about her a lot since back then."

"What do you think would have happened between you if she hadn't disappeared?"

Sutton considered the question as if debating his reply.

"If you'd asked me then, when I was seventeen," he said, "I'd have guessed that we'd have gotten to know each other better, maybe even gone on to get serious, maybe even married. But if you're asking the grown-up me, I think she'd have gone off to college the next year and never come back. She was too smart for this place, maybe too smart for me."

"So what do you think happened to her?"

"I don't know what happened, but I can tell you what didn't happen," Sutton said, his face grim. "She didn't just walk away. She always did what she promised. She was supposed to do the movie routine with the other girls at the football game Friday night, and she and I had a date Saturday night. Plus, the next Monday she had some sort of special test at the school in connection with a scholarship thing Mrs. Whitman had set up for her. There's no way, she'd have just walked."

Twelve.

····●●●●●··· ·

Dinner Surprise

Dinner at Mill House was a different affair that night. There was a documentary on PBS about the decline of the American textile industry that Travis Whitman wanted to watch, and so he had Gladys set up individual tray tables in the library, where one of the sections of books could be pushed away to reveal a TV of impressive dimensions.

Dodger wondered if Whitman would use the show as an excuse to demonstrate his expertise, but he watched without comment, only nodding or shaking his head from time to time. Afterwards, when Dodger asked him if he thought the documentary accurate, all he said was, "It's correct in its facts, but it misses a lot of the underlying truths."

He did not explain further, and Dodger did not press him. He decided he could like Whitman, which wasn't good when you were on a quest like his. It helped to remain detached, to keep an open mind.

They finished third cups of coffee in silence, and Dodger was about to make his excuses to go up to his room when Whitman asked a direct question.

"Have you learned anything useful?"

"If you're asking do I have any better idea of what might have happened to Danielle Standridge, I have to say I don't. I am, on the other hand, getting a better handle on the situation at the time. Danielle seems to have had the kind of personality that attracted strong feelings."

Whitman nodded, as if pleased at the answer.

"My wife thought the sun rose and set in the girl. It just about destroyed her when Danny disappeared. That's the main reason I came to Mystery Mavens. I think if I can learn what happened to Danny it'll be a fitting memorial to Charlotte." He averted his eyes, and brushed at them with his open hand as if swatting a fly.

Dodger wasn't fooled. The man's grief remained fresh and present.

"Why do you think she was so emotionally invested in the girl?" he asked, shifting gears.

Whitman lowered his hand and looked displeased, whether at the question or what it implied Dodger couldn't tell. Whichever it was, he answered without hesitation, his frown relaxing as he spoke.

"Danny's family came to live in Whitman when she was a little girl. When we married and decided to make this house our primary residence, Charlotte took over a lot of what my mother always called the noblesse-oblige stuff. That included handing out prizes at the school, which was when she began to notice Danny. The girl was so bright that, from the beginning, she won anything going. That impressed Charlotte, and she made it a point to meet the girl's mother. When she realized that May Standridge had no particular interest in her daughter's exceptional abilities, she took it on herself to do something about the girl, and Danny became what amounted to a personal project. She bought her books she wanted that weren't in the public library, paid for her to go on field trips, sent her off for advanced testing, bought her a French horn when she joined the band, brought back souvenirs for her when we traveled, that sort of thing. More than the things she gave her, however, she encouraged the girl. No one in the family seemed to have any ambitions for her in spite of the fact that she was a brilliant student. At the time Danny disappeared, Charlotte was already working her network for a good scholarship. Her having Danny do the paper on the North Carolina textile industry was part of that campaign, as I mentioned the other night."

"I hope the girl appreciated what your wife was doing for her," Dodger commented.

Whitman shrugged. "Who knows with teenagers? At that age, you look at things differently. I'll admit I had misgivings. Charlotte spent so much time and money that I began to question whether it was healthy for either one of them."

"What do you mean?" Dodger asked, interested even though he couldn't see where all of this fit into the disappearance other than to highlight how much had been lost for all concerned.

"Well, it wasn't practical, was it? At the end of the day Danny would go to college and take up her own life, which was almost certainly not going to include Whitman. I didn't like to think of Charlotte becoming, in effect, just a stepping-stone for the girl. As for Danny, how would she handle the world without Charlotte there to smooth the way for her? I thought she might feel like a pet that has been abandoned."

"I see what you mean," Dodger said. "You were afraid that one or both of them would sooner or later be hurt by the association."

"It crossed my mind," Whitman admitted. "Still, it distracted Charlotte from the fact that we hadn't been able to have children even though she said she wanted them very much. So I kept my mouth shut and helped where I could without being too obvious about it. I even handled Andrew Standridge when it became apparent he resented the attention Charlotte showed Danny."

"That must have been hard when you disapproved yourself."

Whitman shot him a shrewd glance. "I gather you think my attitude was unjustified?"

"Not at all," Dodger said, shaking his head.

Whitman stood up. "Come with me. In order for you to get an accurate idea of the intensity of my wife's obsession with Danny, there's something you need to see."

To Dodger's surprise, Whitman led the way to the elevator and then along the upstairs corridor to the room that held the mini-museum.

He paused outside the door. "What's in here will give you an idea of how much Charlotte thought of Danny. Just remember, the woman who had it put together was half-crazy with grief."

He flung open the door, flicked a light switch and ushered Dodger inside.

"After Danny's disappearance, Charlotte collected anything she could find connected with her. There are letters, school annuals, art projects, even her French horn, the one that Charlotte had bought her years before, and the band letter she earned with it. I'm not even sure of what's in here – it's been a long time since I took a good look at it."

"Where did she get all of it?"

"Most of it came from Danny's family and the school."

"Figures," Dodger murmured.

"I should probably do something about it, but what?"

"Hard to say," Dodger commented in much the same tone.

"I suppose you're shocked?"

"Not shocked, just surprised," Dodger said. And he was, for the platform that extended between the cases was now empty and the mannequins that had stood on it were nowhere to be seen.

Thirteen.

.··○○●○○○··.

Jess Scores A Hit

So the mannequins are gone?" Jess sounded shocked. "Because here's the weird part. I got lucky with Display Dollies. I not only located them out in LA, but their PR person is a guy my sister was in school with. He likes the possibility of the company being featured in a *VF* profile, which was the story I spun him when I Dropboxed the pic of the mannequins — told him I'd seen them and been impressed. They've already emailed me what's left in their files on this particular order so I can use it as deep background re their process, soup to nuts, so to speak. All I had to do was commit not to use what they sent me in any identifiable form."

Dodger leaned back against the pillows of the four-poster guest-room bed and propped the phone on his chest. "You're amazing. So who ordered them?"

"My new buddy redacted most of the name and card number, but it's pretty clear it was Travis Whitman and he used his Amex. As for what they were given as reference, it was a series of photographs taken of Danielle rehearsing for a school play. At least, that's what it looks like. She's in some kind of evening-type dress. No, wait, there are two different dresses, and she's wearing a necklace with one and a long evening scarf with the other. The set looks like a Chinoiserie-style library. You know, dragons painted on the wall around bookcases and a big brass thingy in the shape of a temple in the middle of the room."

"What about correspondence?"

"There's none of that, just an order form and invoice. The order form has measurements for the mannequins, tied to a numbered photograph. That's why they're not identical. The company was instructed to model the individual mannequins after individual photographs."

"I didn't notice they were different," Dodger admitted.

"No attention to detail," Jess teased.

"That's why I have you," he told her, grinning.

"Anyway, the tag you saw is on the second of the four ordered."

"Okay, Dropbox me the photographs that were used as reference. I've set up a folder for everything I can find relating to the girl. They might as well be added to it."

"Got it. I'll do it as soon as we get off. Now, as to the jerky brother and sister, I don't have much yet. Do you want it?"

"Just give me the gist and email the rest," he said.

"For one thing, they aren't related. Lisa's family name is Ryan, not Sizemore. Her mother married his father when Lisa and Randy were teenagers. After that, they lived in Virginia, in one of those towns that ring D.C. The parents both worked for the government before retirement. They live in London now. Lisa's got a Master's in Library Science and memberships in several professional organizations. Randy has a Master's in Teacher Ed with a specialty in sports. I'm not finding anything to suggest he's been married. She married a Harrison North in 1996, divorced 1999, no children. Get this, it was Harrison who divorced her, citing infidelity with an unnamed correspondent, and she didn't contest it."

"Interesting. Where's Harrison North now?"

"I haven't turned up his address yet. How much work do you want put into it?"

"Not a lot more. I'm surprised you got that much that fast."

"It's thanks to public records and a decent biographical profile with an online article contributed by Lisa to a professional journal," she laughed.

"You've taken all the magic away," he griped. "God, I wish you were here. There's something odd about all this, something disturbing. I don't know if it's because the girl was so young and exceptional, or because there seems to be not that much interest in what happened to her. There's just something *off*. It'd be good to have a second opinion."

"If you find you really need me, I'll come down," she promised. "Just whistle."

"You're assuming I know how to purse my lips," he laughed.

"That I'm sure of," she purred, and a thrill of pure pleasure worked its way through Dodger's muscular frame and to the tips of his disheveled hair. This woman got through to him like no one else. He had to find a way to get back to that night of unexpected intimacy they'd shared the year before. Or, if a rerun proved impossible, accept that their relationship would ever after be no more than a teasing give and take based on a risqué memory. Which was better than nothing, he thought, but not much.

Fourteen.

..·oo**·oo·.

Bound for Blevins

Dodger drove the van into town the next day. If they got back from their rounds while the light was good enough, he'd spotted a street scene the afternoon before that he wanted to paint, and it was easier to bring the van full of supplies than to anticipate what he'd want when the time came.

"Okay if I leave this parked here?" he asked.

"Might be safer out back in the lot," Sutton told him. "That's why mine was in the shop the other day. This drunk came through town and careened off the cars that were parked out front of the station. Cost the town over two grand in bodywork even on my old heap. I'd hate for anything to happen to a vehicle as nice as this."

He gazed with admiration at the shiny white ProMaster.

"Okay," Dodger grinned. "I appreciate it. Just show me where to go."

Once they were both in the police cruiser, Sutton pointed it in the direction of Blevins, the larger town to the west.

"I checked the file and found the name of the guy I remembered from the mall that afternoon — you know, the one who'd been following Danny. It's Bo Carter. I planned on us seeing Mavis Cutliffe, the Standridges' neighbor, first thing this morning, but it turns out Carter lives just a couple of blocks away from her, so we can make a quick stop there first if that suits you."

"Sounds fine," Dodger assured him. "Did the police talk to him at the time?"

"Looks like somebody might have done a phone interview."

"That's all? For a known stalker?" Dodger was surprised.

"Hey, don't blame me," Sutton protested as they rolled out of town. "I wasn't even out of high school."

"And no one's since requested that the disappearance be treated as a cold case?"

"Not that I can tell from the file," Sutton said. "I know nobody's asked me to re-open it since I came on the force, which was seven years ago."

"So," Dodger said, abandoning the line of thought as nonproductive, "what's this guy Carter do?"

"Nothing," Sutton answered. "He was a truck driver. Then he had an accident and was able to claim partial disability. He stays home with the kids while his wife works as a clerk at Bank of America in Blevins."

The street on which Carter lived held small frame houses on tidy lots. Apart from a front-yard assortment of brightly colored plastic toys, Carter's modestly attractive residence was as neat and well maintained as the others on the block.

Bo Carter answered the door at once, as if he'd been watching. His expression showed that this was not a good day, and the arrival of Sutton and Dodger did not seem to be improving it.

"Oldest's got chicken pox," he groused. "You ever tended a kid with chicken pox? How do you get 'em to eat what they're supposed to and not eat what they're not supposed to?"

Dodger shrugged. "No idea."

"I just threw up my hands and called my wife," Sutton said, trying to lighten the moment.

"Is that a dig? My wife works because she wants to." Mrs. Carter's job seemed to be a sore point with her husband.

"Okay, buddy. Your marriage is no concern of ours," Sutton assured him. "As I mentioned on the phone, all we want is to ask you a couple of questions about Danielle Standridge."

"Don't remember her," Carter said, his expression sullen.

"Come on, dude," Sutton said. "I knew Danny. I was there. Everybody knew. You followed her around for months in that junker car of yours."

"I don't know what you're talking about," Carter insisted, turning pink.

"Your name is Frank Carter, known as Bo, right?" Sutton asked. "Well, then, you're on record back in September 1993 admitting that you'd gotten into the habit, as you put it, of 'staying close to her to make sure she's all right'. How can you pretend not to remember talking to the police?"

"Oh, you mean the girl who disappeared, don't you? See, the thing is, I didn't remember the name." He leaned toward them and shrugged with open palms. "Sorry."

"I understand you were at the mall the afternoon she disappeared," Dodger said.

"Was I?" Carter tried to look innocent. "If you say so. I don't remember."

"It was the afternoon the Whitman-Brown majorette squad did a routine in the mall parking lot," Sutton prompted. "There was a big movie-company truck there."

"Yeah, okay, if you say so, I was there. So?"

"What did you do?" Sutton asked.

"Man, I don't remember. That was, what, twenty, twenty-one years ago? That's a lifetime around here. Anyway, after my accident, I don't remember so good. I'm guessing that, if I was at the mall, then I left the mall and came home."

"At the time, you told the police that you noticed an unfamiliar car at the mall, driven by a man who was showing too much interest in the majorettes. Do you remember that?"

"Nope." Carter yelped, his stance defiant. "Told you I have no recollection of any of that at all."

"You don't remember the last time you saw a girl you were so fixated on that you'd been stalking her for months?" Dodger frowned.

"I don't remember being that fixed on her. I just thought she was cute. If I hung around her a little, maybe even sent her mash notes, isn't that what teenagers do? If you ask me, if she didn't just leave on her own, it was one of those movie people who took her off. I sure didn't. Now, I don't have nothing else to say, and it's time to give the kids their mid-morning snack."

"We appreciate your time," Sutton said, rising. "We may need to come back and talk again."

"If you say so," Carter frowned. "Although I don't see the point of it. I've told you everything I know."

"People sometimes come up with additional information once

they've had time to think about it," Dodger pointed out. "If you do, here's my cell number. Give me a call, and you can tell me and I'll pass it along to Deputy Sutton."

Carter looked at Sutton, who nodded agreement, and took the card, examining its front and then turning it over to make sure that there was nothing on the back.

He looked up, and the expression on his sullen face shifted. "Listen, can you do me a favor?"

"Maybe," Sutton said, eyes cautious.

"My wife's not from around here. She's never heard about any of the stuff about Danielle — I believe you said? — and she'd think it's just plain silly that I ever acted the way you say I did. Can you please leave her out of this?"

"Will you promise to call us if you think of anything?" Sutton asked.

Carter nodded.

"Then we'll do the best we can to make sure she doesn't hear about it."

Dodger and Sutton went back to the car, Sutton to check in with the station and Dodger to make notes.

"Well," Dodger said once Sutton was done and about to turn the ignition key, "what do you think about Bo Carter?"

"Typical yahoo back then. Now, who knows?"

"Do you buy that he doesn't remember?"

"Not in a heartbeat," Sutton grimaced. "I'll bet he can describe every time he saw Danny, down to what she was wearing and the weather, maybe even what he had for breakfast."

"Do you see him as capable of causing her disappearance?"

Sutton thought about it. "My first reaction is no way, or at least he wouldn't have been up to it back then. He had to be kind of a doofus with that nickname."

"I'm not too sure," Dodger said. "Even goofballs can be murderous, given the right time and place."

"You said 'murderous' just then," Sutton pointed out. "Does that mean you think Danny was murdered?"

"I don't think anything yet," Dodger said, "but the odds aren't good. Think about it — nobody's seen or heard from her in twenty years."

"Guess not." Sutton looked glum. "It's just hard to process."

"Tell me about this woman we're on our way to see," Dodger said as the cruiser rolled two blocks further and came to a stop on another residential street, very much like the one on which Bo Carter lived with his family, save that the houses here were larger and more substantial looking.

"Mavis Cutliffe is her name. She's married now to James Cutliffe, who works as a manager at the fabrication plant. Back then she was Mavis Karroll. Her husband Harold worked as a manager at the mill."

"And she's the last person to see Danielle," Dodger remembered.

"That's it. There was nothing other than that in the file. I'm guessing that's about all she's going to say."

As it turned out, Sutton was wrong. Mavis Cutliffe, it turned out, had rather a lot to say and seemed relieved at the chance to say it. After confirming that she had indeed seen Danielle sitting on the hood of the Sundance, she provided more detail.

"I wasn't surprised when she slid off. The car hood had to be hot in the sun, especially with what she was wearing. Anyway, I'd noticed her while I was in our car, going over my grocery list. The next thing I knew she was sliding off and waving to somebody."

"Could you see who it was?" Dodger asked.

Mrs. Cutliffe shook her head. "The parking lot was pretty full, with all that was going on, and a couple of big pickups blocked the view toward where Danny was waving."

"What happened next?" Dodger asked.

"My husband Harold arrived back at the car, and we drove to the other end of the mall, to The FoodStop. That was where we always shopped."

"And you didn't see Danielle again?" Dodger persisted.

She shook her head.

"How about your husband?" Sutton asked.

"You'll have to ask him," Mrs. Cutliffe said. "I divorced Harold Karroll in 1995 and haven't laid eyes on him since."

"He left his job at the mill?" Dodger was surprised. That was years before the mill closed.

"Couldn't get out of town fast enough," Mrs. Cutliffe proclaimed. "Good riddance to bad rubbish. Turned out man was a, what is it they call it nowadays when grown-ups like children in the wrong way?"

84

"Pedophile, you mean?" Dodger asked, surprised.

"That's it."

"That's a serious accusation," Sutton said. "What makes you so sure?"

"We lived in one of those brick houses near the mall with a big basement. One day, I was looking for something down there, and I found a stash of tapes, books, and photographs. Filthy things. I was horrified."

"I guess so," Sutton said. "That's bad."

It hadn't occurred to Dodger that plain, old-fashioned pedophilia might have figured in Danielle's disappearance. Even though she was just fifteen, she'd seemed the kind of girl who was older than her years, not younger. Still, this opened new possibilities as to what might have happened to her.

"So I marched upstairs and told Harold he could clear out, right then, and I didn't expect any trouble about the divorce," Mavis continued. "And he didn't give me any, just quit his job, signed everything over to me, gave my lawyer his forwarding address and left. After that, the lawyers handled everything. I haven't seen or heard from him since."

"You didn't report him to the police?" Sutton asked.

She shook her head. "No, I didn't even tell the lawyer. What was the point? I just put the junk in a safe place so he couldn't find it — in case he changed his mind and I needed it for the divorce. Later, after realizing the Standridge girl never turned up, I thought maybe I should have, but by then it was late in the day."

"What about the Standridge girl?" Dodger broke in.

For the first time, the woman hesitated, a troubled look on her broad, pleasant face.

"Maybe I should have made it clear that the Standridges were our next-door neighbors. We lived in the house with the white trim and the big oak by the walk, just to the right of them if you face the houses."

Dodger nodded. He remembered the oak, the largest tree on the block.

"We'd been in our place for a couple of years when they bought theirs," she continued. "That would be about 1985. Debbie, Danny's older sister, was nine or ten and Danny a couple of years younger. I remember they were both cute little things, and at first Andy and May seemed like any other couple. To begin with, I expected we'd become friends. It makes things easier when neighbors get along. But we never did. Not that there were arguments or any sort of problem, but there was something about the situation in the Standridge house that made me uncomfortable from the beginning. Andy was too slick and smooth by half, and May was like somebody who was afraid to close her eyes or turn her back, like she was always waiting for something to happen. And some of the things they let those girls do shocked me, I'll admit it. I know times were changing even then, but it wasn't decent for them to let those girls swim without tops after they started developing. I know their pool was in the back yard, but they had to know we could see. Harold always used to fuss about it, said it wasn't decent and somebody ought to say something. When I asked him why didn't he talk to Andy, he said it would make things too awkward at work. I can't believe I just accepted it, but the job was everything. So we just shut the blinds on that side of the house and never looked out. At least I didn't. I never caught him peeking either, but who knows?"

She stopped, as if still wondering.

"Was that all, about the Standridges, I mean?" Dodger asked.

"No," she grimaced. "I was surprised one day when Harold suggested we try to get friendlier with them, said he'd heard that Andy might be about to get a promotion, said he might even end up the boss of the whole section. It was summer, and Harold wanted us to invite the Standridges to a pool party — most of the houses along there have pools, you know. I didn't want to do it, but he insisted, even had the pool cleaned."

"So what happened?" Sutton urged when she paused.

"Nothing. At the last minute, the Standridges had a family emergency come up that took them out of town. The next time he wanted me to ask them, they had another excuse. By the third time, even Harold figured out they had no intention of ever accepting our invitations, and he gave it up. He thought it was because Andy's dad was a lawyer over in Lincolnton and he thought he was too good to associate with mill people, even though he worked here himself. By then, Debbie was thirteen and looked older than she was. Acted older too. I saw her once when I was working in the side yard. We had what amounted to a forest of big old azalea shrubs there, and I was trimming them when I heard the Standridges' back door slam and Debbie came out, dressed in what my mother used to call a sun suit — just a little halter and tiny pair of shorts. It was way too small for her. By that time, she'd developed so you couldn't help but notice, and she was practically bursting out of it, which didn't seem to bother her a bit. While I was watching, she went to that little garden house next to their pool, took off her top and started playing with herself."

"What do you mean?"

Mrs. Cutliffe paused and blushed, then took a deep breath and continued.

"She played with her breasts, like a grown woman would in one of those porn videos Harold used to try to make me watch. It was unnatural, positively disgusting to see a girl her age act like that. What made it worse was that I happened to look up at one of the windows, and Andy was watching her."

"Was that the only time it happened?" Dodger asked.

"I have no idea. I avoided the side yard after that."

"Did you mention it to your husband?" Sutton asked.

"I'm ashamed to say I did. You have to remember that was before I suspected he had those kind of tastes himself."

"What was his reaction?"

"He made me describe what I'd seen twice, as if he hadn't believed it the first time. Then he said he hoped Standridge was just kidding around and wasn't doing anything bad with his daughters, especially not with Danny."

"He mentioned her by name in that context?" Dodger asked.

"Yes. I asked him why Danny especially, and he said because she was so young and sweet. I said that was an odd thing to say about someone else's child, and he just laughed and changed the subject."

"He didn't bring her up again?" Dodger broke in.

"Not that I recall, but I never forgot what he said and the odd look on his face, almost as if he was imagining something I couldn't see and he liked it."

"Did you ever say anything to May Standridge about the fact that you'd seen Andy watching their daughter act like that?" Sutton asked.

"I tried," Mrs. Cutliffe said. "It was the most peculiar conversation I've ever had with anyone. Maybe I was so embarrassed that I didn't describe it right, but she just blew it off. She said I had to be wrong about what I thought I saw, that the two of them had engaged in games since Debbie was a little girl and whatever I'd seen was just a bit of fun, nothing else, and not to worry myself about it."

"Did you go to the police about your suspicions?"

She shook her head. ""What could I say? That I'd seen a teenaged girl acting inappropriately in her own back yard? That I suspected her father spied on her to see her naked? They'd have laughed at me. You have to remember that Andy was one of the most popular men in town. It would have been hard for people to accept he was this monster who preyed on his own daughters."

"Did you tell Harold you'd gone to talk to May?" Dodger asked.

She nodded. "He hit the roof, said I could cost him his job and I had to promise to stay away from the Standridges, her and him. So I did. I felt guilty at first, but the girls seemed to turn out all right. Debbie was a little wild, but nothing out of the ordinary. As for Danny, she was everybody's dream child. In fact, things went so well for her that I remember thinking my worrying had been for nothing."

"What about after she disappeared? Did her parents say anything to you?"

"Andy didn't. May came over the next day, the first time in years. She told us Danny hadn't come home the night before and asked if we'd seen her. I remember Harold wasn't very nice to her.

Later, when I asked him why he'd acted so mean, he said he resented her assuming he knew where her precious daughter was. I thought he was upset because he and Andy weren't getting along at work or maybe because the Standridges always seemed to avoid us, so I didn't make a point of it."

"What did you think when she disappeared?" Dodger asked.

"'That she was like Debbie after all. Debbie had run off and come back several times, and I figured Danny had gone off with some boy and would show up sooner or later with her tail between her legs, expecting everybody to forgive her no matter what she'd been up to."

"But she didn't," Sutton pointed out.

"No, she didn't," Mrs. Cutliffe sighed. She was clearly embarrassed to admit her true feelings, now that it was years later and the girl remained missing.

"There's something I don't understand," Dodger said. "You mentioned that you regretted not saying anything about Harold's porn to the police once you realized the Standridge girl hadn't been heard from. When was that?"

"A couple of years after the divorce, so 1997 or 1998. I'd already sold the Whitman house and moved back to my parents' place, here in Blevins." She thought about it. "It was 1998. This young man showed up, said he was a reporter writing a feature on the fifth anniversary of the girl's disappearance and wondered if, as a former neighbor, I had any comment I'd like to make. I wasn't interested in raking up any of that again, so I said 'no', that both Danny and her sister Debbie had been delightful girls. It was when his article appeared in the Whitman paper that it hit me that maybe Harold might have had something to do with her disappearance."

"Why would you think that?"

"Because when we went to The FoodStop, after I saw Danny sitting on her mother's car, Harold said he didn't feel well and was going back to our car to sit down. He said he'd pick me up in front of the store in half an hour. After I read the article, I put two and two together and realized that was the exact time the girl disappeared."

"Did he pick you up on time?" Sutton asked.

"He was late. In fact, I was late and still had to wait for him. I was in the passenger-pickup lane in front of the store so long that I wondered if I'd missed him, but then I saw our car turn into the mall from the highway. When I asked Harold where he'd been, he said he'd gone home to get his stomach medicine. Because our house was just up the way, I didn't think anything about it."

"Until you read the newspaper article," Sutton put in.

"And knew by then that he liked young girls," Dodger added.

She nodded. "I thought about talking to the sheriff, but the article made it clear that both her family and the police still thought Danny had run away. The story even had a list of places she might have gone and why."

"What you've told us is very interesting, Mrs. Cutliffe," Sutton said. "I'd like to talk with your ex-husband. If you don't have any idea of where he is, is there anyone who might?"

She thought about it. "His parents are dead — thank the Lord. They were nice people and it would have killed them if they'd known about Harold. He didn't have any brothers or sisters. So, I'm not sure who would have kept up with him."

"You said the lawyers had a forwarding address at the time of the divorce," Dodger remembered. "What were their names?"

"I can do better than that," Mrs. Cutliffe said. "They still send me a Christmas card every year that has contact information. I tucked the last one into my address book."

She rummaged around in the drawer of the big desk that dominated the room and produced a card, which Sutton took.

"By any chance, do you have a photograph of your ex-husband?" Dodger asked.

She shook her head. "Not that I know of. I got rid of everything. I felt as if I'd been harboring a poisonous snake without realizing it. I didn't want any reminders."

"I understand," Sutton said.

"If you do find Harold, please keep my name out of it," she said. "He has a terrible temper."

Fifteen.

.·.∘°🌑⬤🌑°∘.·.

A Mother's Love

"W" hew," Sutton said, wiping his brow with a handkerchief he retrieved from the cruiser's glove box. "That was a can of worms. I can believe that her husband was a louse, but the woman ought to be careful saying that kind of stuff about the Standridges."

"You don't buy her story?" Dodger asked.

"It's hard to," Sutton admitted. "Andy Standridge was a good guy, and Mrs. Standridge is one of my mother's best friends, a real respectable lady."

"So you never saw anything to back up Mrs. Cutliffe's impression that there was something wrong in the Standridge house?"

He shook his head. "I was there maybe four times, twice to collect Debbie for a date and twice for Danny. They were like all the families of the girls I dated. Mrs. Standridge always had some kind of good snack in a glass dish on the coffee table — barbecued nuts, cheese puffs, that kind of thing. She always asked how I was doing and how were my folks. So did Mr. Standridge. They couldn't have been nicer."

"So you never got the idea that the girls were afraid of their father?"

Sutton shook his head. "No way. Debbie teased him a lot, almost daring him to say or do something. Danny, on the other hand, was indifferent. It was like she knew she didn't have to pay attention to him or what he thought. Ever had that kind of experience with a girl?"

"Not exactly," Dodger replied, "but I think I know what you mean."

"Yeah, now that I think about it, it was strange how the girls acted around their old man, but I don't see how that was Mr. Standridge's fault. Anyway, whatever Mrs. Cutliffe thinks, I just don't believe Mrs. Standridge would have put up with anything like that. She was a big churchgoer before her strokes put her in Blevins House."

"Not always a guarantee," Dodger pointed out.

"I know," Sutton admitted, "but it's still hard to believe."

Dodger realized he was hungry.

"Is there someplace around here we can grab a quick lunch?"

"There's a Waffle House up the way if that isn't too basic for you. Then I thought we'd go by the assisted-living place where May Standridge is now to see if she feels like talking to us. After what we've heard this morning, I think it's time to see what she can tell us before we head down a wrong road."

"I'd say so," Dodger agreed.

After lunch, Sutton pointed the cruiser toward a large, two-story structure on a hill outside of town. The sign on its gates identified it as "Blevins House," and the gardens around and beyond the gates justified its comparison with a grand house. The façade of the building sported large, Palladian-style windows and columns. Architecturally, it was a mess, but in terms of comparative grandeur, it succeeded.

"Very impressive," Dodger said.

"This is where well-heeled locals stash relatives they don't want around the house any more," Sutton told him. "Very popular with the country-club set."

"Somehow I didn't get the idea that the Standridges ran to this kind of expenditure."

"I was surprised when I heard Mrs. Standridge was coming here," Sutton admitted, "but then my mother told me that Mr. Standridge had left a big insurance policy, together with his pension from the mill, and also there was long-term care insurance. I guess all of it together pays the $7,000 or so a month it takes for this place."

"It's interesting that Debbie Jenkins spends that kind of money on her mother," Dodger said. "She doesn't seem to like her very much."

"I don't think she has any choice. According to my mother, who got it from May, it was all left in trust when Mr. Standridge died. A lawyer over in Rington is the trustee."

"That makes sense," Dodger said. "How long has Mrs. Standridge been a resident here?"

"About two years. She had a couple of small strokes, then a bigger one, and the doctor said she had to go into assisted living."

"So she doesn't have Alzheimer's?"

"Not as far as I know," Sutton said. "Just the aftermath of the strokes and maybe some other age-related health issues."

"How good's her memory?"

"Comes and goes. I brought my mother to see her a couple of times early on. The first visit, she seemed fine, just a weaker version of herself. The second visit, she looked at Mom like she'd never seen her before, and they grew up together. I hope she feels like talking with us today. They seemed to think so when I called them this morning."

"How do you want to handle it?" Dodger asked as they entered the portico. "Is she capable of answering simple questions if she's having a good day? Any ideas?"

Sutton thought about it, then his frown cleared.

"I don't think interrogation is the way to go. My grandma spent her last year in a nursing home, and she was what the doctors called 'confused' most of it. What we learned was that questions didn't work. She got agitated when she couldn't think of the answers, which she usually couldn't. Once we realized that, we stopped asking her anything. Instead, we'd just state something as a fact. If she agreed, she'd expand on what we'd said. If she disagreed, she'd say something like 'now, that's not so' or 'you shouldn't say such things as that' or 'that's just plain silly'. We'd take it from there. Sometimes we wouldn't say anything — we'd show her a photograph or play one of her favorite songs on the iPod and it'd seem to jog her back to herself for a few minutes. It wouldn't last, but she'd make sense for a little while. Do you see what I mean?"

Dodger nodded, his respect for the deputy notching further upwards.

Sutton opened the door, and Dodger followed him into a lush entryway, complete with wall-sized aquarium. At the reception desk, a young woman worked at a computer. She stood up and extended her hand, which Sutton took with undisguised enthusiasm.

"Jase," she grinned.

"Serena, it's good to see you. This is my colleague Art Dodger, the one I mentioned on the phone."

"Mr. Dodger," Serena said in a pleasantly accented voice, giving his hand a firm shake.

"How is she?" Sutton asked.

"It's still a good day. She was very pleased when I told her you might be coming."

"I gather you were able to reach Debbie Jenkins to get her permission?" the deputy confirmed.

Serena nodded. "I did. It was rather shocking. She said — and I quote — 'I don't care who sees the old witch, as long as I don't have to'. Can you believe it?"

"They never got along," the deputy explained.

A young woman in green scrubs opened the door from the hallway and motioned them to follow. Her tag identified her as *Nursing Assistant Ellen Scoggs.*

"Mrs. Standridge is tickled that you're coming. She doesn't get much company, you know. She said nobody had visited since Christmas, although I find that hard to believe. Christmas was months ago, and I know she has a daughter in the area."

"How is she this afternoon?" Sutton asked.

"Very much herself. She's a pleasant lady, always so grateful for every little thing anybody does for her. I don't think she ever had much attention before she came here."

Dodger began to feel guilty for their errand, guilty, too, for arriving empty-handed.

"Is there a gift shop here?" he asked.

"Back the other way," she said. "Would you like to go there first?"

"Yes. I think a big box of candy would be in order."

"Good idea," Sutton approved.

A few minutes later, armed with a three-pound Gold Ballotin of Lady Godiva truffles, they were ushered into what the young nursing assistant identified as the parlor of May's suite. Well furnished, it sported decorative accents that had to be personal touches, like a piece of competent artwork on the wall and a row of needlepoint pillows done in complicated flower arrangements. Mrs. Standridge sat by the window, staring without expression at a large maple tree ablaze with color a few feet away. A tray table sat next to the arm of her chair, and an old-fashioned cane was propped within reach against the wall.

"Mrs. Standridge," Sutton said quietly. "It's Jase Sutton. You know, we met several times. I'm a friend of your daughters."

The woman shifted around in her chair and stared at him, one side of her face frozen in a permanent leer, the other normally expressive. She wore a plain blue dress and sensible black shoes, like the kind women of an older generation would have favored. At her neck was a chain of gold links that looked real. A ladies' Omega watch slid on her thin, wrinkled arm as she gripped the chair. She stared at them for a moment, and Sutton repeated what he'd said.

This time, in a clear voice, she responded. "Yes, I remember. You're Jason Sutton. Mary is your mother."

"That's right. She hasn't been well, but she asked me to remember her to you."

"That's kind."

She gasped with pleasure as Dodger handed her the Godiva Ballotin. "Oh goody, I love candy. What a kind man. Do I know him?" The last question was directed at Sutton.

"No ma'am. This is Art Dodger, a colleague."

Her fingers worked at the ribbon until it slipped off. She removed the lid and extended the box to both men. Each took a piece, which made her beam. She appeared to enjoy playing the hostess.

She ate several of the truffles, one after the other, with no pause in between, and then dusted her fingertips with a tissue from the box on the tray next to her chair.

"Did you bring my girls with you?" she cried out, looking from side to side in the room.

"No ma'am, they couldn't come," Sutton said. "Debbie is at work, and you know Danny, always busy."

"Yes, Debbie works part time for a doctor over in Rington now, doesn't she? But Danny, what about Danny? I can't remember what Danny is doing. I wish I could see my girls," she fretted. "I don't even have a picture of them."

"Would you like one?" Dodger asked gently.

"More than anything," she said.

Dodger picked up his iPad and motioned to Sutton.

"I'll go downstairs to see if the office has a printer I can use. If they do, I'll be back in a few minutes."

"I'll see if I can get her to talk about the school we all went to," Sutton said in a low voice. "You go ahead."

The office had a printer and Dodger was able to pull a decent print of the two girls in a dance recital from the scans he'd made at the library on his iPad. As an afterthought he signed in to his email account and printed out a couple of the photographs of Danny that Display Dollies had sent Jess. He thanked the office assistant, put the photographs in the folder she held out, and returned upstairs to find Sutton and Mrs. Standridge laughing at the memory of the time the Whitman-Brown music director took a tumble off the podium to fall into the front row of the band.

"It was funny. He was such a stuffy young man," Mrs. Standridge said as she chose another truffle. "Andy always laughed at him."

Dodger pulled Sutton to one side and showed him the photographs. A funny look came over the deputy's face as he studied the images of Danielle in the school play.

"What do you think?" Dodger urged. "Is any of this likely to upset her?"

"I'd start with the one of the girls when they were little. We can decide about the two of Danny when we see how she takes that."

"What are you boys whispering about?" Mrs. Standridge chirped.

"Just something I happened to come across at the library the other day," Dodger said, extending the 8x10" print of the Standridge girls at about the time the family arrived in Whitman. They wore ballet tutus as they danced in a line with half a dozen other girls.

Mrs. Standridge's eyes widened, and she held the photograph as reverently as if it were a holy relic.

"How wonderful! It's from their first dance recital after we moved here. Do you think I might have a copy of it?"

"It's yours. I got it for you," Dodger explained.

"If you like, I'll get it framed," Sutton volunteered.

"No," she said, gripping the print. "I'm not letting this get away. This was when I thought, when I thought, when I thought…"

"That everything would be all right," Dodger prompted, casting a quick look at Sutton, who frowned but nodded.

"That's right," she said, relieved to be understood. "They were such pretty little girls, don't you think? He said that's why it happened. They were just too pretty, and it wasn't his fault. That's what he said. I believed him. What else could I do?"

"Mrs. Standridge," Sutton began. "Are you saying that your husband…"

"Debbie loved her daddy so much from the very beginning," she continued as if he hadn't spoken. "They were always laughing and roughhousing. And then, when Danny got a little older, she came to me and said that Debbie and her daddy were trying to get her to play a game and did she have to? Well, maybe I shouldn't have done what I did, but what was done was done and Debbie didn't seem to care, so I laid down the law to Andy. I told him, told him, told him…"

She gulped, unable to go on.

"That he had to leave Danny alone," Dodger murmured, taking a guess that hit its mark.

She nodded, tears running down her cheeks. "Danny was special. I knew somebody important would want to marry Danny. She had to be kept safe until she could get away to college. Debbie was always tough. I knew she could look after herself."

"Damn," Sutton muttered, half rising from his seat, settling back only at a warning glance from Dodger, who didn't like what he was hearing either but who focused on the fact that they were here to gather information, not to judge this pathetic woman all these years after the fact.

"You did the best you could," he murmured. "But Danny didn't always appreciate that."

Mrs. Standridge shook her head. "She doesn't even notice. She just ignores anything that doesn't suit her and goes on her way. She's my special girl, and I don't even have a picture and I haven't seen her in so long."

Dodger took out the two photographs of Danielle that Jess had emailed.

"Here she is, Mrs. Standridge. Don't cry. Here she is." He handed her the photographs.

"Such a lovely girl in the pretty new dresses," Mrs. Standridge said, stroking the images, one after the other.

"They're from the school play," Dodger pointed out.

Mrs. Standridge began to whimper, confusion clouding her eyes.

"What school play?" she asked. "Can't remember, can't remember, can't remember…" Her face began to redden, and her fists clenched.

She whirled around and, before they could stop her, knocked the Gold Ballotin off the tray table next to her chair, sweeping it away with such force that pieces from it hit the far wall. She began to bang the cane against the floor so hard that it sounded as if a huge drum were being played. The door swung open, and Ellen Scoggs ran into the room, concern making her frown as she shooed the two men out.

Sutton cursed under his breath as they strode back to the cruiser, so angry that he barely managed to acknowledge Serena's parting wave.

"Damn it. People always said he was crazy about those girls, and if you'd known Andy Standridge…"

"Seemed like a good guy?"

"One of the best. Like Mrs. Cutliffe said, he was one of the most popular managers at the mill, which was why I couldn't help wondering, even after hearing her and not exactly doubting her. It was impossible to believe. He was a big, slap-you-on-the-back kind of guy, always had a joke, was always laughing about something, a real man's man."

"But I thought you said how they interacted was weird when you picked up Debbie for dates," Dodger pointed out.

Sutton shook his head. "I thought how *Debbie* acted was weird. I thought she was just showing off. It never hit me that there might be something wrong from Andy's end."

"It sounds as if you liked Andy."

"I didn't think of him that way. There was too much of an age difference, but he was the kind of guy other guys admire. A man's man, you know? Not like my dad, who spent half his life with his nose in a book or a newspaper. Mr. Standridge got out and tossed footballs around with the boys. All my dad did was offer to help us with our homework."

"Your father sounds nice."

"Probably nicer than I realized," Sutton conceded. "I can't get over what we just heard. Son of a bitch."

"Yes," Dodger said, nodding, "but what we have to ask ourselves is what did her family situation have to do with Danielle's disappearance?"

"Could she have been so unhappy at home that she did run off?" Sutton asked, as if he expected Dodger to have the answer. "Have I been wrong all along?"

Sixteen.

. . ₀₀•••••₀ . .

Permission to Rummage

Travis Whitman had plans for dinner in Charlotte, so Dodger, he said, would be left to the cook's tender mercies and his own devices. After telling him this, the dinner-jacketed Whitman handed over the key to the mini-museum.

Dodger looked at it in surprise.

"I keep it locked because Charlotte always did," Whitman explained. "There's nothing in there worth stealing. It occurs to me that you might like to explore it further for your purposes. Charlotte assembled all sorts of things, all of it to do with Danielle Standridge."

"Thanks," Dodger said as he dropped the key in his pocket. "Another look might be useful."

"Rummage at will. Take what you want to examine at greater length back to your room if you like. Just return everything when you're through."

After dinner in the library before the big TV, Dodger decided to take him up on the offer.

Bemusement was the main emotion gripping him as he rode up in the little elevator. The day before, he would have bet money Whitman had shown him the macabre exhibit because he'd learned that Billy had spilled the beans. Also, in the few minutes he'd spent in the room with Whitman, he witnessed what he interpreted as an embarrassment that was neither new nor pleasant to the man who was gripped by it. Dodger was sure Whitman didn't like this demonstration of his late wife's obsessive grief and had no particular desire to share it with anyone. In fact, Dodger would have said the odds were small that he'd ever see it again unless he made an issue of it himself.

Still, here he was, outside the door, key in hand, about to go in, all courtesy of Travis Whitman. This time he'd be on his own with the owner's express consent to explore any aspect of the museum he liked — minus the now-missing mannequins, of course, the mannequins of whose existence Dodger was to be presumed ignorant as Whitman made no mention of them.

The key turned readily, and he reached for the same switch he'd seen used twice before. As before, overhead lights came on, as well as lights for the individual shelves. Dodger walked in and locked the door behind him. He looked at the well-displayed contents of the shelves and wondered if Whitman had removed anything other than the mannequins. The thin coating of dust over everything, however, suggested nothing had been disturbed for a long time.

Dodger surveyed the shelves without delay. He had the feeling this might be the one time he'd have the opportunity, at least when officially sanctioned and could take as long as he liked, and he was determined to make the best use of it. Much of the stuff he glanced at, but then returned to its original position. Some things he put on a nearby table: an autograph album; a couple of Whitman-Brown school annuals; a correspondence folder; and a thick scrapbook with Danielle's name scrawled in childish script below a photograph of her in a latter-day majorette's uniform.

He was opening a pink leatherette jewelry box when his cell buzzed. It was Jess.

"Just checking in," she said. "To make sure you remain un-missing."

"I'm present, but busy. You'll never guess where I am." He told her of his whereabouts and the unsupervised access he'd been given.

"Look around," she suggested. "Maybe he has an ulterior motive. Maybe he's trying to figure out the direction of your investigation. Maybe you're being monitored."

"If I am, it's by something I can't see," Dodger said. "Anyway, if he wants to know about the investigation, all he has to do is ask. In any event, I don't think the guy would bother to wire this place. I'd be surprised if anyone has ever seen this room except for the Whitmans and one or two of the most trusted servants. I get the feeling that, once his wife died, he pretty much shut it up. I think the place embarrasses him. Which isn't surprising, given it's the next thing to a stalking archive.

There's everything here but a wad of used chewing gum."

"Creepy, huh?"

"Creepy disappeared in the rear-view mirror half an hour ago," he told her, bracing the phone between shoulder and ear and carrying the jewelry box to the table, where he dumped its contents. "I'm going through her jewelry right now."

"You can tell a lot about a girl by her jewelry, even a girl that age," Jess pointed out.

"Except for some pins from different honor organizations and a couple of competitions she won, this looks like the typical stuff for a teenager," he said. "There's a charm bracelet, a ruby glass necklace, a mustard seed encased in plastic, a set of rhinestone necklace and brace-let, earrings for pierced ears, that sort of thing."

"Typical schoolgirl it is," Jess laughed.

"Okay, the jewelry box is empty. Now I'm going to try a trick I remember. If this is like a lot of these boxes, the divider will come out and there'll be a fake bottom. That's where my sis..."

He stopped and caught himself. When he continued, his voice was rougher. "That's where some girls store things they want to keep hidden."

Sure enough, the divider came out, revealing a small grosgrain tab at the back he used to pull up the flimsy velveteen-covered cardboard.

"Hold on, there's something here. An envelope with paper in it. It's sealed, but the glue is giving way. Let me work the flap."

He slid the thinnest blade of his Swiss Army knife under a gap, and in a moment had opened the envelope with no visible damage. In it was a folded square of paper; and when he slid it out, a tiny key fell onto the floor. Dodger retrieved it.

"It's a key," he said. "It was wrapped in paper."

"Will it fit the jewelry box?"

"No," Dodger said, trying it. "It's not the right shape, and it's too small. Anyway, why put a key to the box in the box?"

"No idea, but I can remember doing it, maybe so I'd know where it was if I ever wanted to lock the box."

"That makes sense," he conceded. "In a way."

"I'm so glad you condone my youthful organizational protocol," she drawled. "Anything on the paper to show what the key opens?"

101

"Not unless it's in invisible ink. Let me take a closer look at the envelope. No, it's blank too. Any ideas?"

She thought about it for a minute. "Have you come across a diary?"

He looked around. "Not so far, and I'm not seeing anything like that on the shelves I haven't done yet."

"The kind of girl Danielle sounds like would have had a diary. I'll bet that's what the key is for. Girls live in mortal terror of their parents and siblings reading their diary. She probably locked it and hid it in a place available to her but not them, and then hid the key in the jewelry box. That'd be what most girls would do if they wanted to be sure no one read what they'd written."

"She had reasons to hide it," Dodger said. "There are indications her father liked his pretty little daughters too much."

"You mean she was being…"

"Not so much her," Dodger interrupted. "He left her alone, but for some time he'd been interfering with her sister, to use the old legal term, and Danielle may have known about that."

"That's sad," Jess said.

"It's sad," he agreed.

"Do you think the father could have tried it on with Danielle and, when she refused, killed her, either accidentally or on purpose?" she asked.

"I'll admit the thought crossed my mind, and, if that's so, there's nothing further to look into, at least in terms of legal action. Andrew Standridge, the father, died years ago. Anyway, I get the feeling that something different was going on there. May, the mother, is in assisted living because of a series of strokes, but she makes sense enough that she admitted she and the father had an arrangement. He left Danielle alone as long as she didn't get in his way when it came to Debbie."

"She traded one daughter for the other? Gross. Poor Debbie." Jess sounded as appalled as Dodger had felt while listening to May.

"I'm beginning to think it is 'poor Debbie'," Dodger said, "even though she isn't very likable big-sister material."

"What's on the agenda now?"

"Shouldn't take long to finish in here. I see more papers — these seem to be college entrance forms the girl started to fill out. There's a stack of schoolbooks that look new, with a schedule stuck inside one of them. The rest of this stuff looks like clothes — blue jeans, concert tees, shirts, scarves, purses, shoe boxes, even schoolgirl-type underwear. It looks like Charlotte Whitman cleaned out Danielle's closet and drawers and hauled all of it here."

"Charlotte wrote the book on anal, didn't she?" Jess asked sarcastically.

"You think?" Dodger said. "Wait a second. I've spotted something odd over here."

"Odder than the entire concept? I can't wait to hear," she laughed.

"It doesn't make any sense. I see a piece of embroidery with part of a quote stitched on it: 'You get out of life what you put into it.' Here's a plastic case full of what looks like glass beads. Here's a painting that doesn't seem to have been finished."

"It's Danielle's craft projects," Jess told him. "A lot of teenaged girls go through a craft stage. I think you just found hers."

"You did craft projects?" Dodger tried to picture the sophisticated Jessica Hannah, even as a teenager, slumped over sewing or handmade necklaces and failed.

"Sure. I think it began in summer camp with beadwork. I had one of those quote samplers too. Mine said something about every day being the best day."

"Did you finish yours?" Dodger asked, holding the rumpled piece of incomplete embroidery in his hands. He wondered if Danielle had already abandoned it by the time she disappeared or had put it to one side, planning to complete the last few inches of stitching later.

"I don't think anybody ever finishes those quote things," Jess said. "So, no. Mine is probably still lying folded in a sewing box in my old bedroom at my parents' house."

Dodger looked down at the sad remnant of things that had once absorbed Danielle. Were they mementoes of someone who'd been dead for twenty years or things that, even now, she thought of from time to time and wished she'd finished? What had happened to the girl? Were there enough unexplored leads remaining to justify advising Mystery Mavens it was possible her disappearance could be solved?

"Are you still there?" Jess asked, making him jump.

"I'm here. I was just thinking about how sad all this is. Sad for the girl. Sad for Charlotte Whitman. Sad for Travis Whitman. Sad for everyone."

"Isn't it always when something like this happens?" Jess reminded him. "I cried for years over my sister. I'm sure that you, too…"

"Yeah," he said, refusing to go there. "It's beyond sad. All of it."

There was a brief moment of silence as he regretted the cold abruptness in his voice. He hadn't intended it, but survivors each had his or her coping mechanism and his was to keep thoughts of it at bay.

"Are you through there?" Jess asked, leading the discussion back onto impersonal ground.

"Pretty much," he said, more than willing to go along. "All that's left are some framed photographs and certificates." He walked over to the far wall and examined the hanging objects. He could hear Jess breathe.

"Anything interesting?" she asked.

"The girl seems to have taken every school award from third grade on, and she looks good in every picture."

"A winning combination," Jess commented.

"I wonder," Dodger said. "I suspect that whatever happened that day came about as result of who she was, the beautiful girl with the beautiful mind. I had no opinion to begin with, but now I'm not buying this as a random thing."

"If indeed 'thing' it is," Jess reminded him. "Don't try to find a crime where there isn't one."

"That's the issue," Dodger agreed. "The more I learn about this girl, I'm realizing the solution to this mystery is 50/50. Maybe somebody snatched her. Maybe not. Even at fifteen she was probably smart enough to outwit everybody for as long as she wanted."

"Well, if you need anything else… And, Dodger? I'm sorry I made you think about your family. I didn't mean to."

"It doesn't matter," he said, voice colder than he'd intended. "That was then and this is now."

"Of course," Jess said in a formal tone. "If you need me, call." She disconnected in a way that managed to sound angry.

He was sorry he'd hurt her feelings, but she knew he didn't like any mention of what happened to his family. She shouldn't have gone there. Nobody was allowed to go there.

Back in the guest room, Dodger arranged his finds on top of the chrome-and-glass desk in front of the windows, and pulled out the chrome-plated desk chair that was, he concluded as he sat down, stronger than it looked.

He decided to begin with the folder of letters, postcards, and notes. Many of them were to Danielle from classmates on trips, postcards with brief messages of the "Having great time — wish you were here" variety. There were mash notes of an intense, often-inappropriate nature from "Bo" and a Valentine gift enclosure from someone signed "Bryan." There was a letter from Dwayne Simmons on Whitman-Brown High School stationery congratulating Danielle on winning first prize in an essay contest. There were two incomplete letters from Danielle, one headed "My Special Friend" and the other to "Dear Grandma." Dodger wondered how Charlotte had retrieved those, which had to be from Danielle's desk at home. Of course, he remembered, Whitman had mentioned that she'd gotten things from the girl's family, as well as the school.

Finishing with the folder and finding nothing unexpected, he turned his attention to the scrapbook. It was large and thick, 16x20" in outside dimensions, with a cream-colored leatherette cover secured by thick, twisted cord. On the cover were the words "This scrapbook belongs to . ." followed by a space onto which someone, presumably Danielle, had glued a strip of paper with her name printed on it in careful block letters. Below was an inset, grooved frame, intended for a picture of the owner. In the one she'd chosen, Danielle sat in the bleachers, in a majorette outfit skimpier than the one she and the other girls had worn in **Before A Hero**. A sequined cap sat in her lap, and her head was thrown back, laughing.

Dodger's breath caught. She looked so young, younger than in the two photographs in evening dress he'd given her mother that afternoon. More, she looked so alive. He hoped she'd simply walked away from what she considered an unbearable situation. The possibility of that joy, that life, being destroyed was hard to take.

He guessed the photograph was from her first season as a majorette, the fall of 1992. That would explain the obvious age difference in the photographs. Girls could change a lot between fourteen and fifteen. His sister had. It seemed as if one month she was still a kid tagging along after him and the next a young sophisticate who found her older brother too boring to be tolerated.

He pushed the thought away. He had to focus on Danielle Standridge. He opened the scrapbook and saw he was right about the date it was begun. Danielle, ever precise, had dated each object mounted in it, and the first — a mini-poster from a rock concert — was dated August 31, 1992. She must have begun the scrapbook at the start of the new school year. In the pages that followed were other tokens of attendance at one event or another, together with photographs highlighted by drawings that spilled onto the pages on which they were mounted. There was a shot of her in a long, puffy-sleeved dress holding the arm of a gangly boy in what looked like a rented tux, the two of them grinning broadly at the camera as they stood under a banner on which was printed "Whitman-Brown Harvest Dance, 1992." There were favors from parties and a ticket stub from a fair. There were greeting cards from teachers and fellow students, including a birthday card from her mother, in which there was a handwritten message, "Happy Birthday, Danny. You know Daddy and I will always love you." The hypocrisy made his stomach turn, and it was hard not to become angry again with the vague woman he'd met at Blevins House that afternoon. Two facing pages held invitations. Some were formal and engraved — including one to an awards banquet in Charlotte and another to a Christmas party at Mill House. Some were hand-drawn, from other kids, with bad puns announcing the purpose and time of events like Sweet Sixteens and club initiations. There was a May 1993 invitation to become a Whitman-Brown Cool Cucumber.

What on earth was a "Cool Cucumber?" Dodger wondered, reaching for the school annual dated 1992. In its *Organizations* section, he learned that the Cukes, as they called themselves, were girls who'd been chosen to join an elite group whose purpose was to serve the community, but only after they'd been vetted by the current members, who sought the sort of girl who would contribute to the reputation and prestige of the group. For a moment, he wondered if this might be code for a racist thing, but there were several non-Anglo-Saxon faces in the group photograph. What there weren't, he realized, were any girls who could be described as homely, fat or badly dressed. It seemed the formal criteria omitted the fact that only slim, good-looking girls with a reasonable clothing allowance could expect to become Cukes. Well, Danny would have fit in there.

He wondered if she'd accepted. He picked up the 1993 annual to see if Danny had made it into the group picture. No, he thought, that wouldn't work. The school year had just started when she disappeared. He doubted any of the group photographs had been taken. He wondered if the annual would make any reference to Danny's disappearance, and opened the padded cover to find the answer to his question. The first page showed a studio photograph of her with the inscription, "Dedicated to our classmate, Danielle Elizabeth Standridge, who will come home."

Except she hadn't, Dodger thought, and it was pretty clear by now that she never would.

Seventeen.

. . ₀₀●●●●₀₀ . .

When the Last Bell Rings

"Here we are," Sutton said, pulling the cruiser into the semicircular drive in front of Whitman-Brown High School. "Last classes were in May 2005, when the new consolidated school over in Rington opened."

The men got out of the cruiser and paused to look at the big structure.

"It's in remarkable shape," Dodger said, surveying the range of unbroken windows and tidy appearance of the grounds.

"That's because of Roosevelt Jones," Sutton told him. "He's the caretaker, and he's got eyes in the back of his head."

"From what you've said, I'm surprised the school system can afford to pay him," Dodger said.

"It doesn't have to. He's on Mr. Whitman's payroll."

"Whitman keeps his hand in around here, doesn't he?"

"Damned good thing, too. If he didn't, the town would be in even worse shape," Sutton pointed out. "When the school closed, everybody assumed it would be torn down, but then the state threw its hat in the ring to turn it into a retraining center for people losing jobs in the textile industry, which is kind of appropriate if you think about it." He laughed, but there was little humor in his eyes. "The thing was they made it clear the school had to be kept in good repair while all the politics got worked out and the money was found. That was eight years ago, and Jones, who'd been the building supervisor, agreed to stay on and keep everything shipshape."

A tall, handsome black man strode toward them, smiling. He wore a tan windbreaker over khakis and a white shirt.

"Deputy Sutton, good to see you," he boomed, extending his

108

hand. "And this is Art Dodger? Welcome to Whitman."

"It's an attractive town," Dodger commented.

"That it is," Jones agreed. "Could be busier, but that'll come again."

"Mr. Jones is our resident optimist," Sutton explained to Dodger, grinning.

"Optimism is free," Jones stated. "Doesn't cost a penny more than pessimism and gives a much better return."

Dodger laughed.

"See, you feel better already," Jones grinned. "Now, what can I do for you gentlemen?"

"Do you remember Danielle Standridge?" Sutton asked, getting right to the point.

"Sure. The school majorette who disappeared, let's see, was it really twenty years ago?"

"Twenty years ago this week," Dodger confirmed.

"Mr. Dodger's looking into her disappearance for Mr. Whitman," Sutton explained, "and he'd like to take a look around the school."

Jones shook his head. "That was a sad time. If I can help, all you have to do is let me know."

"I don't have anything specific in mind," Dodger said. "I just want to get a feel for the girl's routine." He pulled out a piece of paper. "As far as I can tell, this was her schedule."

Jones lifted his eyebrows as he took the list, but made no comment.

"Well, this is easy enough. Would you like me to walk you through her school day?"

"That's what I want," Dodger said.

"Can you tell me how she usually got to school?" Jones asked. "Did she walk? Was she driven?"

"Her mother dropped her off," Sutton said. "She gave me a lift a couple of times."

"Then odds are she'd have gone in at the end. That was for individual drop-offs." He strode to the door, pulled out a big batch of keys, unlocked the deadbolt, and led the other two men inside a small concrete-floored entryway with walls painted in the two-toned green ubiquitous in public schools of a certain age. A bulletin board next to the door held one poster with the words "Goodbye to Whitman-Brown" in bright yellow against a red background. Below it was a large photograph in which about twenty young people smiled and waved, white and black faces mixed with Oriental and Hispanic, some dressed to the nines and others wearing the ever-present uniform of jeans and sweat shirt.

"I left it there as a kind of memorial," Jones told them. "It seemed like the right thing to do because it was the kids who put those up all over the school. Red and gold were the school colors, and each photograph was a different set of senior and junior students."

He went up a set of shallow steps, through double doors and into a wide hall, and then flipped a switch that turned the gloom into the usual fluorescent haze. Then he stopped and consulted the schedule Dodger had given him. "First, she had History, so she'd have gone this way." He led them around a corner and up stairs to a large room at the end of the corridor, which was dim until he flipped on lights. The room was still full of desks, but the long green chalkboard lining two walls was clean. Dodger stood for a minute, looking around. The room was tidy, devoid of anything capable of providing a clue, which it wouldn't have anyway after such a long period of time and so many students.

"Were you in this class?" Dodger asked Sutton, who shook his head.

"Nope, this was Mrs. Baughman's room. I had Mr. Edwards for History. He was next door."

"What's next?" Dodger asked Jones.

Jones looked at the list. "Chemistry."

"Mr. Baughman was the teacher," Sutton explained. "His lab was down on the first floor."

"We'll use the west steps," Jones said, leading the way around and down to a room at the far end of the building still equipped with lab tables and handsome wooden storage cabinets.

"Danny's seat was over there," Sutton said, indicating a chair on the front row. "I know 'cause I used to wait on her to get through. We both had early lunch, and on days when I had a car here we'd sneak out to Hal's, the hamburger joint on the strip."

"Too bad about Hal's," Jones commented.

"Yeah," Sutton agreed. "He said he couldn't make it without the mill business. I hear he's got a dog-and-juice place in Myrtle Beach."

"Got to check it out sometimes," Jones said. "My wife and I like

Myrtle Beach."

Dodger walked to Danielle's place and leaned on the scarred surface of the long wood table. A plasticized rollout featuring a periodic table of elements still hung on a nearby wall. It looked old. Dodger checked out the copyright date. 1990. It could have hung here then. Danielle might even have studied it.

"All right," he said, moving toward the door. "You said the two of you sometimes sneaked out to Hal's on the strip. Is that the stretch where the gas stations and fast food joints are?"

"Yeah. We could be there in six minutes if I didn't linger and miss the light by the pedestrian mall."

"When was the last time you took her there?"

Sutton thought about it. "Had to be several days before she went missing. My car had been in the shop for almost a week."

"All right, when you returned from lunch, what did you do?"

"Danny went to English with the new teacher who replaced Mr. Simmons after he left for Atlanta, and I had Solid Geometry with Mr. Evans."

Jones took them to the classroom Danny was assigned to on the third floor.

"Her English class was held right over there, through the middle door," Jones said.

Past a long row of lockers, they went inside, but this was a featureless room about which Sutton had no comment, as he'd never come up here with Danny. After a quick glance around, Dodger asked where the girl would have gone next.

"Gym," Jones said, "In the gymnasium building out back."

"All the cheerleaders and majorettes had gym the last period," Sutton explained.

They trudged back down the stairs.

"No elevators, huh?" Dodger commented, wincing as the calves of his legs began to cramp.

"Nope, not even in the new school," Jones laughed, "not for the students. I hear there's a small one for the faculty."

They were walking down a long, locker-lined hall toward the back entrance when a new thought struck Dodger.

"What about her locker? Surely, she didn't carry a stack of books around all day." He didn't mention he'd not only seen the books, but held them in his hands and so knew their weight.

"All of us had lockers," Sutton explained. "That year, I think Danny's was down this way, around the corner, by the stairs. I don't remember the number."

When they went to the location, however, there were no lockers, just markings on the floor showing where they once stood.

"I don't suppose you'd have any idea what happened to these?" Dodger asked.

Jones shook his head. "I think some of them were damaged and they sent them off for scrap. Anyway, even if you found it, it wouldn't do you any good. They would have left her stuff in it for a while, but then cleaned it out and assigned it to another student. Given how long it's been, I doubt there'd be any kind of record."

Sutton looked at his watch. "We'll have to leave the gym for another time. We've got an appointment in Blevins. Thanks for the tour, Mr. Jones."

"Any time," Jones assured him. "It still seems mighty quiet to me around here without all those young ones running up and down the halls. I still miss 'em, and when I think of those days it's just a blur of kids rushing around. Of course, there were a few who stood out, and those you remember."

Dodger stopped cold, and then turned to Jones. "Was Danielle Standridge one you remember?"

"Yes, she was. I noticed her because she was so different from the others."

Dodger waited, expecting him to make a comment about how pretty she'd been or how popular, but Jones surprised him.

"She always seemed to be reading or writing. Everybody else would be messing around and acting up, and that Standridge girl would be in a quiet corner of the library, working on something. She was a real hard worker. I remember because afterwards some people tried to claim she'd been wild, saying she'd run off with some boy. I knew better. The girl was a worker, and workers don't abandon their fields."

Eighteen.

. . .●●●●●●● . .

Sour Grapes

"That was a different perspective," Dodger said as they drove away from the disused school. "I'll bet Jones could tell some tales."

"Sure, he could," Sutton agreed. "But would he? I don't think so. Guy's known for his zipped lip. I'm surprised he said as much as he did about Danny."

"Was it correct?"

"Sure. She read all the time. I don't think I ever saw her without a book except when we went to the school dance right before she... before she wasn't here anymore."

He couldn't bring himself to say "disappeared." Dodger suspected the trip to their old high school had brought back unsettling memories.

"I used to tease her about it," Sutton continued. "I called her the librarian. It was one of the few things that would make her laugh."

"So you could tell she wasn't a happy girl?"

"I thought she was just moody, like a lot of teenaged girls. I didn't think it had anything to do with being happy or sad. Given what her mother said yesterday, it makes more sense. I still can't get over that. It must have been hell to live in their house, especially as everybody thought they were such a perfect family. Poor Debbie."

"Poor Debbie," Dodger repeated, and there was a moment of silence as the two men contemplated what she must have gone through.

"So, what's next?" Dodger said. "You mentioned an appointment in Blevins."

"Yeah, we're going to see Mrs. Ethel Bowland. She's the mother of a girl named Dorothy who was in the same class. When I went through the files again, I saw that she and her husband came in and volunteered information. At first, I didn't remember them, but after I looked through a yearbook it came back to me. From what was in the file, the woman seemed to have it in for Danny, so what she has to say will probably be just rumor and innuendo. Still, you never can tell." He looked at his watch. "If we get with it, we've just got time to make it to Blevins and hit the Waffle House again before we go to see her."

An hour and a half later, the police cruiser pulled into the driveway of a two-story colonial reproduction whose yard was so well cared for that the styling crew from Luxury Landscaping might have just left. The house itself was of white shingle and fieldstone with black shutters. The total impression was of good taste controlled by order, Dodger felt. It was a place you could be comfortable in, but only if you messed it up a little.

Sutton parked to one side, and they walked up to the front door, which was opened on the first ring by a tall, bony woman in her seventies wearing a navy-blue skirt and twin set with a gold chain of high quality. A sizable engagement ring twinkled atop a thick gold wedding band on her finger. It seemed there was, or at least had been, money here.

"Deputy Sutton," Ethel Bowland said with a tight smile. "And this must be Mr. Dodger." Her eyes fell to the Rolex on his wrist, the Lobb brogues, and the camelhair jacket; and her expression relaxed. "Mr. Dodger," she repeated. "Do come in."

She led them from the large entry hall into a generously proportioned living room where all the case furniture was *faux* Hepplewhite and the sofas and chairs covered in faded chintz. A drinks tray was set out on a low table in front of the bay window. Mrs. Bowland indicated they should help themselves, but both shook their heads.

"Now, young men, what can I do for you? On the phone you mentioned Danielle Standridge. I assume that means she's turned up?"

"Why would you assume that?" Dodger asked. "Do you think she disappeared in 1993 by her own choice?"

"Of course she did." Mrs. Bowland waved her hand. "She was a tramp, just like that slutty sister of hers, however well she played the goody two-shoes. She just ran away with someone."

"Who do you think she ran away with?" Sutton asked, and there was a note in his voice Dodger hadn't noticed before. If he were Mrs. Bowland, he'd drop that contemptuous tone. The prune-faced woman was oblivious, however, and continued as if certain those listening agreed with her opinion.

"Some boy she was messing around with. My Dorothy told me boys used to hang around her like flies on honey."

"That wasn't her fault," Sutton protested, but then shut up when he caught Dodger's warning glance.

"Who did Dorothy think she went away with?" Dodger asked, careful to keep his voice casual.

"What do you mean?" Mrs. Bowland gave him a suspicious glance.

"I assume your daughter knew Danielle. She may have had at least an idea of who helped her classmate leave town."

Mrs. Bowland made a dismissive gesture. "Of course, she wouldn't. They were not friends. Dorothy didn't have anything to do with that dreadful girl. I made sure of it. I had to; when she was sixteen, without asking me, she invited Danielle to one of her spend-the-night parties. Boys actually came to the door and hooted for that girl, who was even younger than the other guests. Well, I couldn't have my daughter tainted by association. So I told Dorothy she was never to have her here again and she was to avoid her to the extent possible at school."

"So you didn't feel Danielle leaving town was any particular loss to Dorothy?" Dodger clarified.

"I did not. My daughter was a respectable girl who did not need a bad example. After Danielle left, Dorothy came into her own. At graduation, she was valedictorian of the class, you know, and received the Whitman-Brown Honors Award. If the Standridge girl had still been here, who knows what kind of injustice might have occurred? Dorothy said Danielle always won everything. My husband Frank felt that she did something, well, improper, to be recognized ahead of young people who were her social and moral betters. You know, her father was a mill supervisor. He didn't even finish college. How could he and that hopeless wife of his produce a girl who could be as superior as my Dorothy? Well, I showed how I felt about her; she never darkened my door again."

"Do you have any concrete information about Danny's disappearance?" Sutton interrupted.

"Well," she said, taken aback, "Frank and I were in Atlanta at a law-association conference the week she disappeared, so no. The last time I saw the girl was several weeks earlier in The Darling Shop with Charlotte Whitman. They were looking at dresses, but the store didn't seem to stock the girl's size — she was a puny thing, rail-thin. One of the dresses they were looking at was the same one I was getting for Dorothy, and I was furious the two girls might show up looking like mismatched twins. On top of that, I remember the clerk made me wait while she filled out Charlotte Whitman's special-order form even though all I wanted to do was to pick up the dress we'd chosen for Dorothy. It was most rude, and I said so. The way everybody's always kowtowed to the Whitmans in Whitman is disgraceful, not that it's done the town much good lately." Her smile was grim.

"If you didn't have any information about the disappearance, why did you come to the police in 1993 and make a report?" Sutton asked.

"Because it seemed important to me that the authorities know the kind of girl Danielle was, so they wouldn't waste time looking for some Little Miss Innocent who'd been taken advantage of by someone. In my opinion, they were looking for a runaway, not a victim."

"Back in 1993, did your daughter remain here while you and your husband were in Atlanta?" Dodger asked.

"Of course not. She wasn't even seventeen. She went to stay with her aunt in Rington."

"Do you think there's anything your husband would like to tell us?" Sutton asked as she paused for breath before her next onslaught on Danielle's memory.

"My husband, who was the leading attorney in Blevins, has been deceased for five years," she frowned, her posture stiff. "I would have thought you, as a police officer, would have known."

Dodger noticed that Sutton relaxed his clenched fists only after they were back in the cruiser.

"Talk about a spiteful old cow," he said, glaring in the direction of the house.

"Let it go," Dodger warned him. "It isn't worth it."

"I've placed her," Dodger continued. "I remember Dorothy too. Compared to Danielle, she wasn't any great shakes, but she was St. Theresa compared to her mother. That woman must have hated Danny."

"She still hates Danny," Dodger corrected him.

"But why?"

"Think about it. What did Dorothy look like in high school?" Dodger asked.

"Medium height, I think. A little plump. Fair with freckles. And the reason she made valedictorian was that Danny wasn't around anymore and the boy who had the second-best grades got caught with pot in the gym and was expelled two weeks before graduation."

"There's your answer. Danielle committed the cardinal sin of being not only smarter, but prettier."

"In a way, it's kind of funny," Sutton said.

"What's funny?"

"That old biddy seems to think she scored something off Danny by not letting Dorothy associate with her. Knowing Danny, I doubt she even noticed."

Dodger wasn't so sure.

Nineteen.

·•ₒ•••✿✿✿✿•ₒ•·

Correctional Institute

That night, Travis Whitman had another engagement, and Dodger spent several hours examining the missing girl's school papers. Danielle was brilliant on the evidence of these papers alone. In fact, had there not been notes from various teachers, it would be hard to believe they'd been written by a fifteen-year-old girl.

He wished Jess were here so that he could show the papers to her. She didn't call, however; and when he tried to call her, there was no answer.

The next day, an excited Sutton greeted Dodger with the news that a fresh and unexpected avenue of investigation had opened up.

"There was an article in the paper about an appeal denied a lifer at Scotland Correctional. Get this, he was convicted in 1995 of the abduction and murder of a teenaged girl even though her body was never found."

"Was he living in this area?"

Sutton shook his head. "Over on the coast, but he grew up in Rington, so he could have been here visiting relatives when Danny went missing. He's agreed to talk with us, and the warden's approved. Want to take a ride?"

Two hours later, they found themselves in a special interrogation room at what — Sutton assured Dodger — was reputed to be one of the toughest prisons in the South. The shackled man before them looked as if he would fit right in. Forty-year-old Denton Gilmore had to be 6'6" of overworked muscle. His dark eyes narrowed with a mixture of curiosity and hostility.

"Ya wanna talk? Then talk," he growled.

"You mind your manners," said the armed guard from the corner.

"Screw you," Gilmore snarled before turning back to his visitors. "Now, what can I do you for?"

Dodger and Sutton had agreed up front that in this official setting, Sutton would do the talking unless he indicated he'd like for Dodger to take over. Given that, Dodger leaned back, arms folded, and prepared to watch.

"Where were you in September 1993?" the deputy began.

"I was in Rington."

"How can you be so sure?"

"My daddy died in July and I stayed in Rington with my mama until Thanksgiving, helping out however she needed."

"Did you ever come over to Whitman?"

"Nah, I didn't have no business in Loomtown."

"Did you know a girl named Danielle Standridge?"

Gilmore shook his head.

"You never met Danielle Standridge under any circumstances?" Sutton looked skeptical.

"I told you," Gilmore growled. "I never met anybody named Gabrielle Standridge."

"Danielle," Sutton corrected him. "She was a majorette at Whitman-Brown High School in September 1993."

Realization dawned in Gilmore's eyes. "This is about that girl who did the vanishing act at the mall parking lot, right? I remember my mama going on about that. Did she ever turn up?"

Sutton shook his head as he decided the tack to take.

Dodger, forgetting their agreement, asked the next question.

"Where were you on September 24, 1993, between the hours of four and ten p.m.?"

"Are you fuckin' kidding me? You think I keep a diary in case somebody comes along twenty years later and asks me to account for every minute? Get a fuckin' clue, dude, and stop wasting my time."

"All right," Dodger continued, refusing to be diverted, "let's go at it from a different angle. When you were in Rington helping your mother that September, what did you do in the afternoons and evenings?"

"Depended. What day of the week are we talking about?" Gilmore demanded.

"Friday," Dodger answered. "It was a Friday."

Gilmore didn't hesitate.

"Friday was pizza nights. I always took Mama to the Pizza Hut. She likes to go early, so we would've left the house about 4:30. After-wards, we'd go visit her sister Amis over in Jaster 'cause she had a bigger TV and we'd stay there to watch this show that Mama and Amis were crazy about."

"What was its name?" Sutton broke in.

"Hell, I don't know. Funny home videos. Some kind of stupid shit like that. Then after that came a detective show about this woman writer. It starred that Lansbury woman that Mama and Amis thought was the goods. Then we'd have ice cream, and then we'd go home. Usu-ally get there around ten."

"Is there anyone who can corroborate that?"

"Mama and Aunt Amis — maybe not the exact date but that that was what we did on Fridays. Maybe this old man who was a neighbor of Amis's who'd sometimes come over to watch the funny videos. Amis could tell you."

"Would your mother and aunt lie for you?" Dodger asked.

"I doubt it," Gilmore said glumly, with a sheepish look that under-mined the tough-guy demeanor. "I think they've pretty much washed their hands of me ever since I helped myself to Amis's cookie-jar stash. Mama said that was the frosting on the cake. They didn't even show up for the sentencing on this bullshit charge they pinned on me. But I tell you this right now. This girl you're asking about? Didn't know her. Never saw her. Never had nothin' to do with her. And you can take it to the fuckin' bank."

After that, Gilmore shut up and asked to be taken back to his cell.

On the return trip to Whitman, over coffee in a roadside joint with a refrigerator in the serving area and squashed ants for decoration on the bench upholstery, the two men discussed their impressions.

"It's possible he was lying. Guys like him lie on automatic," Sut-ton said, "but I didn't get that vibe. If he had anything to do with it, he wouldn't draw attention to himself by agreeing to see us." He flicked a suspicious black speck from the table top.

"Not without a lawyer there," Dodger agreed. "I don't see him for this either. You can check out the mother and aunt, but I'm guessing that he was with them, roaring his head off at funny videos or whatever it was."

"That's a long drive for nothing," Sutton griped. "To top it off, I think this is the worst coffee I ever had."

Dodger's cell rang. It was Jess. To his relief, her voice sounded normal when she spoke. "The writer doing the *VF* proposal about missing girls just called. Danielle Standridge is on his list."

"Did he say how he got her name?"

"He didn't say, and I didn't ask," Jess summarized, and Dodger knew his assessment of her mood as improved was false. "Anyway," she continued, "here's his phone number."

The next day was Sunday, and everyone but Dodger took the day off. Except for meals, he stayed in his room, reviewing what he'd come to think of as the Danielle Archive and making lists of questions he now knew would need to be answered. That was always where he started when he decided whether or not Mystery Mavens could be useful in a case's resolution. You had to know what you were after before you knew whether or not you were likely to find it.

That night, he and Whitman ate in the library in front of the TV again. There was a documentary about prep schools, presenting them as bastions of higher thought, strenuous learning, and good sportsmanship, environments capable of producing masters of the universe or, even better, those who commanded them.

By the time it was over and the two men were hoarse with whooping, they poured more drinks and shared reminiscences of what it had been like to spend four years in such a place.

"Some of the boys in my class seemed to be destined for greatness," Whitman conceded, "but those weren't the ones you heard about later. My most prominent classmate was the guy who ran that church-bank scam a few years ago. They'll be sending his reunion notices to the federal penitentiary system for decades. How about you?"

"Most of the boys I knew were dumber than dirt," Dodger said, and Whitman rolled on the sofa with laughter.

It was only later that Dodger realized it was the first time he'd ever thought about his old school without the memory of Joey Farraday and what he'd done wiping everything else.

Twenty.

· ·₀₀●●●●₀₀· ·

Too Much Grief?

At the start of his second week in Mill House, Dodger was finishing his second cup of coffee in the sun-flooded breakfast room on Monday morning when Gladys Tanner appeared to see if he wanted anything else.

"The pancakes were delicious, Mrs. Tanner, and I am stuffed," he assured her. "I'd like more, but I think I'd explode."

She smiled her pleasure at the compliment and corrected him for the way he'd addressed her. "It's Miss Tanner. I never married. But I'd rather you call me Gladys if it's all right with you."

"Gladys it is," Dodger said.

"I hear Mr. Travis took you to the memorial room that poor Miss Charlotte set up for Danny. She was my niece, you know, Danny I mean."

"I believe he mentioned that," Dodger temporized, unwilling to be drawn into a discussion of anything concerning his host with said host's employees.

"Yes, she was my sister May's younger daughter. She was a very odd kind of girl, self-centered and not at all pleasant to be around. Her nose was always stuck in a book. In my opinion, May and Andy spoiled her. I couldn't understand why Miss Charlotte was so set on her, but it was almost like they were sisters or best friends. What did you think of the memorial room?"

"Charlotte Whitman was very devoted to your niece, as you say. She must have been a wonderful mentor for the girl."

Gladys beamed. "She was turning her into a real lady, like her. She lent her things. She even let her use the pavilion for her writing."

"It's a lovely structure." Dodger nodded toward the iron-and-stone pavilion that lay thirty feet or so from the breakfast-room windows, a gleam of cream and black against the bright colors of the trees at the edge of the lawn.

Gladys shook her head. "Not that one. I mean The Library Pavilion, the one out back that had all the books. You know, the one that looked like a miniature of the house."

"I thought that was built later, after Danielle's disappearance," Dodger said, confused.

She shook her head. "You mean the business building. The Library Pavilion is what I'm talking about. If you take the track that leads off to the left from the back road, about halfway toward the gate, you'll see it, or what's left of it. It was a pretty little place. It just about broke Miss Charlotte's heart when those nasty tramps burned it. That was when Mr. Travis had the guard posts put in at the front and back gates. Miss Charlotte didn't like them. She said they spoiled the look of the place, but when he gets a thing in his head, there's nothing for it but that it be done."

"Better safe than sorry nowadays. It's that kind of world," Dodger sympathized.

"I've always thought that was what caused what happened later," Gladys continued. "First, Danny disappeared, which just about did her in, and then The Library Pavilion burned with all her special books inside. I remember she cried and cried. After that was when her problem got worse."

"Her problem?"

Gladys moved closer and looked over her shoulder as if to make sure no one was around to hear. "She drank." She sniffed, and Dodger suspected she disapproved of alcohol in any form or quantity. "She was always fond of a cocktail or a bit of sherry, like the rest of this crowd. But after those two things, it was like she never got enough. At first Mr. Travis just ignored it. I guess he thought she'd get better. When she didn't, he took to fussing at her and…"

She stopped in mid-sentence, and in a few seconds a maid appeared with a trolley to clear away breakfast.

"I beg your pardon, Mr. Dodger, Miss Tanner," the girl said, backing out.

Dodger checked his watch and stood up. "Don't stop on my

account. I'm on my way out."

Gladys's face resumed its usual mask of impassivity. They nodded, and Dodger went upstairs to get his kit for the day.

What Gladys had said explained a couple of things, Dodger thought. When he went out the back door on his way to the garage to retrieve the ProMaster, he looked in the direction that she had indicated to see if he could get a visual on whatever remained of The Library Pavilion. He thought he saw the remnants of a flagged path leading through the woods in the right direction, but wasn't sure. He'd check that out later, he thought. For now, he had to get to the police station where Deputy Sutton waited so they could make phone calls to potential witnesses who lived elsewhere.

At the station, Sutton was writing on a ruled yellow legal pad. "Just questions we ought to ask everyone, for consistency," he said cheerfully. "Also, what do you think about having one of those websites you hear about – you know, something like 'lookingfordanny.com' or 'danny-missing20yrs.com' or something like that? Mrs. Blythe, Mr. Whitman's secretary, offered to do any computer work we want."

"It couldn't hurt," Dodger said. "Before we start on the calls, I've got a question. What happened to Charlotte Whitman?"

The pen fell from Sutton's fingers and rolled onto the floor. "Damn. Let me get that."

When he sat up, he frowned. "Why are you asking about Charlotte Whitman?"

"Someone was talking about her the other day," Dodger answered, "and I realized I ought to know so I don't put my foot in it."

Sutton's face relaxed. "Makes sense. Anyway, it's no big mystery." He got up and went to a filing cabinet in the corner of the room. Opening the bottom drawer, he pulled out a folder, which he handed to Dodger.

"Go on. Open it. They say a picture's worth a thousand words."

Dodger put the folder on the scarred table next to the windows and removed the photographs that were its only contents. One after the other, they showed from different angles a terrible accident, with a small red sports car mangled, its female driver barely visible but clearly dead, the whole enmeshed in bits of tree limbs.

"It happened up on Ceil Mountain. That's the big hill across from the mall. It has an old gap with a couple of dangerous twists. It's so wooded up there that they didn't find the car for several days, and then, I've heard, only because the helicopter boys Mr. Whitman called in spotted some broken trees near the point of impact. Seems Mrs. Whitman flew right off the road. That red Porsche was a total loss."

"DUI?" Dodger asked, examining the photographs with a magnifying glass he took from his kit.

"As far as I know, the coroner didn't go there. He ruled it an accidental vehicular death," Sutton said, avoiding the question.

Dodger shot him a sharp look. "Message received, but just between you and me, was she drunk?"

Sutton hesitated, and then nodded. "Probably. I've heard the old sheriff had to drive her home quite a few times. Her drinking problem was an open secret. She got cut a lot of slack, and not just because she was Mrs. Whitman. Everybody liked her."

"Did you ever meet her?'

"Sure, a few times. When I graduated from ninth grade, Mrs. Whitman presented the prizes and I won one for 'Best Musician', if you can believe it. In high school, she was the sponsor for the Promoters Club when I was president, and she came to a couple of our project days. Later, my mother took me with her to a reception at Mill House while I was in college. And I'd see her around town sometimes. In a place this size, you see everybody sooner or later."

"What was she like?"

"She was beautiful. She had long blonde hair that she wore pinned up and the bluest eyes I've ever seen. My mother always says she looked like this actress named Grace Kelly."

"What kind of personality did she have? Was she outgoing, bashful, what?"

"She had nice manners and you couldn't help liking to be around her, but she wasn't one of those people who tries to take over. She just seemed like the kind of person you could trust. One thing that does seem kind of odd…"

He hesitated, and Dodger had to prompt him to go on.

"It sounds silly to say it, given that she had everything, being so beautiful and rich, but now that I look back, she seems sad. Like Danny, in a way. Neither one of them was what you'd call depressing to be around, but they seemed thoughtful, as if they saw something other people didn't and it made them unhappy. That sounds stupid, but it's the only way I know to put it."

"Maybe that's why they got along so well," Dodger pointed out.

"Could be," Sutton conceded. "I never thought about it that way before."

"I understand Charlotte took Danielle's disappearance hard."

Again came the reluctant nod. "That's what everybody says. But you've got to understand that I wasn't part of that crowd when Danny went missing, and I went off to Atlanta a few months later, to my summer job, and then I was in college. By the time Mrs. Whitman died, I was already in Atlanta. During the middle and late '90s, if I got home for a couple of days every two or three months, it was a big deal, so everything I know is second hand, mostly through my mother, or local gossip or what little's in the files — and a lot gets left out of the official files in cases like this. I know about these accident photographs because I found them in a locked drawer with some other what I guess you'd call sensitive materials, with a Keep Confidential note attached to them. We've digitized most of our old records that relate to fatalities, but not these. I keep thinking I should ask Mr. Whitman what he wants me to do with them, but I haven't got around to it. Truth be told, I've dodged it because I can't get a handle on his attitude toward what happened to her. My mother says he's never gotten over it. She thinks he blames Danny's disappearance for the drinking, or at least blames how upset Mrs. Whitman got when Danny didn't turn up."

"Do you suppose there's any chance that Charlotte's reaction was more than grief?" Dodger asked.

"What do you mean?" Sutton almost gulped.

"It occurred to me that maybe whatever happened to the girl was because of Charlotte Whitman or something she did. Maybe she was already drinking too much, and that caused whatever it was. Maybe what everybody thought was just grief may have had guilt mixed in with it."

"Why makes you say that?"

Dodger shrugged. "Think about it. They weren't related. There was an eighteen-year difference in their ages. Charlotte was an accomplished woman of wealth and position, Danielle a promising student. Okay, so Charlotte was mentoring the girl. I get that she'd be upset, maybe even devastated at the girl's disappearance, but to become an alcoholic over it? Doesn't that strike you as excessive? If she'd caused the disappearance, on the other hand, it would make more sense."

"That's ridiculous," Sutton objected. "Next, you'll be accusing Mr. Whitman."

Dodger considered it. "Well, I can think of scenarios he'd fit into. What if he and Danielle were having an affair, and Charlotte found out and later got into it with her? Or maybe the girl tried to force Whitman to marry her by threatening to go to Charlotte and he was the one who snatched her and did something with her."

"You can take that last one off the table," Sutton pointed out. "Whitman had an alibi for the time the girl disappeared. He was on a private plane with a couple of investors, flying from Los Angeles to New York. He didn't get back to Whitman until the next day."

"How did you remember that? I'm impressed."

"Don't be," Sutton frowned. "I spent part of last night going through the old files on the case again. I've come across several things that may be useful."

"As in?"

"How about the production assistant on **Before A Hero** who spoke to Danny that last afternoon? His name is Justin Richards."

"Then why don't we start the calls with him?"

"Turns out we can't," Sutton said, "at least not right away. His booking agency says he's on a movie shoot in an area where cell coverage is spotty. They claim they'll get word to him, and he'll be in touch, but they won't commit as to when that might be."

"Damn," Dodger muttered.

"Damn," Sutton agreed. "On the other hand, he was interviewed at the time by the Los Angeles police at the request of the Whitman sheriff. A transcript of the interview is in the files. I've made a copy for you." He handed off the photocopy. "Bring it back. This isn't exactly protocol."

"Will do. Have you read it?"

Sutton nodded. "It includes a day-by-day schedule of the production, listing what was shot where and when. Apart from that, it's not very informative, at least not in any positive kind of way. According to the interview, Justin didn't interact with the Whitman-Brown majorettes apart from issuing the costumes they wore in the movie. Moreover, he said that he hadn't heard or seen anything that led him to believe that any of the movie crew or actors were involved with the girls. He said it was an efficient shoot and that they'd been in town just long enough to get local color, which they'd done, on schedule. He said that the only reason he spoke with Danny that last afternoon they were in town was to give her the card of an agent he knew in Hollywood who might be interested in her as a client. He told the LA officers that 'the camera loved her'. In other words, see no evil, hear no evil, speak no evil. It doesn't sound promising."

"Oh, I don't know," Dodger said. "If I were a fifteen-year-old girl with smarts and ambition and a film professional gave me the card of a Hollywood agent and told me to call him, I might see that as a ticket away from an unpleasant situation at home. In fact, that's the first piece of information that suggests Danielle might have a specific motive for going some place else. Did the Whitman sheriff check out the Richards guy?"

Sutton nodded. "From what's in the file, he was the one they suspected she'd run away with. That was the first theory. That's why the locals asked the LA cops to talk with him, but they seem to have given up on Richards fast."

"Any indication as to why?"

"He was with one or more of the production crew not only the afternoon of the entertainment at the mall but for the rest of the weekend and the first two days of the following week. If she ran away with him, she didn't do it *with* him, if you follow my meaning. Also, if you buy into the idea that she didn't run but was snatched, it couldn't have been him. His alibi was rock solid."

"Did the LA police follow through with the agent whose card Richards gave Danielle?"

Sutton nodded and checked the file. "They seem to have called him a couple of weeks after she disappeared. He said he hadn't heard from her."

"Maybe she waited to contact him. Maybe it's time someone called him again."

"Not possible," Sutton told him. "He died a couple of years ago, after selling out to a larger agency. I've asked that agency to search his old records and see if they turn up Danny's name or, for that matter, the name of any under-twenty female who contacted him between September 1993 and September 1994. They're supposed to get in touch within the next few days. That's pretty much all we can do on that front until either Richards or the talent agency gets back to me."

"So, who's on the call list this morning?" Dodger asked, putting the contraband photocopy of the LA police report in his briefcase.

"We're spoiled for choice," Sutton said. "These are the names of the people around Danny for whom we've been able to locate current contact info." He handed a word-processed list to Dodger. "You pays your money and you takes your choice, as the old carney barkers used to say."

Dodger began reading. "Dorothy Hernandez? Who's she?"

"Ethel Bowland's daughter, the girl who won the prizes that should have been Danny's."

"She married a guy named Hernandez?" Dodger laughed. "I'll bet that pleased her mother no end."

"Might be worth calling just to find out," Sutton grinned.

"Andrea Hand? I don't recall that name," Dodger admitted, going back to the list.

"No reason you should — it shows up in police files that you haven't seen. She was, by all accounts back then, Danny's best friend. There was some confusion about where she was that Friday afternoon, which, as far as I can tell, led the sheriff to suspect that she might have helped Danny leave town. They had the girl and her parents in several times. I remember Andrea — cute black girl whose dad was a mill manager."

"Did they live on the same street with the Standridges and the Karrolls?" Dodger asked.

Sutton shook his head. "Even that late in the day, blacks and whites didn't mix much here. The Hands had a house on some acreage between Whitman and Blevins."

"This is an Atlanta number," Dodger said.

"According to her aunt in Rington, who provided the number, Andrea's an executive for UPS."

"Mrs. Johnston is the woman who owned the *Courier Loom*, the newspaper, right?" Dodger asked, going to the next name.

"That's right. She inherited it from her father. I think it was her great- or maybe great-great grandfather who started it, back when the textile business revved up here."

"Last, but not least, who is Joel Harriman?"

"He was the band director at Whitman-Brown the entire time Danny went there. She played French horn in the band, and so he knew her that way. Also, from the file, he seems to have been the main authority over the majorettes. He's music director for a Florida university now."

"What about Harold Karroll? I don't see him on here."

"He's already got a separate file," Sutton explained. "Anyway, so far the lawyers are cagey. They say they've got to get in touch with Mrs. Cutliffe to get her permission to release her ex-husband's contact information because it's all part of her divorce case file."

'Let's call and give her a heads up,' Dodger said.

"Want to start with her?"

"Sure. I've got another question for her anyway."

When Sutton finished updating Mrs. Cutliffe and thanked her for her assistance with the lawyers, he put the phone on speaker. "Do you remember Art Dodger? He has a question for you."

"Mrs. Cutliffe? Art Dodger here. This may be embarrassing, but bear with me. We need the answers to a couple of questions."

"Whatever I can do to help," she said, her voice an echo of itself over the speaker.

"It's about the kiddie porn you found in the basement of the house you shared with Harold."

"Yes." She began to sound more guarded.

"Do you still have it? You said you'd hidden it in case you needed it for the divorce. Did you keep it in case you needed it later?"

"No, I didn't. Once I got my final piece of paper, I took all of it out in the back yard and burnt it in that barbecue pit Harold was so proud of. It seemed like the right thing to do."

Sutton shrugged, but Dodger persisted.

"I got the impression that you glanced at it."

"That's right, quick like."

"What can you can tell us about what you saw? I know it's been a long time."

"That's not the kind of thing you forget," she said. "You're sure this will help you find that poor girl?"

"It's possible," Dodger told her.

"Well, there were a bunch of pictures. The two or three I saw were of little girls and boys doing things to each other and little girls posed without clothes, with their legs spread."

"What about the books and VHS tapes? Can you remember anything about them?"

"In a way they were worse. They had titles like *Big Man Shows Little Girl Everything She Needs to Know* and *Twelve Is Sweet, Ten Is Sweeter*. Oh, and *Deep Throating Dainty Dottie*. I've never forgotten, much as I'd like to."

"Just one more question," Dodger asked her. "Do you remember the age of the girls in the photographs?"

This evidently wasn't what she'd been expecting, and there was a brief pause before she answered. "They weren't babies or anything like that, but they weren't teenagers either. From what I remember, I'd say maybe eight or nine years old."

Dodger nodded and made a note as Sutton thanked her again and rung off.

"What the fuck? You embarrassed that poor woman half to death."

"It was important," Dodger told him. "If Harold Karroll was into kids that age, then he wouldn't be in any way interested in a fifteen-year-old for hanky panky. His ex-wife may have eliminated him from the suspect list without meaning to."

"True to a point," Sutton said, "but it doesn't get him off the hook for kidnapping. What if Danny discovered his little hobby and threatened to tell? We still need to talk with him. If I haven't heard from the lawyers by tomorrow, I'll juice them up." He turned back to his list. "Do you have a preference for who gets called next? No? Then, let's take it in order."

"Works for me," Dodger agreed, getting out his iPad and Bluetooth keyboard to take notes.

Two hours and four phone calls later, they had added maybe half a dozen pieces of solid information to their trove.

Dorothy Bowland Hernandez stated that she had known Danny

and considered her a friend, whatever her mother might say. "Mama had odd ideas that Danny was a bad influence, when she was anything but. As for boys, gosh Jase, I never heard she had any particular interest in any boy except for you." She giggled. "Everybody knew she was sweet on you. 'Course, most of us were then."

Sutton blushed as she continued.

"As for anybody who might have wanted to kidnap or hurt her, unless that crazy guy from Blevins who followed her around went over the edge, I wouldn't have a clue. And I don't know why she would have wanted to run away." She paused for a moment. "Are you saying she never turned up, anywhere? That's sad. She was a terrific girl."

Andrea Hand, it turned out, could tell them more about the situation at the Standridge house. She knew of no one in particular who would have wanted to kidnap Danny — "except for the Dunderhead, of course, and he was too chicken to do anything about it" — and she had no knowledge of any plan on Danny's part to leave town. "Not that I would have blamed her. Those parents of hers were a piece of work. She didn't say much about it even then, but I got the idea toward the last that her dad tried to mess with her and her sister and her mother just stood there and wrung her hands. I felt so bad about it, I asked my parents if she could come and live with us."

"What did Danny think about that?" Sutton asked.

"She was all for it. She was trying to figure out how to tell her parents so they wouldn't try to stop her."

"And that was just before she disappeared?"

Andrea thought about it. "It was while we were still doing the movie — I was a majorette too — so, it was within a couple of weeks of that Friday."

"It's interesting that you remember the circumstances so well," Dodger said.

"That's because she was my best friend." Andrea hesitated before continuing. "Look, you know I'm black, right? Well, when I started at Whitman-Brown, I'd say maybe twenty percent of the student body was black, but there wasn't much friendliness between whites and blacks. There was some trouble a couple of years before when a black girl went to the Harvest Dance with a white boy. That's probably why everybody seemed scared of getting too close. You remember that, Jase?"

"Do I ever," Sutton muttered.

"Well, Danny didn't pay any attention to all that. We tried out for the majorette squad together, and from the first time we laid eyes on each other, it was like we were meant to be friends. She was there for me every step of the way. I'd have done anything for her, and I think she would have for me too. I always think of her as my first friend by choice. You know how most of the people you know when you're a kid you get to be friends with because they live next door or sing in the youth choir with you in church? Those relationships are based on location as much as anything else. With Danny it was different. We met because of the majorette tryouts, but we'd have been friends even if we hadn't made the squad." Her voice caught, but she went on. "There's hardly a day that passes that I don't think of her."

"So you don't remember anything out of the ordinary those last days before she went away?" Sutton asked.

"No. I wish I could help. I really do, but I don't remember anything different. She thought the movie stuff was funny, but they didn't mix with us."

"Excuse me, Ms. Hand. Art Dodger, again. What did Danielle think of Charlotte Whitman?"

"The one who was married to the mill owner? She thought she was great. She was always going on about how she wished she could be like Mrs. Whitman. I'm not sure she liked Mr. Whitman as much, but I think that was because she overheard part of an argument between the Whitmans where he told her that he thought she spent too much time with Danny, that it wasn't fair to turn her into what amounted to a personal pet."

"How do you know that?" Sutton asked.

"Because she told me," Andrea said. "How else would I know? I wasn't one of Charlotte Whitman's pets, so I wasn't part of that circle."

"Did Danielle understand what he meant by that?" Dodger wanted to know.

"She got the idea from something that Charlotte Whitman said that Mr. Whitman was jealous of anything that didn't include him."

"Danielle thought Travis Whitman was jealous of Charlotte?" Sutton interjected.

"Yeah. Sounds screwy, huh? But Danny could be pretty imaginative when it came to people's motives. Back then, she was this weird combination of naïve and smart. For instance, I've never been sure of what was going on at the Standridges — if Danny got it right and if I heard it right. It's a terrible thing to think of anybody, that he'd go after his own kids, especially somebody who seemed normal like Mr. Standridge."

"It's hard to tell about people," Sutton agreed.

"Jase, could I ask you something? Does this call mean that you're looking for Danny again? I hope so, because the police didn't seem that interested before. They did call me and my parents in a couple of times — I guess because she and I were best friends, and I know they came to school and talked to all of the majorettes. Then the investigation seemed to stop. It was as if nothing out of the ordinary had happened. I couldn't figure it out."

"So no one talked to you after those first interviews?" Dodger interjected.

"No. The one time I've had any contact with the sheriff's office was when I called a couple of times about ten or twelve years ago and asked if they'd heard anything."

"What did they tell you?" Sutton asked.

"Nothing. They blew me off, basically told me to stop wasting their time. I had no idea that you're the sheriff now, or I'd have called you before this."

"We are looking into it again," Sutton said, voice cautious, "to see if we can develop any new information or at least get a fresh take on what was provided before."

"Well, I'll tell you who you should talk to if you want to learn more about what was going on with the Standridges — my mother. I know that May, Danny's mother, called her not long before Danny disappeared. Let me give you her number. She's working in Miami now, but it's okay if you call her at the office. And, Jase?"

"Yes, Andrea?"

"If you find her or…" her voice broke. They heard her take a deep breath before she went on. "Will you let me know what you turn up?"

"Sure, Andrea. It's good to talk to you."

"You, too, Jase." She rung off, but not before Dodger heard the suppressed sob. So someone else cared, he thought.

Susan Hand couldn't add much to what they already knew save that, contrary to what Andrea seemed to think, Danielle had already spoken to her mother about moving in with the Hands, and Mrs. Standridge had not taken it well. "I never told Andrea what she said because it was so hurtful. She'd made friends and got good grades in school, and I didn't want her to hear that kind of talk from her best friend's mother. Danny was a sweet girl without a prejudiced bone in her body, but her mother was a racist, pure and simple. She said her daughter wasn't moving anywhere and certainly not to live with a pickaninny and her jungle-bunny parents. I pointed out to her that my husband Franklin was the same kind of manager at the mill as her husband. She said that was just because of EEO and that people like us should be grateful and keep to our place. When I asked her what she meant by that she made it clear she wanted us to discourage the relationship between our daughter and hers. This was just a few days before that awful day at the mall. Franklin and I were still debating about how to handle the situation when Danny disappeared. We weren't going to keep the girls apart, but we couldn't decide how much to tell them of May Standridge's attitude. So Danny still hasn't surfaced? That's a shame, a real shame. She was a sweet girl back then. I hope life's been kind to her."

"Nice lady," Sutton commented after he disconnected.

"Mrs. Standridge, on the other hand, really grows on you, doesn't she?" Dodger grimaced.

"Like a fungus," Sutton agreed. "The further we get into this, the better I understand Debbie."

Next on the list was Janice Johnston, owner and editor of the once-and-former town newspaper, the *Courier Loom*. Mrs. Johnston was willing to talk about the disappearance, and came up with a new tidbit of information as to why the story had attracted little attention. "I'm afraid that was up to me," she admitted. "To begin with, we covered the story as a mysterious disappearance, but then, the very next day, May Standridge called and said that she thought I should know that Danny had simply run off after they'd had an argument and that they'd let me know when she came back or when they heard from her. I called my AP guy, and that update was the story they gave the most column inches to. Then, a few days later Travis Whitman called to say how much he appreciated my handling the story in that way. Then he added that he wanted to take me to lunch at his club in Charlotte to talk about upping his annual advertising budget."

"You thought the two things were tied together — Whitman's advertising and you continuing to treat the story as a simple case of runaway girl?" Dodger asked.

"I did, heaven help me," Mrs. Johnston guffawed, and then stopped. "Look, the financial realities for small-town newspapers were wonky even then. If there had been any hard news, I wouldn't have handled it that gently, shall we say, but there wasn't, and I knew the local cops had looked. On the fifth anniversary of the disappearance, we did do a story — this kid who was interning did the legwork, I remember — but there still wasn't any concrete indication that anything had happened to her. For all I could learn, at the time or later, it was a simple case of runaway girl. Given what her family said, I thought she'd turn up. I gather she still hasn't?"

"Afraid not," Sutton said. "That's why we're looking into it again."

"Good luck," Mrs. Johnston offered. "If you can think of anything else I can…"

"One more thing," Dodger interrupted. "Do you happen to recall how your paper treated the death of Charlotte, Travis Whitman's wife?"

"She died in a car crash, right? Maybe 1999, 2000? I can't cite chapter and verse on the specific wording, but we had a standard format for accidents with fatalities. For starters, we had a policy against printing photographs of the accident scene. All we ever did was publish a brief account stating that an accident had occurred, where and when, involving whom. The individual's obit would say the person had died of accidental causes, no more. Later, once the coroner's report was out, we'd quote appropriate excerpts. The lawyers said that was the best way to avoid liability suits. The *Courier Loom* handled all traffic deaths that way, and hers would have been no exception."

"Well, that answers the question of how Danielle's disappearance stayed under the radar," Dodger said to Sutton after the call was ended. "It was treated as a voluntary absence to begin with. I can see why the Standridges would have wanted it handled that way — who knows what a lot of attention might have turned up about the relationship between Andrew and his daughters? What I don't understand is why

Travis Whitman got involved to the point that he told Mrs. Johnston how to handle the story."

"I may know the answer to that," Sutton answered. "There were some labor issues here back in the 1980s that got a lot of publicity, and Old Man Whitman — Travis Whitman's father — thought the press was to blame for stirring things up. He put out a dictate that nobody talked to the press about anything to do with the mill or the town. Maybe Mr. Whitman picked up that attitude. Other than that, who knows? Unless maybe he thought it would upset his wife," the deputy pointed out. "You know how once those stories get started, they blow up all over the place — newspapers, magazines, TV. Maybe he didn't want her reminded about it for months, given how upset she was about the girl's disappearance."

Dodger made a note of a question he wanted to ask Jess (assuming she was still talking to him), and turned back to Sutton.

"So, who does that leave?"

"Joel Harriman, the music director," the deputy told him. "I'd be surprised if we get diddly from him. I couldn't find where he was even interviewed at the time except as part of the band-majorette group, and he doesn't seem to have volunteered any information."

"Maybe something's occurred to him in the meantime," Dodger suggested.

Harriman sounded hurried but was cooperative. He remembered Danielle Standridge. She'd been a dutiful band member and a better majorette. His recollection was of an attractive, pleasant girl who had never given him or the girls' coach any trouble — he knew because they'd talked about it after her disappearance. When asked if he knew what had happened to the girls' coach, he provided her name and phone number. "We still see each other from time to time at coaching conferences," he volunteered. "She's coached for several years at a private school in Connecticut. I'm sure she'll be able to tell you more about the Standridge girl than I can."

"Patsy Hudnutt?" Sutton said after the call had ended. "I remember now that there was a girls' coach at Whitman-Brown, and the name does sound familiar. It's funny that she didn't turn up in the 1993 interview list. They did a piss-poor job of on-the-ground investigation."

"Well, as you say," Dodger reminded him, "the disappearance was treated more as a voluntary event than as a criminal act that required urgent action."

"But, still," Sutton frowned, "No matter how smart she was or how grown-up she seemed or what her family said, Danny was fifteen years old. Today, it would be an Amber Alert situation and we'd have called in the bloodhounds at once."

He brooded, while Dodger added another item to his "ask Jess" list. Outside, car brakes squealed, and Sutton got up to check the street from the front windows of the big room.

"Want to grab lunch or call Hudnutt first?" Dodger asked, looking at his watch.

"Let's call Hudnutt," Sutton said.

Of all those to whom they'd spoken, the girls' coach was the most surprised.

"You're calling about what?"

When Sutton answered that question to her satisfaction, she was cooperative enough, but it appeared that she remembered very little about Danielle Standridge off the top of her head. Then, with no further prompting, it was as if a light bulb went off, illuminating at least bits of the past.

"She was that extremely pretty girl who was so young to be a senior, right?"

"Correct."

"Gosh, I haven't thought about her in forever. Let me see. She was a majorette, the one who disappeared while those movie people were in town. I remember that, mainly because of the locker."

"What about a locker?" Sutton stopped her.

"You know that all the majorettes and cheerleaders had individual gym lockers?"

"You mean in addition to their regular lockers?" Sutton asked.

Both men sat up straighter as the crisp, clear voice continued.

"Yes. They were in the girls' gym, in a room to the side. Each girl who became a cheerleader or a majorette was assigned her own locker. She was expected to keep her uniform in it, together with her baton, megaphone, or other items she needed for her appearances."

"So Danielle was one of those who had a locker in the gym?" Dodger clarified.

"As far as I know, Danny could *still* have a locker in the gym," the woman laughed, then gulped it back. "Sorry, I forgot the circumstances for a minute, but it was so odd. You see, right after she disappeared, the other majorettes set up a flower holder in front of her locker with a message on the ribbon that said 'Come home, Danny.' When those flowers died, they brought in more. I think one of the girls had an uncle who owned the local florist, and he let her use leftovers."

"Do you recall if the police examined the locker?" Sutton asked.

"I seem to remember the sheriff did come by one day. He must have broken the lock because I remember one of the other girls replaced it 'to protect Danny's stuff' as she put it."

"So the sheriff didn't take everything?"

"I'm not sure he took anything. Those girls would have watched him like a hawk. Anyway, that was when the police still thought she'd just run away and would return on her own. Her fellow majorettes certainly did. So, anyway, when she hadn't come back by the end of the fall term, I intended to empty out her locker and reassign it to whoever we chose to replace her. The other majorettes went ballistic. Replacing her on the field was one thing — they recognized that the line had to be balanced, and the squad alternate filled in all season without any objection from them. Messing with her locker was something different in their eyes. That was Danny's locker, and it would be sacrilege to touch it. They made such a big deal out of it that it seemed simpler to let them keep it locked. They stopped the flower thing after a few months, but they replaced it with a sign. All of those girls had known Danny, so I expect it was understandable that they would defend what they saw as her territory. What was surprising was that, when the last of that group graduated a couple of years later, succeeding squads continued to respect what they'd started. When I left in '03, ten years after she disappeared, Danny Standridge still had a locker at Whitman-Brown."

Twenty-One.

. . ₀₀●●◉◉●₀₀ . .

Back to School

By unspoken agreement, they went back to The Tastee Grill. Lunch today was not only late but more hurried and conversation brief. Afterwards, Sutton called Roosevelt Jones, and the two men returned to Whitman-Brown High School. Bypassing the semicircular arc at the front, the deputy pulled into the rear drive, where the caretaker waited for them at the entrance to the gymnasium.

"I've turned on the lights," he informed them. "The building's been shut up for quite a while. It'll be stuffy, but we can see where we're going." He ushered them through the double, wood-framed glass doors and into an entrance area with empty display cases. "That's where the athletic trophies used to be. They moved 'em to Rington, where I hear they have all of 'em in one big display case with the Whitman-Brown name above it. Sad times. Now, what can I do for you gentlemen today?"

"We understand there's a separate area where the Whitman-Brown cheerleaders and majorettes had lockers where they kept their uniforms."

Jones thought about it. "I think I know what you mean. It's just up here." He led them across still-shiny floor tiles, around the corner, and up a long hall to a pair of doors. "The first one goes into the regular girls' locker room. The next one is what you want." He got out the big ring, selected a key, and opened the heavy metal door to a room no more than twenty-feet square. Along three of its walls was ranged a bank of larger-than-usual lockers. On the fourth was the door into the gymnasium proper, together with a gallery of photographs. Dodger went to the wall. The pictures showed Whitman-Brown cheerleaders and majorettes performing, often on a football field, but sometimes in a gym or on stage. There were gaps in the arrangement, probably due to later members of these elite groups removing images of themselves and their friends. The older photographs, however, appeared to remain where they hung. Dodger studied them. There, in the second photo from the left, in the second row, stood Danielle, arms clasped around a majorette to either side of her, all of them in full regalia, grinning as they stood underneath goalposts, from the crossbar of which hung a banner emblazoned with HEAR US ROAR! From the sidelines a somewhat ratty lion mascot gave them a V-for-Victory sign.

"Here she is," he told Sutton, who walked over and took down the photograph Dodger indicated.

"I'm borrowing this for the time being," the deputy advised the caretaker. "It might come in handy."

Jones shrugged. "As far as I'm concerned, you take anything you want except the windows out of the walls if it'll help find that little girl. My job is to preserve the school's buildings, not keep the police from doing their job."

"I appreciate it," Sutton told him, and Dodger could see that he did.

They turned around. Danielle's locker was easy to find. Not only was there a sign on it proclaiming *Danny Come Home* but also it was the only unit that still sported a lock.

"Do you have the key?" Sutton asked.

Jones shook his head. "We play go fish in desk drawers or call a locksmith, if you want to wait. If you don't, I've got some cutters back in my office that'll go through this like butter."

Sutton opted for cutting the lock, and he and Dodger went through the other door onto the gymnasium floor while Jones went back to the main building in search of the necessary tool.

"That's a hell of a note," Sutton said, a look approaching bewilderment on his face. "Twenty years she's been gone, and I'm about to open her majorette locker. What do you expect to find in there anyway?"

"I'm not sure," Dodger said, "but if we're lucky, I think we'll be repaid for the effort."

They walked onto the center of the court and looked around.

"Was this where your school team played its at-home basketball games?" Dodger asked.

Sutton nodded. "I usually sat up there, about halfway back." He indicated an area. "Danny and Andrea sat down here. Danny liked basketball because the majorettes didn't perform and she could watch the whole game."

"Sounds as if she wasn't crazy about being a majorette," Dodger remarked.

"You know," Sutton said, sounding surprised. "I'm not sure she was. Now that I think about it, she got into a lot of extracurricular stuff at school, more than anybody else I know of. After what we've heard about her family, I wonder now if she did it to stay away from home as much as possible."

"Makes sense," Dodger agreed.

Sutton stood, hands on hips, looking around, and a loud sigh escaped him.

Dodger stared at the bleachers rising toward the roof. "Does it seem strange to you to be back here?"

Sutton nodded. "It's hard to believe the last time was almost twenty years ago. We had some of the senior events in the gym, and I haven't been back since. It wasn't a happy graduation. I remember thinking about Danny the whole time I watched everybody else get their diplomas. Do you know, if she'd been around, she'd be just sixteen when she got out? I didn't think about it much at the time, but she was so young. Now, she's been gone all this time, and I didn't go on to become a jazz musician like I wanted. And all this other stuff has happened, like the mill closing, which would have seemed impossible to us back then, and it's like an eye blink ago that I was last here."

The caretaker hailed them from the door of the locker room, cutters in hand. "It's open," he announced.

Their feet seemed to echo more loudly as they walked across the wooden floor and back into the locker room.

"Okay," Sutton said, "We got to do this a certain way if we expect to be able to use what we find in court. The first thing is to get a stack of evidence bags and some tags. Luckily I carry that in the cruiser."

When he returned, he set an unopened box of bags on a bench that ran down the center of the room, and slit the top with a box cutter he'd also brought with him. "This seems like a lot of trouble, but if we don't do it right, we're wasting our time in terms of evidence collection."

First, he took a photo with his iPhone, of the locker as a whole and then got a close-up of the lock, after which he explained to the other two men the procedures that had to be followed. "So," he said, "the integrity of the find and the witnessing of what we remove is critical. Dodger, here's a pair of latex gloves. Put 'em on before you touch the lock. Okay, now you open the door and hold up each item as you remove it. I'll photograph it and make a list, and Mr. Jones can be the witness. Then you put each object in a separate evidence bag and I'll tag it. Are we good? Okay, Dodger, go to it."

When he opened the locker door, it occurred to Dodger that they were about to look at the unit as it existed when Danielle had last shut the door, barring anything the Whitman sheriff might have moved in his cursory search twenty years before. Except for the thick coat of dust that lay over everything, he guessed that the girl could, from its contents, still outfit herself for a proper appearance on the field. Her majorette's headgear, much smaller than the one she and the other girls had worn for the movie, sat on a shelf at the top. Half a foot underneath that shelf sat a second where he could see a pocket-sized camera and a school binder. Below that was the rod on which a relatively skimpy uniform hung. It had once been sparkly. Now it was a dull red with tarnished gold spangles that didn't glitter even when the flash from Sutton's camera went off. On the floor of the locker stood a pair of knee-high vinyl boots that had no discernible color. Sutton's camera flashed again.

"Got all the pictures you need of the inside before we clear it out?" Dodger asked. "Okay, here goes. First the hat." He rotated it for Sutton's benefit, side to side and top to bottom, and then put it in the evidence bag, which he handed to Sutton, who tagged and initialed it and then handed it to Jones for his initials. The same procedure was followed in turn with each piece of the rest of the uniform until, at last, only the contents of the shallow shelf remained untouched. Dodger removed the camera, held it while it was photographed, and then bagged and handed it over to Sutton. The school binder was the last item that was in plain sight, and once it was processed Dodger motioned for Sutton to move closer to the locker.

"I've got a hunch she may have hidden something in here, and the logical place would be to tape it under one of these shelves. Put the camera under here and point it upward," he said, indicating the bottom of the shallow shelf. "Now, I'll feel around to see if there's any-thing here."

Sutton shot the picture and frowned as Dodger worked his latex-clad fingers over the underside of the shelf. "Nope," he announced. "Nothing."

It was more awkward, but the deputy slid the camera, face-up, across the bottom shelf so that its lens was pointed toward the bottom of the top shelf. The flash went off, Sutton removed the camera, and Dodger repeated the careful groping. After a few seconds, a broad grin spread across his face. "We've hit pay dirt," he announced. "There's something small taped here, at the back, but the tape seems to have solidified. Any ideas?"

"Let's get the bottom shelf out," Jones suggested. "Step back and give me a minute." He used the handles of the cutters to give the underside a sharp knock, and then worked the shelf with his hands. After a couple of minutes, it came free from the notches at the side.

Sutton stuck his head inside the locker and shone his flashlight upwards. "Yeah, it's small, and there seems to be a loose edge to the tape at the far corner. Let me see what I can do." He took out a small penknife, and Dodger could hear a faint scraping. Then Sutton stood up, his left hand extended, a tiny brown leather object no larger than 2x3" in the palm. He rotated his hand and stared at it before looking at Dodger.

"What did you expect to find?"

"A diary," Dodger told him. "A small diary, with a lock. And it looks like you've found it."

"Thanks for the help, Mr. Jones," Sutton said. "I'll let you know what happens."

A few minutes later, they were back at the station with the pile of evidence bags. Sutton left a message with the state forensics lab to call as soon as possible, and then turned to Dodger and asked the very question he'd wanted to avoid.

"What gave you the idea that something like a diary might be in there?"

Dodger hadn't decided whether to tell Sutton about the memorial museum at Mill House in which he'd found the jewelry box with the fake bottom holding the envelope with the key that almost certainly fit the tiny journal's lock. Which was why it was fortunate that a good alternative answer at once came to him. The bonus was that it was almost true.

"Jess Hannah, the researcher I partner with in Mystery Mavens back in Boston, is one smart cookie," he explained. "She was the one who told me the girl probably had a diary and, if she did, she'd have hidden it at school, given what we've turned up about her home situation. It seemed to me that her locker was the logical place if she had indeed done that. Of course, as we saw for ourselves, her regular locker in the school building no longer exists, so I'd given up the idea. Then, when Patsy Hudnutt told us that Danielle also had a locker at the gym, it seemed at least worth a shot. I'm glad it wasn't a waste of your time."

Sutton shrugged. "According to Mr. Whitman, as long as no serious crime comes up, I'm yours. What's on tap for tomorrow?"

"Back in 1993, there was a list in the *Courier Loom* of locations at which the movie crew shot footage. Here's the article. Could we do a drive-by?"

Sutton looked at the scan. "Sure. It should take no more than a couple of hours to make the circuit, depending on how much time you want to spend at each place. What next?"

"I know we still need to talk to Harold Karroll, and there are a couple more people Jess Hannah has turned up I'd like you to call."

"Who's that?" Sutton asked as Dodger rummaged in his Dayrunner.

"First, can you locate a man named Harrison North? He's Lisa North's ex-husband. They divorced in 1999, so he's been gone a while. Given that they married after you left town and he was gone before you returned, you may never have never met him."

"I didn't," Sutton agreed. "But I can start with *North v. North* in the divorce-court records and see what turns up. Why are we contacting him by the way?"

"Jess turned up the fact that it was Harrison North who filed for divorce on the grounds of infidelity with an unnamed other person. I think it'd be interesting to know who the other person was," Dodger said. "What if the affair had been going on for years, and Danielle discovered it?"

"Seems farfetched, but all right, what else?"

Dodger handed him the note he'd made of the name and phone

number Jess had passed along. "I'd like you to call this man and ask him something."

Sutton looked at the paper and frowned. "Hank Gribble?"

"Jess Hannah says he's a writer we should talk to," Dodger explained, adding, "He's working up a proposal for *Vanity Fair* Magazine on a story about teenaged girls whose disappearances were treated as runaways but who have remained missing for over ten years. Danielle is one of the girls he plans on writing about. He may not tell us much because he'll want to protect his story, but, if we can get it out of him, I want to know how he got Danielle's name."

Sutton continued to hold the paper, avoiding Dodger's gaze as he stared down. After what seemed a very long time, he looked up, his eyes troubled.

"Have you mentioned this to Mr. Whitman?"

Dodger shook his head. "Should I?"

"Look," Sutton said, "if I tell you something, will you swear not to let him know you know, much less that you heard it from me?"

"Seriously?"

"Seriously. This town isn't even incorporated any more. We're part of the county now. The only reason we're able to keep town services operating is because the Whitman-Brown foundation subsidizes everything." His gesture included himself as well as his office.

"I get it," Dodger said. "Whitman in effect owns all his eyes survey around here. What does that have to do with Hank Gribble?"

"He called here a couple of months ago, fishing for information on Danny's disappearance. Said he heard about her from a friend of his who'd worked on a movie that was being shot here at the time."

"That explains how she made the list anyway," Dodger said. "All right, so Gribble heard about Danielle, wanted to include her in his article, and called you. What then?"

"When Mr. Whitman hired me, he told me that any requests from the media for information on anything were to be cleared with him before I handled them. So I made an excuse and told this Gribble guy I'd get back to him. When I told Mr. Whitman about it, he pitched a fit. Under no circumstances, ever, under threat of fire, brimstone and anything else you can think of, he informed me, was I to give anyone from the outside any information about Danny Standridge unless he authorized it."

"What did you tell Hank Gribble?"

"Nada," Sutton said. "I didn't call him back. Funny thing is he hasn't called me back either."

"He wouldn't have needed a lot of information on all the girls to do a magazine proposal," Dodger explained. "When you'd have heard from him would be when his proposal was accepted."

"So, anyway, I thought that would be an end to it although I'll confess it did make me take another look at one or two of the old files. The next day, Mrs. Blythe called to ask what I knew about an outfit called Mystery Mavens. I looked it up online and called a couple of people I know who've worked with other cold-case organizations. From what I could turn up, it seemed all right, so I called and told her so. The next thing I knew, Mr. Whitman was headed north to talk to you guys."

"Why do you think Whitman would mind if I knew about Gribble calling?"

"Because he told me not to mention it to anybody. Let me ask you, has he told you about Gribble himself?"

"No," Dodger admitted. "Not a word."

"Why wouldn't he have told you that unless he didn't want you to know?"

Twenty-Two.

·∙•◦◌❀◌◦•∙·

Movie Night

Back at Mill House later that afternoon, Dodger thought about Sutton's question. He couldn't answer it, just as he couldn't answer one that he had asked himself throughout the several days he'd spent in Whitman. Why had Travis Whitman asked Mystery Mavens to look into the disappearance of Danielle Standridge? As a rule, the group was approached by family members or professionals who'd worked on an unsolved case they couldn't let go of. Whitman was neither. At first, Dodger suspected that perhaps he'd had more than a friendly interest in the missing girl, but that didn't seem to be right. He wasn't offering suggestions or showing the kind of curiosity Dodger would have expected if that were so.

Now, sprawled on the sleek four-poster bed, hands propped behind his head, he stared at the mirrored canopy, considering both questions, and realized they might be related. To see if Jess would agree, he called her.

"Jessica Hannah," she said crisply.

"Hey, Jess. It's me."

"If by 'me' you mean Dodger, then that's pretty obvious. What do you want?"

"A friendlier greeting?"

"Yes, well, I'll work on that, when I have time. Now, what can I do for you?"

"I just learned something interesting."

"And that is…"

"What would you say if I told you that Hank Gribble, the writer working on the *VF* proposal, called the deputy sheriff here two months ago asking about the Standridge girl and that Travis Whitman went ballistic when he heard about it?"

She thought for maybe two seconds.

"That it wasn't a coincidence Whitman showed up in Boston shortly thereafter, with a request that Mystery Mavens look into the girl's disappearance."

"That's my take too. The question is why?"

"Distraction, diversion, spin control?"

"Okay," he said. "Distraction and spin control I get, given what I've heard about Whitman's obsession with information containment, but what's with diversion?"

"You should know — it's a writer thing."

"I'm still not with you."

She sighed. "There are writers who won't work on a project if they think somebody else is already on the ground doing the same thing. The people there in Whitman could tell Gribble that someone else is already running that particular rabbit and that said person already has a publishing contract. Let me ask you this — how have they been introducing you to the sources you've interviewed?"

Dodger thought about it. "Deputy Sheriff Sutton and Enid Blythe, Whitman's assistant, know the real deal. Everybody else has been told just that I'm someone looking into the situation with Travis Whitman's cooperation."

"That proves my point. If Gribble bothers to follow through and contact any of the same sources you've been tapping, the message he will get is that they've already been interviewed, and he'll assume it's another writer, one who can scoop him, given the head start."

"Clever. And it rings true," Dodger conceded.

"It seems like a lot of trouble to go through to kill a twenty-year-old story," she observed.

"Normally, I'd agree, but Travis Whitman is like a demi-god around here. It's more than just the money. I like the guy, but it's as if he inherited a crown, and the king is still upset about what happened to his queen, which Gribble or anyone else taking a hard look at this is certain to dredge up. By doing whatever is in his power to get rid of Gribble, I'd say Whitman's exercising the divine right of kings as he interprets it and everyone else accepts it."

"Heavy," she said. "By the way, I've got what you asked for re the four interlibrary-loan books Danielle requested that didn't have anything to do with textiles. You want to go over it now, or shall I email my notes?"

"Send the notes," he told her. "I'd rather talk about something else. Look, about the other day…"

He paused, unable to find what seemed like the right words, and then decided to settle for the unvarnished facts.

"I didn't mean to freeze you out like that when you mentioned what happened to your sister and my family. It's not you. It's just that it's hard for me to talk about."

"I understand," she said, more gently than he expected.

"Maybe sometime I'll get there, but not just yet."

"I know," she said. "I'm sorry if I touched a sore spot."

"I didn't have the right to react that way, given that you've gone through the same thing."

"It's all right," she assured him. "Forget it. We'll talk about all of it later if you want to."

He allowed himself a moment to savor the implications of the comment.

"So," she said, her voice brisk as usual, "what's on for tomorrow?"

He told her, and she said she thought driving around to the movie locations was a good idea. "You can see how they look in person compared to how they used them in the movie."

"I haven't seen the movie," he admitted. "No one's offered to show it to me, and to be truthful, I haven't thought to ask. If I don't catch it here, I'll watch it when I return home."

"Good luck with that," she told him. "I haven't been able to locate a copy. It's in that dead place between classic and straight-to-video, and video was VHS then. Nobody has the movie in a catalogue anymore, so it wasn't popular enough to justify converting it to DVD. If you can find someone around there who has it, that's your best bet."

"What are you doing for dinner tonight?"

"I'm thinking about that little Italian place around the corner. I'll tell them you said hi."

An image of the restaurant's candlelit interior rose before his eyes, and he thought of all the dinners they'd shared there as they reviewed what they were working on, all the conversations that had ended with a wistful goodnight on his part and a half-smile on hers. He'd give just about anything to be meeting her there right now, he realized.

"What are your plans?" her clear voice interrupted his reveries.

"The lord of the manor and I are dining casually tonight. Don't worry, I won't be mentioning you."

She gave the laugh that always did him in, and they said goodnight and disconnected.

He lay on the bed for a few minutes, smiling. Jess made him feel they shared a connection, the first person who'd been able to get inside the protective reserve with which he'd surrounded himself. He wondered if he should make more of an obvious effort to get closer to her. To this point, he'd more or less let things progress as circumstances dictated. He wondered what would happen if he let her see more of what he felt. From that he segued into wondering what would happen if he let Travis Whitman know he'd heard about the writer. Would Whitman grin that boyish grin and say the equivalent of "You caught me — he's why I called you in to be a smoke screen" or would he, as Sutton had put it, "go ballistic" and fire the deputy as the only one (or so he thought) who could have told Dodger about Gribble. Dodger decided that, at this point, it wasn't worth compromising Sutton's position to find out. He'd just keep playing dumb. Maybe, sooner or later, Whitman himself would come clean. For that matter, what did it matter? Odds were Whitman could have opened his presentation to Mystery Mavens with the revelation that a writer was looking into Danielle's disappearance and it would have made no difference in the board's decision to look into the cold case.

Downstairs, Whitman asked him if it suited him to eat in the library before the TV again.

"As it's just the two of us, I thought we'd take pot luck with Netflix," he grinned.

Inspiration struck Dodger. "By any chance, do you have a copy of the film they were making around here when Danielle disappeared?"

"You haven't seen it?"

Dodger shook his head. "Everybody keeps saying it was the biggest thing to hit town in living memory, and I can't help wondering how it turned out."

"Not very well," Whitman grimaced. "It's my understanding that it was considered a complete failure, and not just by me. I remember someone saying if it had cost more and been better, you could almost rank it with **Heaven's Gate** as being one of the all-time bombs. As it was, it sank without a trace."

Dodger almost choked. "How could a movie about a World War II hero based on an award-winning novel be that bad?"

"Let me see if I can find it, and you'll see for yourself. It's pre-DVD, so don't expect much. About all you can say about it is that it has some nice local scenery."

When Gladys Tanner arrived with their dinner trolley, it was to find the two men, cross-legged on the floor, going through stacks of tapes removed from the cupboard underneath the TV.

"Can I help you find something, Mr. Travis?"

"We're looking for that movie that was shot here. I don't recall the name."

"**Before A Hero,**" she said. "There were several tapes of it at one time. I know that one should still be here, on the bookshelves. It came from the movie company in a presentation box, and Miss Char..., well, she said to put it with the book it was based on, which the author had sent her to thank her for giving him that lunch before the movie got started."

Dodger saw Whitman flinch at whatever memory Gladys's comment forced on him. He had to restrain himself from reaching over to pat the still-grieving man on the back, to tell him that it would get better, not much maybe, but definitely better. By the time Gladys retrieved the presentation box from the shelves and turned to hand it to her boss, however, Whitman's usual impassivity had returned to his face, and he handed the box in turn to Dodger without comment.

"You're sure you want me to open this?" he demurred. "This is a custom-made box, and it's never been untaped."

"It's nothing to do with me," Whitman said, "or at least only peripherally. It was Charlotte who facilitated certain things for the movie people here. Open it. It could take us all night to find another copy, assuming there's even one here."

Dodger did as instructed. Inside, fitted into a slot in the box was a VHS tape. On the facing side of the box was an engraved letterhead with a handwritten note from a familiar name dated July 15, 1994, thanking "Dear Charlotte" for "your intuition and grace in knowing what we needed better than we did ourselves" and adding "You are the first person to receive this very limited edition of the tape, which includes something at the end that I think you'll find of special interest."

"There's a note here to your wife from the director." He started to hand it over when Whitman waved it off. "Just put it back in the box. Let's have the tape."

Dodger dug out the cassette, and Whitman took it from his hand and located the correct slot in a built-in unit that seemed capable of playing any format popular in the last half century.

"Now," he said, composure restored, "let's tackle that pizza and start the tape. Just don't let it spoil your appetite."

For half an hour, they watched a film that was as bad as Whitman claimed. The actor playing the hero was handsome but as stiff as if cut from wood. The actress filling the role of the girl he left behind seemed on the verge of giggling throughout, even when he was reported missing in action. The brave nurse from the Midwest with whom he fell in love in the South Pacific spoke English as a foreign language. The script was so predictable in its focus on the maudlin that it came close to pausing the action at key points to allow the audience time to get out its handkerchiefs and shed a few tears. Even the image resolution was bad, suffering as it did from the oversaturated blurriness common to VHS.

"On the positive side," Whitman said, muting the volume, "the town looks good."

And it did, Dodger thought.

"The Clumber House shows up particularly well in that candlelight scene," he agreed. "And the fall foliage is spectacular."

"Yes," Whitman said, "it was a fine autumn for Ceil Mountain." His finger sought the mute button even as Dodger asked when the Whitman-Brown majorettes would appear.

"They're toward the end, in a dream the poor bastard has as he's dying," Whitman explained.

"You're kidding."

Whitman shook his head, unmuting the volume.

A few minutes later, Whitman's cell was in his hand, and he got to his feet even as he once again muted the volume of the video. He listened for a moment, shaking his head and frowning. "Yes, yes. Something else came up. I'll be there shortly." He disconnected and handed the video controller to Dodger.

"Beijing beckons. You'll have to finish without me."

The look on his face gave Dodger a glimpse into the world this man occupied. Powerful as he was, the source of power could demand things of him at any moment that it would be either unwise or churlish to refuse.

Whitman limped as he moved across the room. At the door, he turned. "Sorry the movie isn't better, but maybe you'd like the tape as a souvenir. If so, feel free to take it with you."

"Thanks," Dodger said. "I will. One of my associates is keen to see it and hasn't been able to locate it anywhere."

"Do you wonder?" Whitman grinned, and left.

If anything, the movie grew more sluggish as time passed, and Dodger — yawning and on the verge of nodding off after a very long day — lasted just long enough to see the Whitman-Brown majorettes kick their way into the consciousness of the dying hero as he breathed his last on a sandy atoll on the other side of the world. Curious to see more of Danielle, this time in action, he paused the tape and rewound it several times. It was frustrating to see that the director had used the majorette material in such a way that it was no more than a disjointed series of images — a quick face, a swinging knee, a pointed boot toe, a tossed baton — save for one continuous shot at the last where all the girls were shown together doing a routine in the 1940s costumes. In that very brief bit, no more than a couple of seconds, Dodger could tell which girl was Danielle, but apart from noting that she was smaller and slighter than he expected, not much of an impression could be gathered because the image was blurred, as if a greasy hand swiped across a sheet of glass that covered it. The director had probably been trying for the effect of a dream that faded as the dying hero's eyes dimmed, but it came off more as a mistake. That, he thought, was typical of the film as a whole. It was full of creative ideas that had not quite jelled in the execution.

Yawning, he stopped the tape and rewound it as he drank a last cup of coffee and ate a cookie from the assortment Gladys had provided. He hesitated over the presentation box, but Whitman's offer seemed genuine and so he replaced the tape where it had resided for nineteen years and went upstairs, box in hand.

It was late, and his cell was low on power. Even so, he had an irresistible urge to tell Jess he'd seen the film and was indeed delivering it to her. Now, he'd argue, wasn't that a reason to come to Savannah? Going to his iPad mini, he clicked the familiar blue-and-white Skype icon and then her name.

"Yes, Dodger?"

"So you can ID me on Skype too, huh? I'll have to remember that."

"You do know it's after midnight, don't you?"

"You never go to bed before two. You said so yourself."

"That's true, but it's still a rude hour to call."

"One bit of information and I'll let you get back to your usual pastimes. I saw **Before A Hero** tonight with Whitman. He told me it was bad, but the description was too modest. I swear if it were a cheese, it'd smell like a mixture of Gorgonzola and Limburger."

"Now you have my curiosity aroused. It's hard to find a film with the courage of its mediocrity. I look forward to seeing it."

"That's why I'm calling. Whitman gave me a copy, a presentation copy no less; so don't bother looking for it in the stores, where I doubt you'll find it anyway from what I've seen unless there's a section for *Stinkers*. I'm heading back to Savannah in a couple of days. If you could see your way clear to meeting me there, we could watch it together. I've got a great media room, not to mention a guest room done by the most outrageous, obscenely expensive decorator on the Eastern seaboard."

"You tempt me strangely, I'll admit," she laughed. "I'll think about it."

At least, he thought, she hadn't said no.

Twenty-Three.

. . ●●●●●●● . .

Time and Again

The next morning, Dodger overslept. Skipping breakfast, in spite of Gladys's obvious displeasure, he headed into town as soon as he was dressed. When he arrived, it was to find Sutton hanging up the phone, an indecipherable expression on his face.

"That was odd," he said.

"What was odd?" Dodger asked.

"I just spent a peculiar five minutes fencing with Harrison North."

"How so? How was it peculiar, I mean?"

"For starters, he has to be the most paranoid person who isn't suspected of a crime I've ever interviewed, and that's a lot of people between my old job and this. When I finally got him to say something, what he said made no sense. He told me that he'd done his part and that I could tell Travis Whitman to fuck himself."

"I'll bet you're keen to make that phone call," Dodger grinned.

"I think that's one tidbit I won't pass along," Sutton agreed. "Would you?"

"Don't think so. I gather, then, that Harrison North won't provide the name of the unnamed correspondent who was boffing his wife?"

"Doesn't sound that way," Sutton replied.

"Is there any other way to find out?"

"Apart from asking Lisa North, not with any degree of certainty. It's been a long time, and anybody who'd know has probably left town, like just about everybody else who was in that circle. Their lawyers won't tell, and if the judge who dissolved the marriage was given supporting evidence in his chambers, outside the actual proceedings, it's dead to us unless . . ."

The young female clerk who manned the front desk at the police station appeared in the door, nervously adjusting her uniform collar and beckoning to Sutton, who stopped in mid-sentence.

"You said I was to tell you if that man who hit the police cruiser showed up again. I thought you'd like to know I just saw him walk by, and he looks drunk."

"Excuse me," Sutton said to Dodger, jumping up. "I gotta go." He tossed the paper he held onto his desk, where it hovered for a minute and then drifted to the floor.

"Understood. I'll just work on my notes," Dodger replied, getting out iPad and keyboard. He input for a couple of minutes, and then looked up to find that his eye had landed on the fallen paper. Reaching over, he picked it up to see that it had just two things on it, both in Sutton's neat printing — the name Harrison North and a phone number with an unfamiliar area code. After a moment's hesitation, he input both in the iPad's contacts directory, laid the original note on Sutton's desk, and went back to work. He doubted he'd have cause to use the number, but he could give it to the Mystery Mavens pro who might follow him here.

When Sutton returned, he wasn't alone. Dodger first heard a commotion and then saw the deputy and his young female clerk wrestling a drunk toward the cells at the back of the station. When Sutton came into the office a few minutes later, his face was flushed and his uniform showed signs of a struggle.

'Sorry about that. Where were we?"

"You were telling me that Harrison North wasn't helpful."

"To say the least," Sutton laughed, his good humor restored by the memory. "Unless you count what he said about Mr. Whitman. It seemed to me that North was implying he and Mr. Whitman had some sort of agreement and North wanted him to know he'd stuck to it."

"That's how I read it," Dodger agreed. "Maybe Whitman was the one Lisa North was getting it on with, and he paid off North not to bring his name into the divorce proceedings."

"Maybe," Sutton agreed, albeit without enthusiasm. "The problem is I've never heard about anything like that between Mrs. North and Mr. Whitman, and you usually do in a place like this where at one time everybody was aware of every breath Travis Whitman took."

"She and her brother came to dinner at Mill House my first night in town," Dodger told him. "The general opinion there is that she's 'setting her cap' for Whitman. If the servants knew or even suspected they were already having an affair, that makes no sense — and servants do know in my experience."

"You grew up with servants, didn't you?" Sutton asked.

"What makes you say that?" Dodger protested, the comment louder than he'd intended.

"You can always tell. You're good with getting people to do what you need without making a big deal out of it. No offense intended."

"None taken," Dodger said, calming down. He didn't know why the question had gotten through to him, because the observation was true. He *had* grown up with servants. Maybe it was because he associated them with his mother in happier times. If he were good with people — an observation he doubted — it was because he watched for years how his mother managed a household that, while not as large as Mill House, was nonetheless big enough to operate much like a domestic business. Even now, he could hear her saying firmly to some recalcitrant maid, "Now, Tilda, there's no need for tears. We aren't talking about the end of the world. It's simply that you are such a good worker that I know you can manage your tasks even better, and I'm going to show you how." By the time the training (or re-training) session had ended, they'd be seated with a cup of tea in his mother's library, Tilda still beaming from the glow of extra attention and determined not to repeat the offense that had attracted the attention to begin with.

"What about North?" Sutton asked. "What do you want me to do?"

Dodger thought about it. "I'm not sure the name of the person Lisa was involved with is that critical. It was a long shot. At the time Danielle disappeared, the Norths weren't even married, so for the name to be connected to Danielle the affair would have to be one that began while she was still here, before the North marriage, and continued six years after her disappearance. That's a lot of longevity for that kind of thing."

"Then we'll let that drop for the time being," Sutton agreed. "Now, as to Harold Karroll, the lawyers have come up with contact info. Also, I've had my clerk run a full criminal background check on Karroll. He owns a dry-cleaning business out west. If he's ever been caught doing anything he shouldn't, with little kids or otherwise, we're not finding it. As far as the authorities are concerned, the guy is pure as driven snow. Which complicates how we handle him. The only leverage we have is what his ex-wife told us. We've never seen any stash of kiddie porn that can be traced to him, and she didn't show it to the lawyers. I'm not sure she even told them about it. So we need to give some thought as to the best way to handle this."

From up the hall, the drunk began to bang on the bars. Sutton got up and closed his door.

"Maybe the best approach is to go around the issue, not through it," Dodger said.

"That's a little too cryptic for a dumb cop. What do you mean around and not through?"

"Act as if you don't know about the porn. When you call, tell him that you're investigating a cold case involving a girl named Danielle Standridge, who was, you understand, a neighbor of his at the time of her disappearance in September 1993. Then pause. It'll be interesting to see what he says after hearing that. Then tell him that what you're interested in is September 24th, the afternoon Danielle disappeared, that you understand he drove to his house and then back to the mall that afternoon and that you need to ask him a couple of questions regarding that. Then pause again. See what the guy volunteers."

"And if he doesn't volunteer anything?"

"Say that, given his house is next door to where she lived and the mall is where she disappeared from, you'd like to know if he noticed anything unusual. My guess is that, somewhere along the way, he'll start coming out with something that'll be helpful in one way or another."

"Let's see how good a fortune teller you are," Sutton laughed as he input a number.

He put the phone on speaker, and Dodger heard Harold Karroll's confident "Hello" change into a guarded parceling of words as Sutton went through the scenario they'd devised.

What he said was straightforward enough. He was indeed the Harold Karroll, former manager of Whitman-Brown Mills and once the next-door neighbor to Andy and May Standridge and their daughters Debbie and Danny. He did not, however, understand why Deputy Sutton was calling. The girl's disappearance was a long time ago and had nothing to do with him.

Dodger reflected to himself that this remark came up a lot in cold cases, as if distance and ignorance provided a shield.

Sutton lifted his eyebrows and continued. "We're seeking information about the afternoon of September 24th. That was the Friday that a movie company that had been in town during the preceding month gave the reception at Whitman Mall at which Danielle Standridge performed with the other majorettes. We understand that you had occasion to drive from the mall to your house and then back to the mall at approximately four p.m., which is a time frame of interest."

"You've been talking to that crazy ex-wife of mine, haven't you?" His voice began to rise. "You can't believe anything that bitch says."

"The source of the information is irrelevant, Mr. Karroll. As I said, all we're interested in is whether or not you noticed anything unusual as you drove back and forth to the mall that afternoon."

"Oh."

It came out as a release of breath, and they could sense his relief.

"Uh, let me think about it. You say it was a Friday? Yeah, I do sort of remember, some of it anyway. I remember the movie truck and the majorettes were doing something in the middle of the mall parking lot. Other than that I don't recollect much of anything except that crazy Mavis jumping me 'cause she thought I was fooling around with this woman who worked with me at the mill and she accused me of leaving the mall to meet her. Yeah, yeah, it's coming back to me now. I left Mavis in the grocery store and went back to the house for my stomach tonic, but all I did was pick it up and go straight back to the mall, whatever that nut case told you."

"Did you see Danielle Standridge?" Sutton asked.

"No." The answer was short and definitive.

"You don't remember anything out of the ordinary that afternoon, either at the mall or coming and going?"

"Just the stuff at the mall. That whole month, I remember people were all excited whenever those movie people showed up with their cameras, acting all important. The locals would get a sight of one of 'em up the way and act flat-out stupid. I'll bet if you checked, you'd find there were a lot of accidents while they were in town 'cause people drove crazy, just crazy. I remember I had a scare when I pulled out of my driveway to go back to the mall. This little red car almost rear-ended me, chasing one of those damned movie vans a little way up the road. Then, when I got back to the parking lot, that bitch Mavis jumped me." He paused, giving Sutton a chance to say something. When he didn't, Karroll continued with more confidence.

"After we got the groceries in the trunk, we headed back to the house. That's what I remember about that afternoon. That night and the rest of the weekend, I stayed around the house nursing my stomach, which was dealing me fits, so I wasn't out and about to see anything. Like I said, it was a long time ago, but if I remember anything else after I think about it, should I give you a call?"

"That'd be a good idea," Sutton told him. "Let me give you my cell number so you can reach me directly."

"You said your name is Jason Sutton. Are you local? Are you the same one who used to have that high-school group that played parties back then?"

"That's right," Sutton said, blushing.

"I remember you. Now you're back there as the sheriff. Life's a funny thing, isn't it?"

"Sure is."

"So," Karroll continued after a moment, "has Danny Standridge turned up?"

"Unfortunately, no," Sutton told him. "That's why we're looking into it again."

"She was a nice kid," Karroll said in a low voice. "I hope you figure out what happened to her."

The guy actually sounds as if he means it, Dodger thought. Of course, a lot of pedophiles presented a sympathetic façade.

"Well, he got to be Mr. Helpful real quick," Sutton remarked after hanging up the phone. "What do you think?"

"That he's got maybe the best alibi of anybody we've talked to, assuming his ex-wife confirms that he was around the house all weekend. Even if she doesn't remember, I don't buy him as connected with this."

"How so?"

"His only concern was whether or not you knew something you weren't saying. He was afraid that the ex had told you about his stash she found in the basement. Once you passed the point where he expected that to be the reason for the call, he was more than willing to be helpful. I didn't get any sense of resistance, did you?"

"Nope," Sutton said. "So I guess that takes care of Harold Karroll."

"Unless you want to take a survey about who did and didn't like having the movie production in town," Dodger laughed.

"Yeah, he didn't take to those movie people, did he?"

Twenty-Four.

·.·····

On Schedule

Dodger's phone buzzed. Looking at it, he saw Jess's image. His heart leapt. Had she decided to meet him in Savannah?

"Hi, Jess." He listened for a minute, as Sutton watched. "Sure, thanks for the heads up. Let me review status with Deputy Sutton, and I'll get back to you."

When they disconnected, Dodger turned to the policeman.

"Trouble?"

Dodger shook his head. "By no means. When we start one of these exploratory visits, we set up a calendar, and tomorrow is the date, Jess Hannah just reminded me, by which I am to offer a preliminary assessment of the situation."

"I know Mr. Whitman told me some stuff up front about you and your bunch and what you do," Sutton said, half-apologetically, "but he made it clear I was to go along with whatever you want while you're here, providing any assistance, so I didn't see there was a lot to think about. Will you tell me what it is that you intend to have accomplished when you leave here?"

"I hear what you're saying," Dodger told him. "My role — my only role — is to make an assessment as to whether enough remains of official records, surviving sources, and existing information to make a formal investigation likely to succeed. What that means is that I go to the source of the event and spend a few days, always with the cooperation and agreement of the local authorities, just talking to people and looking things over. Then I report back to the Mystery Mavens board, with our standard case checklist completed, and give them any notes I've developed, as well as my opinion. They ask me a few questions, and then they decide whether the organization proceeds."

"So it isn't your role to develop theories?"

"Not my role as such, but it's been known to happen. If it does, then I pass them along as well, with the caveat that all I did was scratch the surface, which they know anyway. I mean, what we've done in the last few days would have taken much longer in a standard investigation mode where everything is checked and cross-checked."

"That's true," Sutton agreed, "but still we turned up some stuff the sheriff didn't back then."

"The difference," Dodger reminded him, "is you and your expertise, especially your knowledge of the area and the people."

"Thank you," Sutton said, blushing, "but I've got to say that the big difference this time around, compared to 1993, is that Travis Whitman is promoting the idea of an investigation and before he supported the family's statement that Danny had run away."

"That's a key factor," Dodger conceded. "But by any standard, from what I can tell, you're much more on top of this after a week than the original sheriff was during all those years it sat in the files before he retired."

"Well, to be fair, things are a lot quieter around here nowadays. I don't have as much to deal with as they did back then," Sutton pointed out. "They had to handle a larger number of general incidents, and with the town getting emptier every day, my case load keeps dropping. I wonder sometimes how much longer it'll be until Mr. Whitman looks at the quarterly stats and decides our little department isn't necessary any more."

"How would you feel about that?" Dodger asked.

Sutton shrugged. "It's been okay here, but I'd survive. I've had offers to go other places, even back to Atlanta. I stay here because of my mother. You know how that goes." He hesitated, giving Dodger a chance to speak, then continued when it became clear that nothing would be forthcoming. "Anyway, if it wasn't for Mama, I'd be happy enough to go back to the city. What I like is the work, and you can do that anywhere. I'll tell you something though…"

"What?"

"It'd make me feel a lot better about leaving Whitman if I could work out this business. I've thought about Danny's disappearance off and on over the years. The idea of her up and leaving never made any sense to me, but I couldn't see that anybody had any real reason to snatch her unless it was a sex-murder thing. I guess I thought she'd either turn up alive and tell us how she'd fooled everybody or else we'd find whatever was left of her body. That majorette outfit was pretty distinctive. But in all this time… in all this time, there's been nothing." He hesitated, eyes cloudy with unshed tears. "I guess you think it's sick that I can't let it go."

"I'd be the last person to think that," Dodger told him, shifting his gaze to the window, where he could see clouds of an improbable white against an autumnal sky so blue it looked artificial.

They sat in silence while each man contemplated memories he wasn't inclined to share, but then Dodger's mood went into action mode more or less on its own.

"Well, now that we know where we're both coming from, why don't we see how much we can turn up today?"

"Works for me," Sutton said, blowing his nose. "What's on the agenda?"

"First, do you know where Andrew Standridge is buried?"

"Probably in the Whitman Memorial Cemetery, but I can double-check that with Tonya Powers — she's the woman who keeps the cemetery's plat up to date. Used to do it for the town and keeps it up now for the town's churches. If he's there, you want to go?"

"Whitman Memorial – that's the cemetery in the movie they shot here, right?"

Sutton nodded.

"Then let's go, whether he's there or not. I'd like to see it for myself."

Half an hour later, they stood under the roof of the tiny porch attached to the cemetery's entrance lodge while Sutton consulted the directions he'd written down as he traced where they needed to go on a large laminated map attached to the exterior wall of the lodge. As he waited, Dodger looked around with interest. It was a bigger place and the monuments of a wider range as to size and style than he had expected from the brief scene in the movie for which some of it served as background.

"Okay," Sutton said at last, "as far as I can tell we follow this main drive as it curves toward that hilltop, then you see that little white mausoleum right at the edge of the drive?"

Dodger nodded.

"We park there, work our way around the mausoleum and head toward the perimeter fence." He looked at the map that Tonya gave him. "According to this, Andy Standridge's grave should be about the third one back from the mausoleum. You want to go up there, or did you just want to verify where it was?"

"I'd like to go up there," Dodger told him. "He died ten years ago, right? I'd like to see what the family put on his tombstone and who he's buried next to."

Sutton thought about it and nodded. "I see."

It hadn't rained recently, and the footing was good as they worked their way across scraggly grass, through other, smaller stones before reaching a large double stone, one side of which bore the identification *Andrew Jackson Standridge, May 19, 1938 – November 6, 2003*. Contrary to custom, the other side was blank — no name of a following spouse, no birth date, no empty space for a death date. Running all the way across the stone at the bottom was the most ambiguous epitaph Dodger had ever read: *Mere words cannot describe his life and works – May he have the rest that he has earned.*

"Whoa!" Sutton recoiled. "That's a double-edge sword, huh? Especially given what we've learned about Andy Standridge."

"I wonder who chose it — Debbie? The grieving widow?"

"I never heard. Could have been either one of them, I suppose. That's cold language, isn't it? My guess would be Debbie, but who knows? What I can't get over is the fact that Mrs. Standridge pretty much went along with whatever he wanted to do."

"I'm not sure that's so unusual," Dodger said. "Trading the daughter who's the object of the incestuous relationship for peace in the family or even the continuation of a marriage. I've heard of more than one case where a rich man made access to the daughter a condition of marrying the mother or staying with her."

"Gross," Sutton said, shaking his head as if trying to rid himself of a bad taste. "One thing's for sure, May has no intention of being buried next to him, but given that stone they won't put anyone else there either."

Dodger walked around the stone, examining it from all sides. Then he fell to his knees and pulled back the dead grass from the base to make sure that nothing was inscribed there. All he found, however, was a small, incised logo for the memorial company. Back on his feet, he brushed off the knees of his pants.

"My dad's over there," Sutton said, pointing toward the center. "He's got one of these double stones too, but my mother's name is already next to his. All they've got to do is put in her date of death. That's how most people do it around here these days. Is that how your parents handled theirs?"

Dodger closed his eyes as a wave of pain washed over him. His parents' cremains lay in a family vault in the old cemetery near Hartford where most of his mothers' ancestors lay. Their inscriptions were unambiguous and straightforward, just like that of their daughter who lay between them — names, dates (birth different for each, date of death the same) and a shared sentiment: *Much loved they lived, much lamented they died. May they rest in blessed peace.*

He felt a touch on his elbow and opened his eyes to see Sutton looking at him with concern. "Dodger, you all right? For a minute there, I thought you were about to keel over."

"I'm fine," Dodger said. "It was just an odd feeling."

"Goose walked over my grave," Sutton said, then stopped himself. "Sorry, that sounds stupid. It was just something my grandma used to say when a funny shiver caught her unawares."

Recovered from the near-panic attack (and it reassured him to think of how long it was since he'd had a full-fledged one), Dodger headed back to the police cruiser, followed by Sutton.

"Where'd they shoot the burial scene that was in the movie?" he asked.

"Back down close to the gates is my understanding," Sutton said. "Have you seen the movie?"

"Last night. Whitman showed it to me."

"Pretty bad, huh? I remember I was a freshmen, sophomore, something like that, in college when it hit the campus multiplex, and I took this cute girl who was the sister of one of my frat brothers to see it. It was so bad that I didn't admit I was in it. Luckily, it was a crowd scene they shot at the high school, and you'd need a magnifying glass to find me."

They shared a quiet laugh, and then got back into the cruiser.

"Where now?" Sutton asked.

Dodger consulted his notes. "I'd like to run by Ethel Bowland's and get her opinion about something."

"Better you than me. Should we call her?"

"I think it'll be easier if I just drop in on my own," Dodger said after thinking about it, his mood now back to normal.

The mood swing didn't surprise him. He knew that was how such episodes proceeded. He'd be fine, and then something would remind him, and he'd be back there again. Then, faster now than at the beginning, he'd catch hold of himself and grab onto the present moment, back into a world that offered the distracting complications of other places, other lives.

Twenty-Five.

. . ₒₒₒₒₒₒₒₒₒ . .

Social Judgment

In the cruiser, as they drove toward Blevins, Sutton pointed out things he thought would interest Dodger.

"I grew up on Second Street, the next street over from Main, just up there," he said, pointing in the opposite direction as they drove past the brick-paved pedestrian area which today had maybe half a dozen people taking advantage of its ornamental-iron benches. "My mother still lives there. If you have time before you go, you might want to talk to her. She and May Standridge were girlfriends all the way through school."

"Maybe this afternoon," Dodger promised, "if that'd work for her."

"I'll call her and make sure before we go. I haven't told her about what Andy Standridge was doing with his girls, by the way. I didn't see any point, and it would disturb her."

"Got it," Dodger said. "No talk of the Standridges at all except as it relates to the disappearance."

"I'd appreciate it," Sutton said.

"Where do you live?" Dodger asked, embarrassed that he hadn't inquired before.

"On a small farm the other side of town. When I brought her here, my wife had the idea she wanted to do a truck farm; you know — take produce into the city and sell it to restaurants or at the Farmers' Market. That lasted until the tomato fruitworms, potato aphids, and stink bugs showed up. Now, the garden's all marigolds and Joe Pye plants, but that's okay as long as she's happy."

"Sounds idyllic," Dodger said. "I think everybody thinks they'd like to farm at some time."

"So she tells me," Sutton laughed. "I have to say that thought has never crossed my mind. Now, up here, this is the old Masonic Lodge. My grandfather was Master, and my father was Senior Deacon. Never joined myself. Over there is the Presbyterian Church. That was for the people who thought the Baptists, Methodists and Evangelicals were too lower class but who didn't want the bother of driving to Blevins to attend the Episcopal. There's a Catholic church there, too, but not many people who worked in Whitman Mills were R.C. Now, up here, is the Gem. I took my first date there when I was twelve. I still remember how my mother scrubbed my ears and combed my hair."

Dodger's attention wandered as he remembered his first date. He'd been at Salisbury School, and the girl was at Hotchkiss, where the dance was being held. It had been difficult to arrange the car, and he hadn't wanted to bother his father who thought he was too young to be taking girls to serious events.

"And up here," Sutton was saying, pointing to a derelict Victorian mansion, "was where Old Lady Brudnell lived. Her family was a holdover from the farm families that were here before the mill. Her grandmother's father was a Yankee banker, and it was her money that built the house when she married Brudnell after the Civil War and came south. Her granddaughter went to Whitman-Brown, but she was a couple of years ahead of me. Back up that way is where the old town spring used to be before the mill put in the water system."

Dodger marveled at Sutton's command of his territory and wondered if he could be happy somewhere else. He wondered, too, what it would be like to have that kind of continuity, but knew it was a pointless conjecture. He'd have to be content with what worked for the moment, and be grateful for the opportunity.

About halfway to Blevins, Sutton indicated a narrow paved road that wound through fields to a farmhouse about a thousand feet away. "That's where the Hands lived. Danny spent the night there sometimes. It's interesting that Andrea Hand seems to be the only one she let have any idea of what was going on with her father and Debbie, unless she put it in her diary. Oh, and that reminds me…"

"What?"

"The forensics people called. They collected the locker material from us last night, but they can't start processing it for several weeks. I'm not surprised. Cold cases aren't top priority, given how busy they stay. I did, however, call in a favor with a girl I know there and got them to agree to scan the diary and email it to me later today. I'll let you know when it comes in, and you can tell me where to send a copy to you."

"Use the email address I gave you before," Dodger told him. "That had to be a heck of a favor you called to get that done today."

Sutton smiled. "I haven't always been a boring, happily married man with children."

"You dog," Dodger grinned. "What did you play anyway?"

"Play?"

"In that high-school band of yours that did gigs around here."

"Oh, we ranged further than that. We did the Southeastern bar circuit a couple of summers, even had our own bus. We called ourselves The Whitcats, and our thing was we all dyed our hair blonde, wore white tees and skintight black jeans with black boots, and had sunglasses with Roy Orbison frames that we wore while we performed."

"Sounds striking," Dodger laughed.

"Hey, dude, don't knock it. We were the second-hottest act on the circuit, and at least no one ever threw stuff at us except for the occasional pair of panties. Also, for your information, I can call in favors in a wide range of Southern cities."

"You still haven't told me your instrument."

"Saxophone or clarinet, depending on the need that arose. I started taking piano when I was six and went on from that to any instrument I could get my hands on. I was in the Whitman-Brown band by junior high and stayed in it all the way through high school. That was how I met Danny, when she came to play in the band as a seventh grader. She was so small she could barely hold up that French horn. Of course, once they tapped her for the majorette squad, after she started growing up, she hardly ever played with the band any more and then only for concerts, never for games."

By then, they pulled into the outskirts of Blevins, and within minutes the cruiser moved up the well-tended drive that led to the colonial-style home of Mrs. Ethel Bowland. Through the bow window, they could see her walk toward the front of the house to confirm that it was a vehicle she'd heard. By the time Dodger reached the stoop, she had the door open. Today the sweater set and skirt were a different color, but that was the only change. Her good jewelry was in place, and her coif was perfect, as was the subtle makeup. It seemed that Mrs. Bowland did not allow herself off days.

"Is Deputy Sutton coming in?" She stared over Dodger's shoulder as if ready to use the power of her gaze to keep the policeman at bay.

"No ma'am," Dodger told her. "My base is Mill House, and Travis Whitman asked Deputy Sutton to chauffeur me, as a courtesy to a guest. I wanted to see you again, and your beautiful house of course." He nodded toward the house and fiddled with the Rolex on his wrist. "I told the deputy to wait in the car."

It was the right note. Sutton was put in his place as a servant of sorts, while Dodger was positioned as a man worthy of being entertained at the grandest house in the area but who was keen to pay a second visit to Mrs. Bowland and her worthwhile surroundings.

"Do come in, Mr. Dodger," she said, ushering him through the door. "May I offer you some refreshment? I was about to have iced tea." She nodded toward the goblet that sat on the coffee table, centered on a large coaster.

"Iced tea is exactly what I'm in the mood for," he assured her. "It's a warm day."

She returned almost at once, with a second goblet on a small black-lacquer tray, which she sat on the side table next to the chair she'd indicated he should take.

Dodger picked up the glass and admired its cutting. "Nothing shows off Waterford like well-brewed iced tea, I always say," he remarked.

"Why, that's what I've always thought," she told him, smiling more pleasantly than she'd managed at any time during his first visit. "Now, to what do I owe the pleasure of this call, Mr. Dodger?"

"First, I'd be much more comfortable if you'd call me, Art, Mrs. Bowland."

"Then you must call me Ethel," she told him.

"Well, Ethel," he said, "I wouldn't bother you with this, but I'm trying to clarify something and of all the people to whom I've spoken while I've been in the area, you struck me as the one with the best social memory, not to mention judgment." It sounded like bullshit even to him, but she leaned forward, lips parted, eyes bright, totally buying it.

"Yes, Mr. Dodger," she almost gasped. "I'm still not clear on what you're doing in Whitman, but anything I can do to help, of course I will."

He took out his iPad mini, and located the Dropbox folder with the four images sent Display Dollies for mannequin reference in 1994, the images subsequently sent to Jess and, via Jess, to him. He clicked the first image full screen and went to sit beside Mrs. Bowland.

"May I?"

"Of course," she said, her smile gracious as she shifted to allow him an extra inch he didn't need given that the Chippendale-style sofa was at least six feet wide.

He held up the iPad between them. She frowned when she saw the image of Danielle in the formal dress posed against the stage setting.

"Isn't that the Standridge girl?"

"Yes ma'am, it is."

"Well, I don't know what you think I would know about..." She pursed her lips.

"Now, Ethel," he said, his voice soft and ingratiating. "I know the girl isn't up to the standard that you — or for that matter I — are accustomed to, but even so I'm sure you agree it's our responsibility to rectify injustice. Whatever her shortcomings, Danielle Standridge was just fifteen, and she hasn't been seen or heard from in twenty years. It seems to me that somebody ought to be conscientious enough to bring that girl home, one way or the other. Or at least explain to the people who cared about her why she isn't coming home. Don't you agree?"

"Well, I suppose so," she said reluctantly. "What is it that you want me to do?"

"It'll only take a moment. I want you to examine this photograph and tell me two things. First, is that how Danielle looked the last time you saw her? By that, I mean, does she look the age she looked when she disappeared, as far as you remember? Also, is that the dress like the one you bought your daughter for the next school dance?"

She took the iPad in her hands and, to her credit, gave the image a thorough examination, even asking if there were a way to make it bigger.

"It's how I remember the Standridge girl looking just before, you know, she went away. As for the dress, I don't think so."

He leaned over and clicked onto the next image, which showed

Danielle still in the same setting but in a different dress.

Again, Mrs. Bowland examined the image with care. Dodger watched, thinking that, while he didn't like the woman, he admired her conscientiousness.

"This seems to have been taken at the same time as the first one," she pointed out. "Her hair's the same, and she's wearing the same bracelet although the necklace and dress are different. The scarf's only in the first picture."

"You see, I knew you were the one to consult," he beamed. "I hadn't spotted that."

"This dress, I think, might be like the one Dorothy wore to the prom. Let me get my album, and we'll see."

"I'd appreciate that more than you know," he told her.

She went to a side table and opened a deep drawer, from which she extracted a photograph album that, on inspection, seemed to consist solely of images of Dorothy from nude infant to elegant bride. Mrs. Bowland turned pages until, about two-thirds of the way through, she came to a page-sized photograph of her daughter with a pimply-faced young man beneath a skimpy Harvest Dance banner. Dorothy was indeed wearing the same dress that Danielle wore in the stage setting.

"Yes," Mrs. Bowland pronounced, "they're the same. Dorothy looks much better in it, of course. Don't you think so?"

"Certainly an elegant and appropriate presentation," Dodger assured her.

There was a pause as she contemplated the photograph of her daughter as she was twenty years before. In between, judging from the pictures, a lot had gone on, and Dodger would wager that she was thinking how not all of it was as she wished. Still, she'd been kind to him, and he regretted making her think on unpleasant things. Even unpleasant people shouldn't have to do that, he thought. If nothing else, what he'd been through tended to make him more tolerant of the foibles and fears of others.

To make conversation, he commented, "You'd think that the school that could come up with a stage set like this" — he indicated the Chinoiserie background of the Danny image — "could have devised a setting for these Harvest Dance photographs that would be more appropriate for girls like your daughter."

Mrs. Bowland looked at him in surprise. "Stage set?"

"The background against which Danielle is standing," he explained. "I assumed it was from a school play."

"That isn't a stage set," she corrected him. "It's the interior of The Library Pavilion on the Mill House estate."

It was Dodger's turn to be nonplused. "I assumed it was from a stage production."

"Oh no," she said. "Charlotte Whitman was chairman of the Whitman History Foundation — of which my mother was a founder, I might add, so I conceived it my duty to remain involved after her death — and she held receptions there for the committee several times. I think there may be a photograph of it in the other album. Give me a moment."

She rose and went to the side table on the other side of the bow window. From its drawer she pulled an album that in external appearance was identical to the one that lay open before them. In the second album, she found the page she sought, and slid the heavy book over to Dodger's lap. As she'd said, there she was, perhaps twenty years younger, cocktail glass in hand, standing next to the same dragon-like figure as Danielle. Behind her, as behind Danielle, other dragons circled the walls. Dodger stared at the image. So Danielle hadn't been in a stage set? That put a different slant on the situation. He wanted to think about this revelation and decided it was time to go.

"I cannot begin to express how much I appreciate your graciousness to a stranger," Dodger said, rising, "but I don't wish to abuse your hospitality."

"Not at all, Art. I hope you'll call again." The diamonds on her fingers flashed as she extended her hand.

Back in the police cruiser, returning Mrs. Bowland's smiling farewell wave, Dodger found a bored Sutton.

"I was about to go to sleep, but I take it you survived the monster mom. On the other hand, maybe not. You look like a man who's had a surprise."

"I did," Dodger told him, "and I'm not sure what to make of it. Could we go by Debbie Standridge's place? I need to ask her something."

"Back and forth, back and forth. We'll turn into yo-yos at this rate," he grinned. "Do you want to call Debbie or just surprise her?"

"Surprise," Dodger said, mind chewing on what he'd just learned. Something wasn't adding up here, and he wasn't sure what. He had an idea that Debbie might be able to correct the error.

The return trip, without commentary, seemed faster, and in less than half an hour they turned into the wide drive to the Standridge rancher, to stop behind the ancient Buick.

Debbie was home and she was, moreover, sober, perhaps because she was dressed for work.

"What are you doing here, Jase? Better make it fast. Dr. Purefoy called me to come to work, and he's a demon when it comes to being on time." She didn't invite them in, but stood on the stoop, car keys and purse in hand.

Sutton gestured to Dodger, who at once opened the iPad to Danielle's image in the prom dress against the Chinoiserie background.

"Do you recognize this dress?"

Debbie frowned, eyes narrowing. "I've never seen this picture before. Where'd you get it?"

Dodger ignored the question. "What I want to know is if this dress is one you recognize as belonging to Danielle?"

"My God, no. I mean, I don't remember Danny having anything like that."

"What about this one?" He flipped to the next image and got the same reaction.

"I don't remember everything in her wardrobe," Debbie admitted. "I don't remember everything in *my* wardrobe back then. But I know neither of us ever had anything as nice as those dresses." She looked harder at the image. "They probably came from The Darling Shop downtown and I don't think I ever set foot in there unless I was with a girlfriend who was buying something. Mama had real nice clothes that she went to Charlotte to buy, but she always took Danny and me to the Episcopal Church's thrift shop in Blevins or, if we were lucky, the discount store. Daddy didn't like her spending money. At least Mrs. Whitman bought Danny some pretty, new things, but nobody did that for me and I always felt like everybody was thinking how bad my clothes looked. 'Course, I have to admit that Danny was generous. She'd let me borrow anything of hers I wanted, so that helped sometimes."

To Dodger, it seemed as if Debbie's comment summed up the

Standridge household — bad father, indifferent mother, ill-used daughters, one envious of the other. He wondered if May Standridge's practice of going to Charlotte for her "nice" clothes, in spite of her husband's stinginess, was part of the payoff for turning a blind eye as Debbie was molested. For that matter, was the payoff continuing with the insurance proceeds and annuities that made it possible for May to live, cossetted and protected, in a luxurious facility instead of sharing a ward at some anonymous nursing home?

"I need to see anything you've still got of Danny's," Sutton's voice broke the awkward silence.

Dodger looked at him in surprise. For the most part, Sutton had up until now volunteered little in the way of investigative independence. He'd been told by Whitman to assist, and he'd done it – and he'd done it well, Dodger admitted. He couldn't have asked for better logistical support. Now, here he was, suddenly acting like a cop.

"Are you fucking kidding me, Jase? Mama and Mrs. Whitman cleared out just about everything years ago. What little was left, we got rid of when we moved in. We needed Danny's old room for Ash, and we could barely get her stuff in there, much less hang onto anything else. I'd be surprised if you can find anything left in this house of Danny's."

Sutton frowned. "Charlotte Whitman came to the house and helped your mother clear out Danny's things?"

"Isn't that what I said? Now, I gotta go."

Sutton held up his hand.

"Wait up," he told her, "I'd like to see Danny's old room."

"Shouldn't you have a search warrant or something to do that?" she asked, beginning to look sullen.

"We can do it that way, if you want," Sutton told her. "It'll mean more attention and it'll be more than just me and Dodger in your house, but if that's what you want…" He turned to go, but she laid her hand on his arm.

"All right, but you've got to do this fast. I'm not kidding, Dr. Purefoy will fire me if I give him the least chance."

Sutton nodded. "I understand. Now, which way is Danny's old room?"

She looked at him in surprise. "I thought you knew."

"How would I know? The only parts of this house I've seen are the living room and the kitchen, and the kitchen was just the other day."

Debbie looked disbelieving, but said nothing further as she led them into the entry hall with its built-in planter and skylight intended to bring sun to the drooping plants, past the living room on the left, through a door, and right into a long hall that ran the width of this side of the house. There, she led them to the first door on the left, which she opened to reveal an average-sized bedroom with windows that overlooked an overgrown rear yard. Clearly a girl's room, it was painted bright pink with big cutouts of Justin Bieber and Selena Gomez on either side of double closet doors. The long dresser held trays of makeup and costume jewelry. The unmade bed was covered with flowered sheets, and the spread, which lay half on and half off the floor, was citrus yellow.

Sutton walked to the center of the room and looked around. "Was it like this when Danny used it?"

Debbie shrugged. "The furniture's the same, except Ray refinished it 'cause Ash thought it was too ratty. It's even pretty much arranged the way it was — it has to be to fit in here. The room's been painted. When Danny had it, it was a pale peach color. The rug's different. Before, there were just a couple of bedside area rugs over hardwood. The window coverings are new."

"How about the closet?" Sutton asked. "Is it the same, on the inside, I mean?"

Debbie strode to the double louvered doors and, with a sigh, threw them open. Inside was a row of white metal hanging devices, with several stacks of white wire boxes. What could be seen of the walls showed them the same color as the bedroom.

"We stripped out everything and started over. Satisfied?"

Without answering, Sutton walked over to the windows and looked out, then turned back to Debbie.

"Why would you think I'd know where her room was?"

"I guess I figured she sneaked you in. I know I would have, given the opportunity, but Daddy watched me like a hawk."

Dodger and Sutton exchanged a glance. It was little more than a flicker, but Debbie caught it at once.

"You know something, don't you? Did my dear mama spill the

beans or have you come across someone Danny blabbed to?"

"Now, Debbie…" Sutton started to say, but she rushed ahead as if unable to stop.

"She walked in on us, you know. He always took me to the guest room, which was next door to this one, just bigger and nicer and with a small bathroom attached. When I was little, he'd set me on the edge of the dresser and we'd play how many times it'd take before he could get all the way in. If I was a good girl and helped him do it in less than five tries, he'd give me a treat. When I got older, he liked for me to lean over the back of this chair so he could go in from behind." She indicated an antique-style chair with a shaped back and curved legs, her expression indecipherable. "He said it'd go deeper that way and that was what he liked. He usually locked the door. I guess he forgot that day 'cause there he was, going away like a pile driver when I heard this scream and I looked around and it was Danny, standing in the door. I just always figured she knew. He never took much care to hide it. I guess I was wrong. Her hand was over her mouth and her eyes were as big as saucers. I've never forgotten the look on her face."

There was a moment's silence before Debbie continued. "That was about a month before she took off. I always figured that was why. Maybe she was afraid he'd go after her next. Maybe she just thought she was too good to live in a household where her dear daddy was getting it on with her dear sister in one way or another all the time. Fuck, who knows why she left? All I know is, I got to go right now. If I floorboard it, I may make it in time yet if I go in the side entrance."

Back in the cruiser, the two men avoided each other's gaze.

"I've got a daughter, you know," Sutton said finally. "I can't even imagine what kind of monster would do that to any little girl, much less his own kid."

"It's hard to fathom," Dodger agreed, remembering his father's protectiveness toward Abby, who'd been just seventeen when she died.

"To think that Danny saw that just breaks me up," Sutton added. "I can't believe she hid it so well. We were dating, for God's sake, and she never let on. Why didn't she say something to me?"

"Because she was embarrassed. Or maybe she didn't see any point. When you get right down to it, what could you have done?"

"I'd have told my dad. He'd have put a stop to it."

"Maybe, maybe not. The point is, you were just a kid yourself."

"Do you suppose it upset her enough to make her want to leave?"

"Could be," Dodger admitted. "If she didn't suspect up until she walked in on Debbie and their father — and people as smart as Danielle are often the last ones to register what's going on in their immediate environments — it had to be the shock of a lifetime. Who knows how that would have affected her?"

Twenty-Six.

·· ◦₀₀🌑🌑🌑₀₀◦ ··

Shared Girlhoods

Mary Sutton looked with affection at her son Jason as he leaned down to kiss her cheek, resting his hand lightly on her shoulder as he did so.

"Why, Jase, aren't you nice to bring Mr. Dodger by to see me."

She was the mother of movie casting, Dodger thought — pretty, soft and round in a pale pink dress, her hair in soft curls, her blue eyes wide and alert. He could see traces of her son's smile in her face and also the source of his no-nonsense approach, for the blue eyes were shrewd and the hand she offered steady.

"It's a pleasure to meet you," he said, leaning down to take her hand. Sutton had explained that she'd suffered a bad fall the month before and had to stay off her leg while she was in therapy.

"My, you are big," she observed, looking up into his face. "Your mama must be proud of what a fine, strapping man you became. And you have kind eyes. Such an attractive combination, I think, great physical presence combined with sensitivity."

"I hope so," Dodger said, trying to ignore the flash of painful frustration that overcame him whenever anyone assumed his parents were alive and part of his life, trying also not to blush at the unwarranted compliment.

"Jase says you're here to look into Danny Standridge's disappearance. At first, I don't think he was too much in favor of dragging it up again, but I can tell that now he's pleased you're making such good progress."

So Sutton hadn't wanted the case re-opened? He'd hid it well, Dodger thought.

"I don't know how much progress we're making," he told her,

"but your son has been a big help."

"Jase is a good boy," Mrs. Sutton beamed.

"I understand you know the girl's mother."

"I surely do. Gladys and May Tanner and I grew up together. My father was the mill bookkeeper, and theirs was the machine-shop supervisor. We lived next door to each other over on Managers' Street on the way to the mill. I'm closer in age to Gladys, but she was always a weird girl while May was more fun. About the only negative thing you could say about May was that she liked pretty things too much; she'd obsess over some ad in a magazine until the page was wrinkled. She was always scheming how to get her father to buy whatever it was that she wanted. The funny thing was, after she got it, more often than not somebody at school would trick her and take it away. She was very easy to manipulate, I'm sorry to say. We were best friends, or at least I thought we were until she visited her aunt in Lincolnton and met Andy. It was a whirlwind kind of situation. I think he swept her off her feet. He was very good looking, you know, better looking for a man than May was for a woman. Anyway, before anybody here had any idea of how serious May and Andy were, we heard she was engaged and then married without so much as an invitation being sent out."

Mrs. Sutton leaned over, clearly about to impart what she considered confidential information.

"We all wondered, in fact, if they had to get married. Nowadays, if a girl like May gets pregnant, she just announces the date of her 'single mother shower' but then things were different. If you were a 'nice' girl from a 'good' family, which May was, babies came after marriage, not before. Nobody would have been surprised if there'd been, in short order, an invitation to a baby shower and then word of a 'premature' birth. We were wrong, of course. It was years before Debbie was born. After that, she was different, at least to me. I mean, we stayed friendly. If I went to see her right now, you'd never guess that we'd ever been closer, but once she met Andy, she put everything else on the back burner, including me. She didn't ask me to be godmother to either of her girls or even to attend their christenings. I heard that some distant cousins of his stood up with both of them. Friendships are like that as you grow up, I suppose — they either get closer or weaker. Nothing stays the same."

She looked thoughtful for a moment, and then turned her sweet smile toward Dodger. "But I've nattered on long enough about me. Jase says I might know something that would be helpful."

The truth of it was that Dodger had come only because Sutton had wanted him to, and he had no expectation that Mrs. Sutton could assist. If she could, he was confident that Sutton would have brought him earlier.

"Well," he temporized, casting about for a question, "what can you tell me about Whitman Mall, where Danny disappeared?"

"Oh, the mall," she said, clapping her hands. "The mall was fun. They opened it when Jase was just a little boy. Just about everybody in the area came here to shop. The FoodStop was the biggest grocery store for miles — it was the biggest store in the mall. At the far end from it was Delk, the second-biggest, which before the mall came was downtown for years. It was our local department store. You could buy anything in there, from bed sheets and towels to shoes and underwear. Next to Delk was The Princess Shop, which was like a rival to The Darling Shop. It never caught on. Most girls still went to The Darling Shop for their formals for the school dances. Going down the row, back toward FoodStop, there was The Choo Choo Hobby Shop — you can still see the painting of a train on the storefront if you look hard, Cones 'o Fun — that was the local ice cream shop, FootFit — that was a shoe shop that specialized in athletic shoes, Candles 'n More — I used to go in there to buy dried flower arrangements, HealthOn — that's where you could buy vitamins and food supplements — and they did acupuncture in the back, as I recall. At the end, next to Delk's, was Sally Sue's, which sold casual clothes for girls and women. That was my favorite store. There was even a Chinese takeout around the corner from The Princess Shop, on the side of the mall."

She sighed. "But it's all gone now. The last of the good jobs left years ago. Most of the people still in the area are on some kind of assistance. There aren't many people around here who can afford to shop in those kinds of stores anymore."

"Did the mall just shut down?"

"Oh, no. It was sad to see, but it died store by store. The last store in the original part, inside, managed to hang on the longest — that was a shop that sold fabric, clothes patterns and what my generation calls sewing notions. It closed down five years ago. Do you know I have to wait until I go into Raleigh to visit my sister to buy decent thread?"

"Is the mall where most of the high-school girls shopped?" Dodger asked.

"It's where a lot of them hung out," Mrs. Sutton said. "I'm not sure how much shopping went on. There was a snack stand on the inside, with some tables in the middle of this half-open court, and that's where a lot of the girls liked to gather after school. I remember I'd go in for thread or yarn and see them there, talking and giggling, nursing Cokes and cookies so the guard wouldn't run them off."

"Did you ever see the Standridge sisters there?'

"Not Debbie so much, but sometimes I'd notice Danny. She was such a friendly child. She always waved. Once, I recall, I even gave her a ride home. There was this young man who was bothering her — I guess you'd call it stalking today. Her friends weren't ready to leave, and she asked me for a lift."

"Do you know his name, the stalker?" Dodger asked.

"No, but the other youngsters didn't seem surprised to see him there. Some of them were teasing and laughing at him."

"The Dunderhead," Sutton told Dodger. "Ten to one."

"Probably," Dodger said. He turned back to Mrs. Sutton. "This is very helpful, ma'am. By any chance, were you at the mall the Friday afternoon that Danielle disappeared? That was the day the production company gave the going-away celebration in the parking lot, and the Whitman-Brown majorettes repeated their routine from the movie."

Mrs. Sutton shook her head. "I don't recall why, but I know I wasn't there. I remember because May called a day or two later and asked me the same thing."

"Mrs. Standridge called you?" Dodger asked.

"Why?" her son added.

"She wanted to know if I'd seen Danny. She knew I'd given her a lift a time or two and she thought I might have again. She was rather rude about it, as I recall. She didn't seem to believe me when I told her I wasn't there and hadn't seen Danny in days."

Dodger had a sudden inspiration. He got his iPad from his case, input the security code and clicked onto the image of Danny in prom dress against the Chinoiserie background.

184

When he showed it to Mrs. Sutton, she gasped with delight. "It's Danny, and she looks wonderful. What a lovely dress, and it suits her so."

"That's the photograph you showed Debbie," Sutton said. "You never did say where it came from."

"It's a circuitous tale," Dodger answered. "Too long to go into here." He turned back to Mrs. Sutton. "Do you recognize the background, ma'am?"

She looked at it for a few seconds and shook her head, then frowned and looked again. "You know, I think it's the main room in The Library Pavilion at Mill House, but that's impossible. Didn't it burn?"

"That was later, as I understand it," Dodger told her, "around '98 or '99 as I recall."

"You know, I think you're right. I know it was about the time Jase graduated college and before Charlotte Whitman died because she sent him a graduation card on account of his being in the Promoters. I remember the Pavilion burned that summer. They said it was some of those tramps that hung around the area. Yes, that must be The Library Pavilion. Sarah Whitman, Travis's mother, hosted receptions there sometimes for the Clumber House volunteers, and my mother and I went. She was instrumental in saving the Clumber place, you know. The more I look at the picture, I think it's The Library Pavilion, but we can find out for sure right now. Jase, get me that book on North Carolina cultural treasures – it's the big one in the red cover on the bottom shelf over there."

She began to flip through the large glossy pages and then gestured to Dodger. He looked over her shoulder at a professionally lit and photographed version of the room in which Danielle had posed. It was beautiful, an elegant pastry of a room, all golds and reds with gilt fretwork in the corners and a big chandelier in the form of a fanciful temple. The space was lined with big bookcases that gave it gravitas, which was somewhat undermined by the black dragons that climbed the walls around the cases. On the next page was a photograph of the exterior which, unlike the interior with its Chinese-inspired décor, was Gothic in style.

"Do you mind if I scan these two pages, Mrs. Sutton?"

"Of course not. How handy that you can. Is there anything that little device won't do?"

"Very little, ma'am," Dodger laughed, clicking onto ScannerPro.

"You need one of those, Jase," she told her son.

"Mr. Whitman doesn't like what he calls gadgets," Sutton laughed. "He says they're just time wasters and don't do anything that's necessary."

"Then we'll just have to get you one for yourself."

"I've been thinking about it, Mama."

After he'd finished, Dodger re-shelved the book and began to tell Mrs. Sutton how much he appreciated her seeing him and how helpful she'd been.

"If you can think of anything else you'd like to ask me, you call, you hear? Now, Jase, Suellen left this week's grocery list over there on the sideboard, like always, and this time please get the Breyers Mint Chocolate Chip and not that Breyers Girl Scout Mint — it tastes better."

Dodger saw the briefest hint of resignation wash over Sutton's face. Clearly, being the dutiful son was not always easy.

They were back in the car, Sutton with the shopping list folded and tucked into his shirt pocket and Dodger checking his notes.

"Well," Sutton said. "Where now?"

"How do you feel about following me out to Mill House to see what's left of The Library Pavilion?"

"What's there?"

"Probably nothing. I'm just curious. Call it tying a bow on top of the package."

"Well…" Sutton thought about it.

"Unless you think Whitman wouldn't like it," Dodger said.

"I doubt he'd care one way or the other. Anyway, he's out of town for the rest of the week. I got a heads up from Roberta earlier this afternoon. So I'm game if you are."

Twenty-Seven.

Beautiful Ruins

Sutton waited as Dodger retrieved the ProMaster from the lot behind the police station and then followed him to Mill House, where — at the direction of Joe, the driver cum ruler of vehicles — they parked in the stone-paved courtyard behind the house.

Dodger saw Gladys at a first-floor window, and waved. She waved in return, a potholder in her hand.

"Shall I tell Ms. Tanner you want tea?"

"Not just yet, Joe," Sutton told him. "We're going to walk around the estate for a few minutes."

For a moment Dodger thought Joe would try to stop them, but after a brief pause he stepped back and waved them on.

Sutton led the way toward the flagstone walk Dodger had noticed earlier.

"I'm guessing, but from the map, it looks as if we follow this path through the woods, the site should come up to our left."

The woods were golden with strong sunshine, and Dodger became aware that all he could smell was the acrid fragrance of autumn. Underneath, the ground was soft with fallen leaves and needles from the tall trees overhead. The silence was surprising.

After a few minutes of this quiet walk in which even the sound of their feet was muffled by leaves, needles and damp soil, they emerged onto a circular courtyard paved in stone. No more than twenty feet in diameter, it nonetheless had presence with its defined edges and center fountain in the shape of a dragon wrapped around a book. Behind it stood an excellent representation of a Gothic gate through which could be seen a rough rectangle approximately twenty by thirty feet of what looked like old pasture growing up. On closer inspection, Dodger found the remains of a stone foundation.

"So that was The Library Pavilion," Dodger said.

"It would appear so," Sutton agreed. "I was never here. This wasn't the kind of place The Whitcats were booked for."

Their laughter was deadened by the trees that closed in on the site.

"It's grown up more than I would have expected," Dodger commented.

"It's verdant around this area," Sutton told him. "They say it's the water table. Anyway, if you take 1998 as the date of the fire, it's been fifteen years."

"Time flies," Dodger replied, poking along the foundation.

All that remained intact were the square alcoves on either side of the arched gate. Each of the alcoves had a narrow door and a round window. The doors were locked; and when Dodger tried to peer through the windows, all he could see was a stack of charred chairs in one and a pile of ruined books in the other.

He pulled out his iPad and looked at the image he'd scanned of the structure from Mrs. Sutton's book.

"That must have been some fire," he said, "to have destroyed that much stone and glass."

"Doesn't take as much as you might think when a place is full of flammable materials. Anyway, I expect that Mr. Whitman's grounds guy would have had the fire debris hauled away."

"It's funny that he didn't rebuild it, given that his mother and wife used it in connection with their civic and charitable commitments."

"I'd agree with you except that my guess is that, even then, Travis Whitman was already looking for the right time to clear out of here," Sutton said.

"Especially now," Dodger agreed, "given that the mill has been closed for so long."

"I mean, he could go anywhere in the world, and there isn't anything left in Whitman to hold him as far as I can tell," Sutton continued.

"Wonder what the right time would be for him?" Dodger asked, looking around at the quiet woods encroaching on the stone courtyard and the Gothic remnant. "His family has been running things around here for, what, over a hundred years? How do you time a departure from that?"

"Who knows?" Sutton shrugged. "Maybe when the last of the mill structures is gone or the state settles the business of the high school and that retraining center they've talked about for years. That was Whitman's special project."

"What do you suppose will happen to the town if he does pull out?"

"He's chairman of the board of the family foundation that underwrites just about everything around here. Unless he appoints someone with strong local or at least state connections to head the foundation, my guess is that in short order the town will sink back into little more than a crossroads of scattered houses."

"And the downtown?"

"There's a rumor," Sutton lowered his voice in spite of the obvious isolation of the situation, "that a developer has been sniffing around who wants to turn it into a themed shopping destination."

"That'll bring in jobs," Dodger pointed out.

"Yeah, but most of them will be minimum wage, and the others won't be filled by locals. When the mill closed, it was the beginning of the end for middle-class employment in Whitman."

"Sad," Dodger said.

"Changing times," Sutton responded. "And there's nothing to be done but to figure out how to deal with it."

Overhead, high above, an unseen jet traced a precise trail against the brilliant blue sky. The men stood and watched for a moment, and then they turned to go.

Twenty-Eight.

..∘∘●●◍◍◐∘∘..

Up in Dodger's Room

In the room that had been his for over a week, Dodger sat at the desk before the large casement window — Bluetooth keyboard in front of him, iPad screen glowing, Pages app ready for input — and thought about what he would recommend to Mystery Mavens. After a few minutes, he began, fingers moving across the keyboard with a facility borne of his father's belief that every boy should learn how to type and cook just as every girl should become comfortable with tire-changing and the basic principles of electricity.

First, there'd be the summary of the situation, which was easy enough.

> *Danielle Standridge, beautiful fifteen-year-old girl who is star student and active in many school activities, disappears in September 1993 in crowded mall parking lot within sight and sound of people who've known her all her life. Her family says that she's run away. The police and the community's leading citizen – who knew the girl – go along. It's days before a serious search is begun, and it isn't well conducted even then. The investigation, which was slow to begin, never catches up. The case grows cold quickly and stays cold for twenty years.*

Then there'd be the trigger, which was to say, what in his opinion was the motivation of the person who'd appealed to Mystery Mavens – not necessarily the motive provided during the initial presentation to the group, but the motive on the ground. That, too, was easy.

> *Travis Whitman (the applicant) – whose wealthy family has a*

long-time reputation for information containment – learned that a writer named Hank Gribble is trying to sell a proposal for a lengthy profile in Vanity Fair magazine about missing girls and that he intends to include Danielle Standridge. Whitman did not mention this information in the presentation he made to Mystery Mavens. It's my opinion that Whitman involved us as a distraction and diversion. I believe that Travis Whitman's basic motivation in coming to us is that he doesn't want Gribble poking around what he very much views as "his" town and "his" business, almost certainly in part because any such exploration will turn up the fact that his late wife was an alcoholic who died in 1999 in a single-car accident. He may think that our involvement will muddy the waters for Gribble (which it probably will).

Then there'd be his assessment as to the amount of resource remaining available. Here he could be somewhat more positive.

Assuming that Mystery Mavens chooses to continue to the professional-investigator stage, there appears to be enough resource remaining to support a closer look. There are challenges, namely (1) the length of time that has elapsed; (2) the scattering or death of many people who might know something of value about the girl's disappearance; and (3) the fact that some of those who remain have very real motives for not wishing to remember that time or to address it honestly, even at this remove. On the other hand, there are significant logistical advantages: (1) the police records – such as they were – appear to remain intact; (2) there is a better-than-usual local library run by a professional with the capability and resource to be of significant help; (3) at the time of the girl's disappearance, there was an active local newspaper (no longer in business) whose archives are now held by the local library; (4) the local police authority in the person of a well-trained and willing deputy has provided enough assistance during the past week and a half that I have observed or been part of multiple interviews with people who can provide background or suggest

*a path forward; and (5) the area's leading citizen — Travis
Whitman — is providing every possible support and encourag-
ing others to do the same.*

Then there'd be his opinion as to what had likely happened to the
missing girl, which must of necessity be inconclusive, to say the least.

*In my opinion, it's 50-50. The girl may be alive. She may be
dead. My reasoning is based on the following: (1) the girl had
a motive strong enough to make her want to run away, with or
without help, and she's smart enough to stay hidden; and (2)
there were people who felt strongly enough about her to have
kidnapped and killed her.*

Finally, there'd be his recommendation. Should Mystery Mavens
send in the pros?

*I think a professional investigator, with the cooperation of the
local authorities (which he or she can assume as a given) is
likely to learn the truth of what happened to Danielle Standridge. Because of that, I would recommend this as a project
likely to be capable of a successful conclusion.*

He read the report, made a couple of minor changes (had he actu-
ally misspelled "Mystery"?) then slid it over to Dropbox for retrieval by
Jess, who'd review/edit and pass it along to the Mystery Mavens board.
Then he texted her it was done.

For some time after that, he stood before the large window, gazing across the crimson-and-gold-tinted landscape, trying to pinpoint
what was bothering him. It had something to do with those photographs of the dressed-up Danielle posed in what he now knew was The
Library Pavilion. Was it something someone had said or something
he'd noticed? Did it have to do with Display Dollies and the mannequins modeled on the photographs? Or was it some key difference
between the dress as it appeared on Dorothy Bowland and the version
worn by Danielle? Had Danielle's sister Debbie told the truth when she
claimed never to have seen it before?

Or was this sense of oversight something else entirely? Mrs. Sutton had said the dress was becoming to Danielle. Every woman who'd seen the photograph thought the dresses were "nice," which translated to expensive. A couple of those had even said with a high degree of confidence that the dresses had come (or must have come) from The Darling Shop. Had the dresses been a gift from Charlotte Whitman to the girl? If not, the name of the person who bought them might be key. Would there be any way to retrieve the information after so much time? He thought about it. It was a long shot, but Enid Blythe, Whitman's assistant, had struck him as both thorough and efficient. He looked at the time on the iPad — 6:30. She might be gone for the day, but it was worth a shot. He navigated to his contact directory, located her name, and clicked *Call*. He expected to get an answering machine, but the businesslike voice answered almost at once.

"Enid Blythe."

"Ms. Blythe, it's Art Dodger."

"Yes, Mr. Dodger. Did you find the note Mr. Whitman had me email you? He regretted leaving during your visit, but business called him elsewhere."

"I got the email. Thanks. Look, can you check something for me?"

"Mr. Whitman said you are to be given every possible assistance, Mr. Dodger. Of course, I'll be glad to do whatever I can."

"By any chance, would you have charge records for Charlotte Whitman in your database that go back to 1993, when Danielle Standridge disappeared?"

"Charlotte Whitman? That depends on the records you mean," she answered.

"I want to pinpoint when Danielle got something that I suspect Mrs. Whitman may have given her. What I need is a copy of Charlotte Whitman's charges for the months of August and September 1993 with a particular store."

"Do you know which charge card?"

"I'm afraid not, but I can tell you the name of the store. It was The Darling Shop in Whitman."

"Oh, yes," she said, "a very nice little establishment. It was a real pity when they closed. If you'll give me a minute, I think I may have what you're looking for."

She put him on hold and was offline for several minutes. He wondered if she were calling to get permission from Travis Whitman and
decided probably not. She'd been told to assist by Whitman, in front of
him no less. If she could assist, she would. He didn't see her contacting
the continent-hopping Whitman with something so trivial.

"Mr. Dodger? I've located the records, which show several Darling Shop charges made by Mrs. Whitman during that time frame.
Shall I email them to you?"

"That'd be terrific. I'm impressed you were able to find information that far back, much less that quickly. Very few people computer-
ized records twenty years ago."

"I certainly wasn't quite to that stage in 1993. We didn't input
current records until 1997. As for older records, the fact that you asked
about Mrs. Whitman made it faster to locate what you wanted. When
she died, Mr. Whitman instructed me to take all my files that related
to her, plus everything that he gave me from her personal records, and
put them into permanent storage. I think he wasn't sure what might
be needed and found it too painful even to give me instructions as to
sorting and retention."

"He seems to have taken her death hard," Dodger remarked.

"He was very devoted," she acknowledged, her manner cooler. He
had, he suspected, crossed some line.

"Well, thanks again," Dodger said, sensing that he was about to
wear out his welcome.

"I'm glad I was able to help," she responded, her voice returned to
its original crispness.

He disconnected, and went into the black-and-white bathroom
to relieve himself. The toilet tissue was the softest he'd ever felt. As
for the towel with which he dried his hands afterwards, it was thick
enough to double and use for a pillow. Even the soap bore a distin-
guished logo, and it was changed several times a day. Unless his eyes
and touch deceived him, the fittings were gold-plated and the large
mirrors distortion-free. Everything about the guest quarters was the
best that could be had. This was a household obviously run on the
principle that nothing was too good for Travis Whitman and his guests.
It was not a mindset with which Dodger was unfamiliar. Babe, one of
his great aunts, the widow of a Texas oilman, not only had a home in

which *Fracas* was used as air freshener but kept a personal shopper on call at Bergdorf's and became such good friends with the designer who handled her account at Bvlgari that she remembered him in her will. She'd left her jewelry collection to Dodger's mother, her favorite niece, who'd enjoyed it for the two years she lived following its inheritance. After her death, still shell-shocked by what had happened, Dodger put her favorite pieces in a safety-deposit box, where they remained, and authorized the lawyers to sell the rest and donate the proceeds to her favorite charity. His great aunt had a motto of sorts —"Enough is never enough" — and he suspected that Travis Whitman and Babe were soul mates. Her tastes might have been more flamboyant, but he had more money with which to gratify his, which would make them pretty much even in the ostentatious display department. Still, in spite of Dodger's initial concerns, Mill House had served him well, and it would be churlish to complain that he'd never slept better or had hotter showers or better food.

Well as the guest quarters had served him, however, he had a sense that it was time to go. The report was away. Jess would use it to complete the checklist. All that remained to be done with Sutton was to give him a heads up as to what would happen next if Mystery Mavens decided to proceed. Then he could head back to Savannah and do his damnedest to see if he could get Jess to fly down.

His eye fell on the box of items he'd removed from the mini-museum Charlotte Whitman had created as a memorial to Danielle. He might as well return them now. He picked up the box and headed down the corridor. The door to the museum room was locked, as before, and he had to pull the key from his pocket, juggling the heavy box with his other hand. It was then that he realized how quiet the house seemed. He might be in this large place alone.

Once inside, he turned on the light, put down the box on the sorting table, and began to return items to the places from which they'd come the week before. He realized that something was different at once. The shelves were free of dust, and the marks on the floor of the platform where the mannequins had stood was clean. Also, perhaps it was due to the unusual silence of the big house, but he was aware of a low hum that he hadn't noticed before and remembered Jess's amused warning about the possibility of a security camera or recorder.

He shook his head. Why invent menace in this place, sad reminder of so much unhappiness? Of the cold-case preliminaries he'd scouted, this one was the least likely to generate hazard. He had not had a single threat thrown his way the week and a day he'd been here. No one had questioned with any persistence what he was doing, nor had anyone shown undue interest. Truth be told, however special Danielle might have been, the only two people he'd come across who still seemed interested in her disappearance were Deputy Sutton, who'd been on the verge of becoming her boyfriend, and Andrea Hand, her best friend, the one person outside her family who'd known even a little of the truth of what went on behind the placid brick façade of the Standridge house.

Dodger was tired, and it made him antsy. The thing was he didn't understand why. He'd slept well; he'd eaten well; he'd encountered no real obstacles. Maybe it was the intensity of what he'd been doing and the fact that he had come to like this girl who'd been gone so long. It was odd, but he felt bereft, knowing he was closing a chapter, knowing he'd never again see Charlotte Whitman's macabre tribute.

Back in his room, he decided it was time to pack. In the fitted closet, he opened his bag on the center island and began to pull clothes from the racks. Most of it would go straight to the cleaner in Savannah, but for the drive he held back a once-worn pair of khakis and a patterned shirt he normally wore while painting. The suitcase closed easily. There weren't many clothes because he hadn't planned to stay long. This time, he had to admit he'd broken one of his cardinal rules about this avocation into which he'd drifted as an antidote to his personal pain: he'd gotten emotionally involved. From the first time he'd looked into Danielle Standridge's eyes, he felt he owed her the truth.

He was packing his business kit when the cell buzzed. It was Jess.

"I got your message. I take it you're through?"

"To the degree I need to be. The experts can take it from here. I've got a quick meeting tomorrow morning, then I'm on my way."

"You sound tired," she said.

"I am," he agreed, "and I don't know why. It's been a productive week, and I can't complain about the accommodations. I think I'm ready to get home, take a good, long nap, and polish off the collages for the San Francisco show."

"That'll be good for you."

"It will, but I know what would be better. Come down to Savannah, Jess. I'm not sure what time I'll get back tomorrow, but I could meet you at the airport first thing Thursday. That'd give us Thursday, Friday, Saturday and Sunday, even if you can only stay through the weekend." He heard the pleading note in his voice and hated himself for it. Jess didn't like men who clung; she'd made that clear.

"I don't know, Dodger. What happened last year was a matter of the moment."

"You think I don't know that? That's not why I'm asking you."

"Really?" she sounded skeptical.

"I need you," he said simply. "I need to talk. I think I'm ready to tell you about it, about what happened."

He was surprised when the words came out of his mouth. That wasn't at all what he'd intended to say, but now that it was out there, he realized it was true. He did feel ready.

There was a moment's silence. He was prepared for her to brush him off, but he was surprised.

"Let me check the flight schedules, and I'll get back to you."

Twenty-Nine.

..oo•Q•oo..

Sutton's Farewell

Dodger awoke early Wednesday, ready to go. He allowed a few moments to enjoy the charcoal-gray canopy on the mirrored four poster, the dove-gray carpeting, the mirrored bedside tables and chests, and the armchair that was upholstered in a metallic fabric that glittered black and silver in the bright light from the windows, themselves covered with metallic blinds that he'd forgotten to close the night before. He doubted he'd ever again have quarters this stylish on a Mystery Mavens go-fishing expedition, and it had been exceedingly pleasant.

Getting out his phone, he hit the number in Savannah for Barbara Archer, his studio assistant. She sounded so sleepy that he knew he'd wakened her.

"Hi, Barbara, Dodger here. Sorry to be so early. I'll be home this afternoon, around dinner, but don't hold me to that. Before I do anything else, I'd like to take stock of what's left to be done with the collages. Can you meet at the studio at, say, eight? Good, I'll look forward to it. Also, can you call Mrs. Lorenzo and give her a heads up?"

Mrs. Lorenzo was his housekeeper and, obliging as she was in other ways, she didn't like surprises.

He checked his messages, hoping there might be something from Jess, but there was nothing from anyone. It had been a quiet night.

In the breakfast room, he put down his bag and business kit beside the sideboard and took time to savor a couple of Gladys's cranberry-and-pecan muffins and have an extra cup of coffee. When he'd finished, he got out the gratuity envelopes he'd prepared the night before, each with its handwritten "Thanks" and rang the bell.

As he expected, Gladys herself soon appeared.

"I'm leaving today, Gladys, and this is for you. I enjoyed these wonderful meals, and I must say you run a well-organized household."

"That isn't necessary, Mr. Dodger," she beamed, taking the envelope, "but I thank you."

He handed her the second envelope, the one with Billy's name written on the front. "I'd appreciate it if you'd give this to Billy."

"Certainly, sir," she said, tucking the envelope in a pocket.

"And this," he said, handing over a third envelope, "will you divide it among the rest of the staff as you see fit? I know that it takes quite a household to keep an establishment like this going."

"Of course, Mr. Dodger, and may I say that we've enjoyed having a real gentleman, all of us? You're welcome here any time — Mr. Travis said so, and I agree, for you've been a pleasure to have at Mill House. Some of these people Mr. Travis brings home, you'd think they'd never slept under a roof before, much less in a bed, and the things they do with a knife and fork make you shudder for the Coalport. As for the uses to which some of them put our lovely towels, well, it's a disgrace."

"Times change," Dodger said, and it occurred to him he'd said that rather a lot this past week, maybe because Whitman was a town in which too much had changed.

"Will you tell Mr. Whitman I'll call in a few days? I understand he's away. Do you know when he's returning?"

"Not until Tuesday is my understanding."

"Then I'll give him a call on Wednesday. Now, if you'll excuse me, I've got a long drive ahead of me."

"Then you just wait a minute and I'll do you a poke." She giggled. "That's what our grandma called the bags she used to give us full of cookies and fruit when we'd be leaving her house to drive home."

As usual, the ProMaster, key in the ignition, sat in the middle of the motor court. As Dodger put the bag of muffins and his bag and case in the side door, he looked around and spotted Joe inside the garage, under the hood of the Beemer in which Whitman had driven him around town the week before.

Seeing his gesture, the garage man came forward, wiping his hands. "Yes sir?"

"I'm leaving today, and I want to thank you for your help." He handed Joe his envelope, and received a wide smile in return.

"Yes sir. That's a fine piece of equipment you have there. Very unusual how you have it fitted out."

"It serves the purpose," Dodger smiled.

"You're some kind of artist, aren't you? If you don't mind me asking. I noticed all the paint and drawing stuff."

"You hit the nail on the head. Again, thanks, and I'll be going."

Joe and Gladys waved him off, the first from the courtyard, the second from a kitchen window, and he was on his way.

Back in Whitman he risked parking in front of the police station, and inside was waved on by the rosy-cheeked Roberta, who was on the phone, taking down what appeared to be a yet another burglary report.

Sutton looked up with a smile. "Well, sleepyhead, ready for a big day?"

"In a way," Dodger answered, grinning. "I'm headed home as soon as we finish here this morning."

"What prompted this?" Sutton asked.

"I filed my report with Mystery Mavens last night, so I've fulfilled my mandate here, which I could in no way have done without your expertise and assistance."

"Can you stay long enough to hear a few things I've turned up?"

"Sure. I assumed we'd have some things to wrap up. What's happening?"

"First, I found another police file from 1993, with detail that was never entered into the computer database. Some of it didn't make a lot of sense, so I called an old Whitman-Brown friend whose dad was a part-timer in the department in those days and he put me in touch with his father. I don't know if any of this will be of use at this point, but this is what I found out. To begin with, the local police assumed Danny had left town with some of the movie people. It was just so damned coincidental. She disappears one day, and they leave town the next. When you combine that with the fact that her parents kept saying she'd run away, it made sense. Then, when the movie people didn't pan out, they looked at Andrea Hand and her parents. At one point, they even went out to the Hand farmhouse and looked it over, with the Hands' permission, thinking they'd find Danny there. The next theory was that something bad had happened to her when she went to the stadium for the majorette practice that was scheduled just before the game that night. One of the other majorettes said she saw a couple of suspicious guys hanging around under the bleachers. The chief thought maybe Danny was sexually assaulted by them and had run away rather than face her parents and classmates. They found the lurking bleacher guys and brought them in, but got nothing. So, one by one, these theories got tossed as polygraph tests were passed, ironclad alibis were produced, and/or conflicting evidence turned up."

"Did they ever consider the most obvious possibility?" Dodger asked. "That she'd been kidnapped and murdered, probably within hours of when she disappeared?"

Sutton shook his head. "Not that I can tell. They didn't even do a physical search for almost a week."

"It's surprising," Dodger said, "that this theory, which experience predicts is by far the most likely, wasn't considered at the time."

"Putting together what's in the files, what the old cop said, and what we've heard this last week, it's almost as if they kept exploring other possibilities," Sutton pointed out, "just so they wouldn't have to consider the worst-case scenarios. They hoped she'd turn up alive, give them the bird, and show everybody they should have known she could take care of herself, thereby absolving them from any blame in whatever had happened. It was total community denial."

"Or maybe it was just because they didn't want to face the possibility that a murderer had, at least for a while, walked — maybe even lived — among them," Dodger added.

"There is that, too," Sutton agreed. "In any event, I need to tell you also that the scans of Danny's diary arrived, and I've sent them to your email."

"Thanks," Dodger said. "I'll look forward to reading that. Anything else on the investigation?"

"Just that Bo Carter called here this morning."

"The Dunderhead?" Dodger grinned.

"The one and only. He is mighty curious about any progress we've made and reminded me about three times not to tell his wife about what he was up to back then. Anyway, that's what I've got from the official front on the disappearance. I did turn up a file on the fire that took out The Library Pavilion in '99. The police were sure that the arsonists were three boys from the high school. They had a good tip, and the right amount of the right stuff was missing from the chemistry lab that the boys all had access to. The boys had no credible alibi. They even had motive. One boy's father was fired from the mill the week before for coming to work drunk."

"That's interesting," Dodger said.

Sutton shook his head. "What's interesting is that Mr. Whitman said he didn't think local boys would do that, that he was positive it was some of the tramps that he'd run off from the grounds before, and that he would feel obliged to share his opinion with defense counsel, assuming the boys were charged. Needless to say, the whole thing got dropped."

"Now, that is interesting," Dodger agreed, "but is there any indication the fire was tied to Danielle's disappearance?"

"Nah. I just thought you'd like to know, given that we were out there yesterday."

"All right," Dodger said, "you've shared. Now it's my turn. As I think I mentioned, I've turned in my Mystery Mavens report."

"Which I don't suppose you're able to discuss?"

"Not at this stage," Dodger admitted. "But I thought it'd be helpful for you to know what'll happen next, whatever the organization decides to do. First, you should know that I painted you and your expertise in glowing colors, so if this goes forward, they'll be depending on you. I hope you'll extend to them the same terrific support you've afforded me."

"Goes without saying," Sutton replied.

"Whether they decide to go forward or not — and they don't always follow the recommendations — the applicant, in this case Travis Whitman, is notified. I'll ask them to copy you so you'll be sure to know the outcome. If they decide not to go forward, they'll hold on to everything I reported. If you or Whitman, or anyone else for that matter, reapplies in the future, the new information will be factored in with the old to decide what to do at that time. If they decide to go forward, you'll have some high-powered experts at your command — professional investigators, evidence analysts, forensics experts, the works."

"They'll come here? Great. How long does it take before they make a decision?"

"It depends on how quickly they can assemble the board that makes the call. From my experience you won't hear their decision before a month, but you should hear in less than two months."

"I wish you were coming back," Sutton said. "It's been a real pleasure to work with you and see how your mind spots things I hadn't thought of."

"I could say the same," Dodger smiled, "but, trust me, you'll find the pros much more useful to you. My guess is, with your help, they'll be able to turn up the truth, whatever it may be. And I hope it's that Danielle did leave on her own and is off in some beautiful place, doing worthwhile things with that great brain of hers."

"She got through to you too, didn't she?"

"I won't deny it," Dodger said.

There was a moment of silence as the two men contemplated the young and lovely girl and the possibilities, good and bad.

"So you don't think there's any way word will come from your people in the next few days?" Sutton asked.

"Not a chance," Dodger told him.

"Well, if you're sure I won't be needed, I may take off Saturday on this trip to Disney World that we promised the kids. The vacation was scheduled months ago. We've already got the reservations and everything."

"You won't be needed in connection with the cold case," Dodger assured him, "at least not as far as we're concerned."

"Then I'm calling my relief to confirm it's all his next week. He's a retired cop from Blevins who comes in part time when I need him."

"Convenient."

"What are you going to do?" Sutton asked.

"Right now, I'm headed for Savannah. Then I've got a guest for a few days. Then I'm going to finish this series of collages I'm working on for a big show in a couple of months."

"I'll bet you're a good artist," Sutton said.

"I'll send you something one of these days, and you can judge for yourself," Dodger grinned. "Now, it's me for the open road."

The return drive took less time than had the drive north, Dodger thought, but maybe it just seemed that way because his mind stayed busy second-guessing itself. It wasn't Danielle that occupied him, but Jess. His invitation to her had been so impulsive a gesture that he was shocked when he heard the words issuing from his mouth. It was true that something seemed to have shifted, at least a little, in the power of the old tragedy to affect him in this present moment, but did that mean he was ready to talk about it, all of it? He never had, with anybody. Could he, with Jess? Of course, it might not be an issue, certainly wouldn't unless she came down. He was almost to Florence South Carolina, where he'd have lunch before getting on I-95, when his phone buzzed, and he saw that it was a text. The message was short and, to him, sweet:

Ar Sav Thurs 10-02. DL 1265 2:48pm. Jess

He was pleased that she cared enough to share what he thought he was ready to do, even as he continued to wonder if he could do it. Not only had he never spoken of what had happened with full truthfulness to anyone, even the therapists, but he'd tried to avoid its terrible ramifications even within himself. For that, and other reasons, the horror remained undiluted. He wasn't sure, even now, that it shouldn't remain untold. The die, however, was cast, and he thought he cared enough about Jess and trusted her enough to accept if he would ever be able to talk about this, it was with her.

From the moment they met, he'd sensed a special connection, and it wasn't just that she was sexy and good-looking. It went deeper, as if she could hear something inside him that he did not yet know how to express himself.

There was no point in thinking about it further. His immediate goal was to get home intact and take things one step at a time. He could do that. It was how he'd made it through the last twenty-five years.

His throat felt scratchy, and he reached in his jacket pocket for the box of Cinnamon Altoids. The first one helped, but not much, and he hoped he wasn't catching something. Coming down with the flu was all this week required to make it complete. As he pulled out the box, a key came with it, the key to Charlotte Whitman's mini-museum. He'd have to remember to send it back.

More to distract himself than because he was in the mood to listen to rock, he clicked on the iPod, preloaded to a thundering playlist of which the Stones were a prominent part, turned the volume up as loud as he could stand it, and forced himself to concentrate on the road.

The drive on I-95 to the intersection with I-16, where he'd make the turn east toward Savannah was tedious but uneventful. The drive on I-16 into the city was tedious but filled with the usual examples of the inability of many drivers to stay in a lane and sustain a legal speed on the expressway. Then, at last, in the late-afternoon sun, five-and-a-half hours after he'd pulled away from the Whitman police station, he saw the top of the bridge over the river, pulled off the expressway onto West Bay Street, and began to work his way toward the tall red-brick house on the square that he called home.

Thirty.

. . ·●●●**●●**●●· . ·

Art Goes Back to Art

Dodger sat at the glass-topped breakfast table in the bow window overlooking the side garden and allowed plump, motherly Mrs. Lorenzo to fuss over him.

"You've lost weight," she complained. "Have you been drinking your orange juice every morning?" Mrs. Lorenzo, like the late Linus Pauling, was a firm adherent to the principle that high intakes of Vitamin C could cure every complaint.

"Not always," Dodger admitted.

"You will have a fresh pitcher tomorrow morning," she assured him. "Now, you must eat the nut cutlets I've prepared from the new recipe. They will rebuild your strength."

Dodger smiled, lacking the heart to tell her that he'd been fed very well while away. He was fond of Mrs. Lorenzo and would not hurt her feelings for anything.

After finishing the nut cutlets, which were, to his surprise, tasty, Dodger went upstairs to the studio, which occupied the top floor of the house and began to assess his progress toward his goal of forty new collages for the San Francisco show.

He gazed at his work with more satisfaction than usual. He didn't think any of it was perfect — he never did — but he thought that collage, a new medium for him, at least allowed more flexibility than oils, watercolors, or acrylics used singly. He liked being able to incorporate any of them at will in any piece, using them to highlight, obscure, or otherwise manipulate the collage's core content, which was often photographic or printed.

By count, he'd completed thirty, eight lacked final touches, and two were barely begun. As was his practice, the thirty that were complete hung side by side in rows of two along the corkboard-lined interior wall. The eight that were almost ready, waited on the facing wall, also corkboard-lined. The two that were just begun stood on easels positioned so that the bright lights above shone directly on them, revealing in unforgiving detail just how much remained to be done.

It would, he thought, take little time to apply finishing touches to the eight that needed them, maybe three or four days for the whole lot. As for the ones just begun, that was more problematical. To be safe, he'd estimate three days for each. That meant, allowing for drying and perhaps a change of mind or two, everything should be ready to pack by the first of November.

He heard the sound of the small elevator behind him and turned to see a young black woman of substantial size emerging from it, her free-flowing sleeves threatening to be become entangled with the grillwork. Spying him, her handsome face broke into a wide grin.

"Dodger, you old reprobate, you're back! Was the trip successful? Has your giant brain already leapt to the conclusion of the killer's identity? How many hearts did your break? Have you found the girl of your dreams? Are you fleeing the law?"

It was a running joke, and he grinned in return.

"Nope, but I did recommend that Mystery Mavens proceed with a professional investigation. Now, Barbara, I've reviewed status, and it seems to me we can schedule the packers for the beginning of November."

"That soon?" She raised her eyebrows.

"I think it's reasonable. Anyway, given that everything's supposed to be in San Francisco no later than the fifteenth, we almost have to have the lot packed and on the way by the eighth or ninth."

"If you say so," she grinned. "Just don't blame me when the packers hit us with a rescheduling fee."

"We can make it," Dodger assured her. "Let's go over the whole show and you'll see what I mean. Now, this lot over here," he began, indicating the finished collages that hung on the interior wall, "as far as I'm concerned, they're ready to be packed once they've been checked for surface flaws, so if we…"

He walked her through the show, indicating what he was going to do and what he wanted from her in connection with the concluding phase of preparation for this new kind of show.

When they'd done, he pulled a couple of bottles from the refrigerator in the small studio kitchen, kept the Diet Coke for himself, and handed a Cheerwine to her.

"Here's the deal for tomorrow," Dodger said. "I'm working in the morning, but I must collect a friend at the airport around two. My visitor is interested in art, and I may want to show the studio Thursday or Friday. The studio will, however, be clear for you tomorrow afternoon and then from Saturday on. That'll give you several days to check the finishes on the thirty over there, touching up anything that's not right, before we start the final stages on the other ten at the end of next week. Will that fit into your school schedule?"

She thought for a minute, and then nodded. "I'll blitz the school projects this week."

"That sounds good, and if you need me, don't hesitate to call my cell."

"I will, but it'll help if you remember to keep it on," she laughed.

"I'll try," he promised.

He walked her to the elevator, said goodnight, and stood for a moment, listening to the smooth whirr of its mechanism as it took the gifted young artist down three flights to the rear entrance where her VW would be parked next to the ProMaster. The sound made him think of the elevator at Mill House, which made him think in turn of how similar and yet how different the house was from the one in which he'd grown up. He found himself yawning and looked at his watch to see that it was almost eleven. It had been a long day. No wonder he was wiped. A quick shower, he thought, and he'd pass out for the night.

That wasn't how it turned out. The shower was fine. The soft cotton pajamas felt great. As for his bed, it was good to be back on the mattress selected because it felt good to him. He lay there, eyes half closed, and looked at the soft glow of the street light filtered through shutters over the big front windows. He knew that, if he got up, he could open a shutter and see the trees of the square as almost black, the walks disappearing between large leaf canopies, the statue honoring the Revolutionary War general a gleam of white visible in bits through the foliage that surrounded the square's center.

It pleased him to know the familiar scene was at hand, but he remained in bed, eyes half-closed, hovering on the brink of sleep.

Half an hour later he remained on the brink, and felt frustration beginning to build. Reaching for his iPad, he clicked onto Netflix and then *Midsomer Murders*. He liked the show, but for some reason, viewed the last thing at night, it worked better than a sleeping pill.

An hour later, realizing he was more awake than ever and that, moreover, he'd seen (or heard) this episode of the show so often that he found himself mouthing the lines with Barnaby, he gave up.

Out of bed, he threw on a sweatshirt over pajama bottoms, slipped into his painting shoes, grabbed the iPad, and headed for the studio. If he couldn't sleep, he might as well work. The schedule he'd laid out for Barbara was ambitious. Maybe, it was just as well to get a head start, given that Jess was coming and he wasn't sure for how long.

Climbing the stairs rather than waiting for the elevator, it took a couple of minutes to leave the relative darkness of the bedroom hall and move one floor up, toward the soft glow of night lighting in the studio. Once there, he paused for a moment, smelling the satisfying aroma of paint, glue, lacquer, paper, canvas and wood, before flipping on the bright overheads.

He walked around for a couple of minutes. Was he in the mood to work on finishing touches? He didn't think so. He wasn't even drawn to the pieces just begun. He needed a new project to occupy his mind, to take away his reservations of having more or less promised Jess to tell her what he hadn't told anyone before. Also, he had a niggling feeling that he'd left something unfinished in Whitman. He needed not to think about these things, and work was the best diversion of all.

Going to the multi-compartmented bin on the rear wall where he stored canvases of various types and sizes, 8x10" canvas board in a stack cheek by jowl with 8x10" gallery-style canvases at one end and custom-made 5x8' stretched canvases at the other. After a moment's decision, he pulled out a 20x20" with a 2" gallery frame and carried it over to an empty easel.

It was blue, he thought. It had to be midnight blue, almost black but with a tinge about which there could be no mistake. He began by removing the canvas from the easel and placing it flat upon the large table under a bright light. First he poured a stream of white gesso, then began spreading it with a long-handled 4" brush, dragging it back and forth, back and forth, across the canvas's smooth surface, careful to coat both front and sides. As it dried, he played *Quell* on the iPad. Checking the surface with his finger, he decided it was dry enough for a second undercoat, and squeezed gobs of gold-colored acrylic onto several places, proceeding to spread the paint roughly over the smooth white gesso, adding more in places, which he roughed up with a small spatula. When he'd finished, he repeated the drying process except this time he watched an episode of *The Big Bang Theory* while he waited.

When the canvas was dry, he carried it back to the easel and propped it on the stand. Under the working light, what he saw was an irregularly textured surface of mottled gold with white flecks showing in places, which was exactly what he wanted.

Getting out a big tube of deep midnight blue, he applied a thick coat over the entire canvas, front and sides. When it was almost dry but still just damp enough, he sprinkled glitter at random, shaking off the excess. The end result made him think of a night sky, dark but with bits of light and color that were in reality stars.

Was that what it looked like the night Danielle Standridge had disappeared? Had she been fleeing under that kind of sky, perhaps looking out of a window in a hotel or friend's bedroom as she contemplated her next step and hoped no one would be able to trace her before she reached where she wanted to go? Or had she been imprisoned, tied up and gagged, barely able to get a glimpse of a midnight sky through tree limbs or the crack in a wall, regretting whatever it was that had brought her to this place? Or had she already been dead, a limp form barely discernible in the dark?

All of which was ridiculously fanciful, Dodger told himself, but as the canvas had made him think of her, perhaps the canvas was meant to be hers. He took the iPad over to the Bluetooth printer and located the photos of Danielle in various majorette outfits. First he printed out the vintage getup as big as the printer allowed. Then he went to the scan he'd made at the library of one of the newspaper photographs and printed it as well. Looking at the two of them together, he decided he'd rather use the shot of the girl who hadn't known she was being photographed, a girl unaware of her surroundings, unaware of what was to come. He took an Xacto blade and cut away the other girl in the picture. Then he sanded the back of the remnant and carried it over to the canvas he'd prepared. Moving quickly, he smoothed it over the still-damp surface, using a burnisher to force paper into grooves left by the dried base coats. From his case, he selected two of the postcards Lisa North had given him, one of the Whitman-Brown Mills and another of Whitman-Brown High School. From the trays of odds and ends that Barbara had collected from area flea markets and antique shops just for the purpose, he chose an assortment of beads, die cuts, dried flowers, tiny photo images, jewelry, coins, old lace and cord. Back at the canvas, he began placing things, juxtaposing large against small, color against black and white, seeing where he'd put a slash of white or a dot of pale blue.

He was so tired that his arms grew heavy and his eyes dull, but still he kept on, in a frenzy, trying to capture what he'd felt about the girl — a slash of brilliance against a murky background. When he looked up and saw that the wall clock showed five a.m., he was shocked. He'd been working for hours and hadn't realized it. It was time to go to bed; and if he didn't sleep right away he'd take one of the pills Dr. Francis had prescribed for emergencies. Today definitely qualified. He didn't want to meet Jess at the airport looking like someone coming off a bender.

Thirty-One.

..•●●◎◎◎●●.. .

Angel in Jeans

Having set the alarm on the iPad mini to wake him at noon, Dodger just had time to do what could be done to look appropriate for what was maybe the most important airport run of his life. It was, he reflected as he showered and shaved, certainly the most stressful. In his fitted closet, he decided on conservative, keeping in mind Savannah's propensity to become much warmer on very little notice.

Jeans, white shirt, tan jacket, topsiders – he glanced at himself in the full-length mirror and felt discouraged. He hadn't aimed for any particular effect, but preppy was evidently his default mode. Should he change? What the hell, he thought, there could be worse looks than preppy artist. At least it was authentic. He was what he was. Pretending to be a mountain guide or a Silicon Valley mogul or a hiphop artist would be both pretentious and hypocritical. Anyway, this wasn't a date. Why was he even thinking about this?

> *Because Jess is on her way, here, to see you, just because you asked her to. Because you like Jess more than anyone you've ever known. Because Jess understands.*

The whisper in his head had no sooner finished than a second served as a cold reminder.

> *But she's not coming for the purpose of romance. She's coming as a friend, to help a friend.*

He felt like asking the second voice why he should he listen to it any more than the first. All that mattered was that Jess was coming, was even now in a Delta jet whose pilot was about to announce initial descent into Savannah, was perhaps even now thinking about him.

If he were lucky, he thought, very lucky, maybe she had come to realize she cared about him as he'd come to care about her. Well, he'd know soon enough. In fact, he'd better get going, or he'd be late.

Jess came through the outward-bound side of the security gate, and he watched with genuine pleasure as she paused and began to look around. Her long legs were encased in tight, faded-denim jeans that ended in, he was amused to see, metallic topsiders. She wore a white tee, a dark-blue denim jacket, and a hip-length gray cape that at first glance looked like a short trench coat. Her long sun-streaked brown hair, parted in the middle, curled loosely over her shoulders. Instead of a purse, she carried an enormous soft-leather bag in a shade that reminded him of the color he'd been trying for in the collage on which he'd worked that morning. When she saw him, she smiled and waved, and began to walk faster as he in turn walked toward her.

When they met, he leaned over to brush her cheek with his lips and took the bag.

"My God, what's in this thing?"

"My wardrobe, not to mention incidentals," she laughed. "You can't expect a girl to travel without a supply of lead."

"It must have taken you forever to get that past Security."

"I have my ways," she grinned, and he believed her.

As they walked through the terminal, she told him an amusing story of a man who'd fallen asleep partway through the flight and begun snoring so loudly his embarrassed wife had tried to wake him, only to have him sock her in the jaw as he was regaining consciousness. As she talked, he caught a glimpse of the two of them in a store window and had to smile. They looked staged, as if a photo stylist lurked just off camera. Two preppies on casual day. Even so, they looked natural together. He began to feel buoyant, almost light-headed. He liked the graceful way she moved, her legs keeping pace with his even though she was several inches shorter. He liked the warmth of her laugh. He liked her hand on his arm. Hell, he liked everything about her.

The good feeling lasted until they were through the terminal and on their way to short-term parking. She tapped his arm, and when he turned, her smile had been replaced by a look of genuine concern.

"You look exhausted, Dodger. Are you sure you're ready to do this?"

"I worked late," he said, the defensiveness of his answer sounding like a whine. "In the studio."

"All right, you worked late, and it's a look of creative fatigue, nothing else," she snapped. "All I'm trying to say is if you've had second thoughts about going into what happened to your family, it's all right. You should do it when you're ready, and not before."

Because he *had* been having second thoughts, he knew he should be grateful, but he felt almost cheated. He'd geared himself up to do this because he thought she expected it, because that was why she'd come. Now, she'd let him off the hook, or at least shown him the hook could be released. But hadn't he been counting on her expectation to give him the nudge he needed? He was too tired, and it was too confusing, especially as the scent of her perfume made him want to reach out and grab her and hang on for dear life.

He stopped at the car, and she whooped.

"My God, Dodger, a Prius?"

"It's very convenient for town. What's so funny?"

"I don't know. I guess I never think of you as practical."

"Call it logistical efficiency," he said somewhat coldly.

"Don't be like that." She grinned, patting his arm with affection. "Now, show me Savannah."

As he retraced his drive of the day before — I-95 to I-16 to West Bay Street — he told her something of the city, founded in 1733 by General James Oglethorpe, a battleground during the Revolutionary War and occupied during the Civil War, an important river port, a center of cultural activity, all of the usual tourist-level information.

"You give a good history lesson, but that's not what I mean, silly. I read John Berendt's book, and I want to see the murder place."

So he drove her past Mercer House — where antique dealer Jim Williams had lived and where he'd shot his boyfriend — and around several of the squares that featured in the book, ending with The Olde Pink House on Reynolds Square.

"This is where I thought we'd have dinner tonight," he told her. "It's cliché and not as nouvelle cuisine as your usual preferences, but it's Savannah to the core."

"Looks wonderful," she said, "and a little formal. I'm definitely changing. And I must say I love these squares."

"Then you'll really love my place," he promised her.

When he pulled into the small parking area behind his house, he had to work to park the Prius between the ProMaster and Barbara's VW. He pulled Jess's bag over the seat, wiggled to get out and joined her on the pavement, where she stood, gazing upward at the house's back side.

"This is one big house," she told him. "You always make it sound like a glorified artist's loft."

"The top floor is nothing but studio," he pointed out. "The floor below has bedrooms. The next floor down is where the living room, dining room, library, kitchen, and breakfast room are. The ground level is what may be the world's best guest suite, apart from the one where I was put up in Whitman. Mill House was something else."

He shifted the heavy bag into his other hand. "The door just there, next to the big rosemary shrub, leads into where you'll stay."

When he unlocked the paneled door that led into the tiny entry, he opened the drawer of the small table that was the only furniture and pulled out a key on a ring.

"This is the exterior door for the suite," he explained, "and this is the key."

She put it into her jeans pocket.

"It's on a separate alarm system," he explained. "The printout in the table drawer here explains how it works if you want to activate it."

"After Boston, Savannah seems pretty unintimidating," she laughed. "But I'll put it on once we're in for the night."

"Through here," he said, continuing into the bed-sitting room.

"This is beautiful," she exclaimed.

"Thank you," he replied. "The previous owner remodeled it, but a friend of mine decorated it. Our goal was comfort."

"I'd say you succeeded," she assured him. "That sitting area could lure me in a second." She nodded toward the deeply cushioned love seat and armchair and cream-and-rust Oriental rug. "And there's a fireplace! I'm surprised you ever get anyone to leave."

He was pleased to see that she liked the place, pleased, too, that Mrs. Lorenzo had thought to turn on the gas fire. It was, he thought, the crowning touch.

He went to a door at the far side of the bed and opened it. "This is the bathroom for the suite. There's also a half-bath in the stair hall. As I understand it, this one is kept stocked with the usual amenities, but if there's anything else you want, let Mrs. Lorenzo know and she'll take care of it."

"I must say, Dodger, you know how to treat a girl," she teased.

"I appreciate your acknowledging that fact at last, Ms. Hannah. Now, let me show you the hall. The elevator isn't accessible from the suite, but to come upstairs, go through this door and straight up and you're in the first-floor hall. There, you turn to your left and go toward the front of the house. The library will be on your right."

"How elegant it all sounds," she giggled.

"Once you're settled," he told her, ignoring the comment, "come up anytime for your choice of afternoon tea or a drinks tray. Or maybe you'd rather just crash for a while."

"The latter, please," she said. "I feel grungy and I want to take advantage of that fabulous shower in the bathroom. What time is our dinner reservation?"

"Eight," he replied. "We'll need to leave about a quarter 'til. It'll take less than ten minutes to get there, park in the deck, and walk over to the restaurant."

"Then why don't I come up around seven, ready to leave? You can pour me that drink and show me your studio."

Leaving her to it, Dodger climbed the stairs, surprised at how tired he still felt. The burst of adrenalin generated by his reaction to Jess's arrival had dissipated, and he was glad to see the drinks tray set out in the library and the gas fire already blazing on the hearth. Lights were adjusted so that the spines of books standing on shelves that lined much of the room provided no more than a faded mosaic of color. He pulled drapes over the shutters that covered the big bay window and opened the doors of the armoire behind which was mounted the biggest flatscreen that would fit into the huge Victorian piece. He picked up the controller that lay next to it and navigated to Netflix, where he resumed a movie he'd been watching before he went to Whitman. It was about superheroes, a topic that reminded him of his childhood. His father had also been a Marvel Comics fan and would bring him the latest when he returned from business trips. They'd made a ritual of opening them together on the following Saturday, sitting before the fire or on a porch to read while they had breakfast. Of course, that was before he'd learned that the man he thought was his father wasn't, which he supposed was the start of everything bad. Even so, reading Marvel comics together was one of the most pleasant memories from his childhood. As for now, a Marvel movie should keep him awake while he waited for Jess.

Outside and below the big bay window, someone was driving too fast around the square, and he could hear the squeal of tires as the vehicle rounded the curve onto Abercorn. Ordinarily, he would have found the sound borderline irritating. Now, it seemed normal, and normal was reassuring. Whitman had been quiet, too quiet, with too much ambiguity in an environment that hid too many unanswered questions, that spoke of too many unhappy endings.

He went to the table that held the drinks tray and poured a stiff vodka and tonic. Then, tumbler in hand, he adjusted the movie's volume and settled back on the sofa to watch the exploits of *The Avengers*. It was good to be home.

Thirty-Two.

.．.．..●●○○○●●○.●..

Tourist Talk Gone Bad

Something was wrong. Dodger woke to find himself, fully dressed, under an afghan on the long library sofa, a streak of light escaping through a chink in a shutter that hadn't been quite covered by the drapes. The armoire doors remained open, but the flatscreen was black. He could hear voices and laughter from the breakfast room.

Struggling to sit up, he looked at his watch. It read 8:10, but that made no sense. Wasn't that daylight coming through the shutter? He got up, walked over to the bay window, and pulled back the drapes. It looked like daylight coming through all the shutters. Opening one, he saw before him the usual morning activity — business people hurrying toward the big building on the opposite side, SCAD students with rainbow hair sketching the statue in the center, and the old man and little boy who always came out to feed the usual mix of pigeons and gulls along with any other birds that showed up.

He'd slept through the night. *Wow, Dodger, great way to make an impression.* He started to go to the breakfast room, where Jess and Mrs. Lorenzo seemed to be getting along like sisters under the skin, but then caught a whiff of male funk and decided not to deduct more brownie points from any score Jess might be keeping on his hosting abilities.

Upstairs, he made short order of shower and shave, then put on khakis and a plaid shirt and headed back to the first floor. When he opened the door into the breakfast room, he found Jess on the long seat of the built-in nook beside the big window, reading a guidebook, while the housekeeper, having heard his approach, poured another cup of coffee.

"Thanks, Mrs. Lorenzo," he said, taking the cup.

Jess looked up and grinned.

"What can I say?" he told her. "I'm a lousy host. Can you forgive me?"

"There's nothing to forgive. You had a busy week. You needed the sleep."

"The last thing I remember," he admitted, blushing, "was sitting down on the sofa with a drink to watch a Netflix movie. The plan was to kill time until you came up."

"I'd say time killed you," Jess grinned, and Mrs. Lorenzo giggled. "When I came in, the glass was on the floor, and you were stretched out on the sofa, snoring I might add. I watched you for a minute — you wrinkle your nose when you sleep, did you know that? You seemed okay, so I covered you up with the afghan and came back to the kitchen. Mrs. Lorenzo and I talked it over and agreed that we should wait for a while to see if you woke up and, if you didn't, to assume you were out for the night."

"You missed dinner," he said.

She shook her head. "Nope. Your studio assistant Barbara showed up about 7:30 to ask you something. She didn't have any plans, and it seemed a shame to miss dinner in that interesting-looking house, so she and I walked over. You didn't tell me you could walk it faster than you could drive it."

So much, he thought, for the romantic, candlelit evening he'd envisioned. He hoped they'd had a good time.

"Barbara is a smart girl," Jess continued. "And yet you have her brainwashed. She thinks you're a fabulous artist. Are you?"

Dodger turned to Mrs. Lorenzo, who grinned as she waited to ask him something.

"Mr. Dodger, where would you like breakfast served? It's a beautiful morning."

"Then why don't we do the porch?"

"It's one of the perks of living here," Dodger told Jess as he led her to the sun-washed porch. "It can be miserable in the summer but from about the beginning of September until May, you can eat outside as often as not."

In a few minutes, Mrs. Lorenzo appeared with a tray of cutlery and dishes, which she proceeded to arrange on the black wicker table.

"I will bring muffins, fruit, and orange juice in a few minutes.

What else would you like?"

"Given that I've already had toast and coffee, that'll be plenty for me," Jess told her.

"We'll have an early lunch somewhere, Mrs. Lorenzo, so I think that'll be enough," Dodger added.

She looked displeased. He guessed she was already debating whether to do shrimp and grits or whole-grain pancake stack or even cheese breakfast soufflé with honey-glazed Canadian bacon, all part of her standard breakfast-menu rotation. She loved feeding people.

When she left to get the muffins, Dodger turned to Jess and tried to apologize again for going MIA the night before.

"Forget it," she shrugged. "All will be forgiven if you take me out to the beach."

"This time of year, as warm as it seems, the wind means it'll be a little brisk for swimming," he warned her.

"I don't want to swim," she assured him, "just to see the ocean."

As it turned out, they made a day of it. First, the beach at Tybee Island, where they walked on the shore until they grew hungry and went in search of crab cakes, which they at last found in a place that was fun but much too noisy for more than the most casual conversation. After that, they walked the ramparts at Fort Pulaski, where Jess — who showed more of an interest in the Civil War than Dodger would have expected — was fascinated to see the first project on which youthful engineer Robert E. Lee worked fresh out of West Point. Then she expressed a desire to see Bonaventure Cemetery.

"But only if it won't bother you," she told him. "I know graveyards do some people who've gone through what we have."

"It won't bother me. It's been photographed so much that it's almost like a mortuary theme park to a lot of locals. That's a shame because it's a beautiful place. I know you liked the book, but did you see the movie Clint Eastwood made of *Midnight in the Garden of Good and Evil*? Remember the opening aerial that swoops over the marshes to end in a cemetery? That's what it looks like."

When they reached Bonaventure, Dodger slowed the car to a crawl, heart thudding but not unbearably so. For some reason, having Jess here made everything seem more normal, even a place like this, which was a relief given that he'd exaggerated more than a little when he claimed it didn't bother him.

"It's beautiful, but it doesn't look as spooky as I thought it would from the book. It's like a park, but there isn't much color contrast, is there?"

"That's because the hanging moss and most of the trees here don't change color, which means there's a lot of gray, brown and green. Now, when you come back in the spring, you'll see it at its best. The azaleas will be in bloom, and it's spectacular. I'd advise mid-March."

"What makes you think I'm returning in the spring?"

"That's my goal for the next year, didn't I tell you? I'm going to get you to Savannah for visits as often as possible."

He said it like a joke, and she laughed, but it lingered between them all the way back to the Historic District, where he took her to Leopold's on East Broughton and she opted for Greek Yogurt Parfait while he succumbed to a Banana Split.

By the time they reached his house, things were as easy as they'd been before he'd stated the ill-conceived goal. When they got out of the Prius, he took her into the side garden, where a tiny gazebo, just big enough for two people and a table, sat in the middle of a small maze of low-growing boxwood. Mrs. Lorenzo showed up almost at once, bearing a tea tray. She'd been waiting for their return, and Dodger, seeing the little cakes and carefully arranged tea set, didn't have the heart to tell her about the Leopold's stop.

They watched as the housekeeper poured tea into paper-thin cups and left. They each took a sip, and then sat in a companionable silence.

There was traffic on the square, but not much, so when Jess turned to him and said in a low voice that she had to fly back to Boston the next day, he heard every syllable clearly.

"Tomorrow?" he asked, unable to conceal his disappointment.

"There's a do tomorrow night for the latest Maxcliff. That's one of the reasons I told you yesterday that I'd understand if you didn't feel up to talking seriously. I know from my own experience that it can take working up to."

Dodger nodded, staring at the toes of his topsiders, but then looked up into her eyes.

"How many people have you told about your sister?" he asked.

"Only a handful — mostly therapists or members of the board at

Mystery Mavens when I joined. I assume they've told you, given that they asked us to work together, although now that I think about it, they didn't tell me much about you."

He shook his head. "I don't think the board ever tells. The reason they ask as much as they do — and this is just my opinion — is because they don't want people joining to exploit the organization."

"That makes me feel a little better." She hesitated. "In a way, this trip was a test for me as well as for you. Given how much we've gotten to know each other and how well we get on, not to mention your own past experience with the same sort of thing, I hoped I'd be comfortable talking about it with you."

"If it'll make you feel better, I wish you would," he said, reaching out to touch her hand, which lay between them, next to the tea tray.

"It's hard," she said, voice subdued, face solemn. "Still, it's been fifteen years. You'd think I'd be more sensible."

"It isn't to do with how long it's been or being sensible," he said. "It's so traumatic when it happens, it's like you're shell shocked, like a soldier who's seen or been involved in something particularly terrible. Some soldiers never get over it, and I'm not sure survivors do either. For years, I couldn't even think about it."

"Me either," she confessed. "I think it's getting better, but I can't promise if I start that I can finish. You know?"

"I know," he assured her, wishing more than anything he could wipe the pain from her face.

"Elaine was my kid sister, you see, just four years younger. She'd always been very protected, very trusting. Our parents didn't want her to go so far away, at least not for the first couple of years, but she was determined to go to college on the coast with Nick, her boyfriend. My parents liked him. He and our dad had even devised a fantasy investment portfolio together. They considered Nick part of the family. I guess they thought he'd look after her, so they agreed. Everything was okay as long as they were a couple, but then when she was eighteen, the year she became a sophomore, they broke up and Nick transferred the next term. She still seemed to be doing okay, and I remember my dad saying that maybe it was for the best because she was too young to get married. The next thing we knew, she was calling about this boy named Jerry in one of her classes who was harassing her, following her around, posting mash notes on bulletin boards for everyone to see, carving their initials on a tree, calling her apartment in the middle of the night. My dad was very concerned. He urged her to drop out at once and transfer someplace closer for the next term. When she refused, he called the campus security head, who brushed him off. The security guy said the way Jerry was acting was just silly crush stuff, that this kind of thing went on all the time in schools, that my dad had to accept that Elaine was growing up and could look after herself. Daddy was furious. He called Elaine again and leaned on her so hard that she agreed to transfer starting with the upcoming term, but she refused to drop out. She said she wasn't going to lose a term's worth of work and credits over one idiot who didn't know how to act."

"She sounds like a sensible girl," Dodger said.

"She was. She filed the transfer paperwork and was waiting to hear back from Bennington when the police from the town next to the college called and asked to speak to the parents of Elaine Hannah. I took the call, and I knew something horrible had happened the second I heard that wording. I told them I was her sister and asked what they wanted. They refused to tell me, so I had to give the phone to my father. I've never forgotten the look on his face. It was as if his bones were dissolving. I guess my mother suspected what was being said from his expression, and she collapsed on the spot."

Jess paused, clenching her fists, which were now propped on the side of the iron table.

"We were all on the first plane west. At first they tried to tell us that Elaine had died after falling and hitting her head on the pavement. They said she was drunk. My dad refused to believe them, and he insisted on a full autopsy. It showed that she'd been raped so viciously that she'd regurgitated and drowned in her own vomit. It was as she was dying that she fell and got the bruise on her head."

"Jess, I am so sorry," Dodger told her.

"The irony is that witnesses said, and the autopsy proved, that she *was* drunk. I guess that was what gave the police the idea that they could brush it under the rug. However she'd died, they could claim it was because she'd been drinking and put herself in harm's way. Anyway, they tried to end it there, just turn it into a run-of-the-mill suspicious-death investigation so the school wouldn't be involved."

"That's rough."

"It was pretty obvious that the investigation was at a standstill when my dad remembered the guy who'd been harassing her. When the police claimed they hadn't been able to locate him, Daddy hired a private detective who had his full name, class schedule and contact info after about half an hour of interviews with some of Elaine's friends. When my dad gave the police the information, they backtracked on what they said before and claimed they'd already checked the guy out and cleared him. It was obvious they would do anything in their power to keep the school clear, even if that meant letting the guy get away with it. Then my mom had a heart attack."

"Damn," Dodger exclaimed. "Sorry."

"It was horrible. She couldn't even attend Elaine's funeral. Anyway, everything else was put on hold while we got her to Johns Hopkins and then back home. I don't think Daddy left her side for months. He got first one specialist and then another, but it was almost as if she didn't care if she got better. She got weaker and weaker, and then she died just over a year after Elaine's death. That was when Dad went back to California and kicked up such a fuss about their lack of progress that he got the police to admit that there was DNA evidence to show that Jerry had had sex with Elaine. When he asked them why Jerry hadn't been charged, they said it was because the guy claimed the sex was consensual and she was fine when he left. After what they'd claimed before, he didn't trust them. He hired another private detective and gave him the information he'd just received. The detective turned up a witness who provided a timeline for part of the evening that showed it could only be the Jerry character who was having sex with Elaine when she died. Daddy took the information to the police, who said they'd pass it along but it wasn't enough to give a prosecutor reason to charge Jerry. Daddy went ballistic and started talking about lawyers and press interviews and his friend the governor, which wasn't like him at all. All of a sudden they got interested in at least making a gesture. And that's all it was, a fucking gesture."

All through her account, Jess had gone faster and faster as if momentum forced her to get through it as fast as possible, but now it was as if her spring ran down, and she sat, mute, staring at her hands, a frozen look on her face.

Dodger didn't know what to do. After a few minutes, thinking he needed to break the trance in which she'd put herself, he reached out and touched her hand again.

"Jess?"

She jumped as if jolted by an electric shock. When she looked at him, it was as if she'd forgotten he was there.

"I'm sorry," she said, making an obvious effort to sound as usual. "I'm a lousy storyteller."

"Don't make excuses," he told her, suddenly angry. "You don't ever have to make excuses with me. You think I don't understand you can think about some of it, maybe even get to the point where you can talk about it, then you round some corner and it hits you like it was yesterday? You do whatever feels natural with me, Jess. If you want to talk, talk about it as much as you want. When you need to stop, you stop. If you need to cry, cry. If you feel like jumping up and down and screaming — God knows I do sometimes — you do it."

Surprised, she looked at him with an expression on her face he'd never before seen there.

"You don't have to tell me anything you don't want to. Stop right there if you need to. You've earned the right to share or not, and it's not up to anyone even to think you're not being appropriate."

"*Appropriate* — that's a funny word, isn't it? I'll tell you what's appropriate. *Appropriate* is when the police don't treat the victim like the one at fault. *Appropriate* is when the one at fault is tried for the crime that occurred, not sentenced to a couple of years (suspended) for a bullshit misdemeanor count that his lawyers get him to plead to. *Appropriate* is when the police and prosecutors understand why my dad got so mad about the fact that the guy got away with it. *Appropriate* is when my dad doesn't go home and blow his brains out. *Appropriate* is when I don't feel like this the rest of my life every time I think about it."

Without realizing how he got there, Dodger was next to Jess, gripping her shoulders as she sobbed as if she'd never stop. Looking up, he saw Mrs. Lorenzo coming from the house and lifted his hand to wave her away. She hesitated, and he wondered what she thought. Then she turned and went inside.

Jess cried for a long time, but then he realized her shoulders weren't shaking as much. He continued to hold her until she shifted in his grasp. He moved back and handed her a handkerchief.

"Thank you," she murmured, voice shaky. "I am so sorry. I never intended to subject you, of all people, to that, but once it started, it was as if it took over, as if I couldn't stop."

"I understand," he said. "If I can't understand, who can?"

Thirty-Three.

Admitting Fault

They were in Dodger's studio. After regaining her composure, Jess asked to see what he was working on, and he took her up the stairs to the top floor and turned on all the lights. She walked from piece to piece, studying each, not saying anything. He began to get nervous. He had no illusion they were perfect, but he thought there were elements of interest.

"I didn't know collage was your medium," she said at last, standing back to survey the entire wall of finished pieces.

"It wasn't. I did one almost as an afterthought and included it with the oils I sent to my last show at this gallery. It was a surprise when they called and asked for an entire show. I've been working on them for several months."

"They're wonderful," she said, turning to look at him with shining eyes. "There's something I don't understand, though."

"What?"

"The one on the easel, the one with the dark blue background and all the odd bits and pieces, why does it look so different from the others?"

"It isn't part of the series done for the show," he explained. "It's a one-off piece I started the night I returned here from Whitman. It isn't finished. I can't decide whether to incorporate any of the other photographs of the girl. I know I want to add slashes of red."

Jess looked at the collage more closely. "I see. It's Danielle Standridge, isn't it?"

He nodded. "I couldn't sleep the first night back, so I came up here and the canvas spoke to me. It had to be hers." He stopped, realizing how odd that sounded.

"I know what you mean," she agreed, continuing to stare at the piece. "Sometimes when I'm writing, the characters take off in their own direction, dragging me with them."

He looked at her in surprise.

"She was beautiful, wasn't she?" Jess said.

Dodger nodded. "What I couldn't decide was whether that was her undoing. It's good that it isn't mine to resolve, just to say 'loose the hounds of truth'."

"I passed the report on," she told him. "I hope they take up your recommendation. It's so horrible to think of a girl like that just evaporating."

Dodger nodded. "Terrible as our knowledge is, at least we know what happened."

Jess understood at once what he meant, for she came over and squeezed his arm. "We do, for good and bad. Listen, Dodger, I want to thank you for bearing with me in the garden. You'll never know what it meant to me. Painful as it was, it helped. I just hope that sometimes you'll be able to release at least some of your pain."

She reached up on tiptoe and gently kissed his cheek.

He felt tears rise in his eyes, and he realized that if he'd ever be able to share even a little of all that had happened, what he'd never before admitted to anyone, it was now, with her. He knew she was looking at him, realizing what was going through his mind, waiting. The moment stretched out, then snapped.

"I'm not sure I can do this," he said, leading her to the studio's sitting area. "But I've got to try."

She hugged him, then watched as he paced up and down and began, with false starts and cracked voice as he fumbled for words, to unwind the truth as he had always feared it, telling what he knew and what he surmised, trying to unravel for himself as well as for Jess the story of what had happened to his family.

Thirty-Four.

Truth Telling

"Until I was thirteen," Dodger said, "I had a normal childhood. Nice parents and a sister three years younger who was sometimes bratty, but okay all in all. I never thought about whether we were happy, which in a kid I guess is proof that we were; and when I look back on it, those days seem like a kind of golden dream. Then I started at the prep school where my dad had gone. One day I got into an argument with another boy in my section, and he taunted me with the fact that my dad wasn't my dad. I guess his parents had told him. Maybe a lot of people knew."

"Little monster," Jess said. "What did you do?"

"First I hit him, and then I ran away from school and headed home. Dad was out of town on a business trip, but my mom admitted it. She said they'd planned to tell me the next year. My real father was a man she married while she was in college. It lasted for a few years. All she told me at that time was that it wasn't a very good relationship and that she should never have married him. I think she was surprised when she discovered she was pregnant with me, and she decided to end the marriage. That seems to have suited him as well and he didn't kick up any fuss at giving her full custody, was even generous with child support. My mother remarried as soon as the divorce was final, when I was a year old. After some negotiation, my birth father allowed my mother's second husband to adopt me, which was why I grew up with the same family name as my sister and never had anything to do with him."

"That was the first you'd heard? You never guessed?"

He shook his head. "There was no reason to. My mother's parents never told. As for my dad's, they treated me the same way they treated

229

my kid sister, and none of the aunts and uncles ever hinted at it. Ours seemed like every other family I knew, and to learn that it wasn't really got to me. I hit the roof. When I calmed down enough to ask her who my real father was, she got angry. She said I was never to say that to my dad, that he was the only father I had, the only 'real' father I'd ever had. I called her a name I didn't know I knew and said I didn't have to listen to her. She slapped me, and I ran off and spent the night with one of my friends without telling my parents where I'd gone."

"It's understandable. You were shocked."

"I didn't take it well, then or later," he admitted. "I blamed my mother. All I wanted to do was to punish her. I skipped school. I shop-lifted. I started running with a bad crowd. I was a big kid and I got into a lot of fights. I got into just about every form of trouble open at the time to a teenager with a good allowance. First, my parents tried rea-soning with me. Then they sent me to therapy. Then they got my birth father to contact me and tell me how lucky I was. That really made me mad. The one time the guy contacts me in my whole life, and it's to give me what I considered a crap sermon. That was when I went on my first bender and tried coke. I think the final straw was when I stole my dad's Amex and used it to charge a suite at the best hotel in the area, which my buddies and I then proceeded to trash."

"That doesn't sound like you. What happened?"

"The management called the cops, who called my parents. Dad squared the management, who dropped the charges, but the next school term, I was sent to a prep school with a reputation for dealing with 'boys with issues'. I hated it. They were always talking at you and throwing good examples in your face, which I thought was much too uncool for a world-wise type like me. All that made it bearable was Joey Farraday. He was a couple of years older, a big guy even taller than me, with short blonde hair and bright blue eyes. He was captain of the football team, played lacrosse, starred in the school play, and looked like Patrick Swayze. I thought he was just about the coolest guy I'd ever met, and I hero-worshipped him. He was very popular at school. He knew his way around. He could get just about anything anybody wanted — booze, drugs, cheap electronics. Of course, even then there were rumors about him. Some people noticed that anyone he didn't like tended to have problems — schoolbooks stolen, papers cut in two, room trashed, computer screen scratched — so nothing all that serious, just kid stuff, but enough to make the others want to stay on his good side. Anyway, I put a lot of the talk down to jealousy. In spite of that, it seemed like everybody wanted to be buddies. For some reason, he liked me, and I thought he was the greatest thing going."

He stopped pacing and looked at her. "I guess you think that sounds stupid."

She shook her head. "I think it sounds like being a teenager. I pledged a sorority in college because the president, who was probably the prettiest girl in school, as well as the most popular, made me feel as if I would be the star in their crown. As soon as I signed on the dotted line, of course, she forgot my name. So what happened with Joey?"

"He graduated prep a couple of years before me and got thrown out of two of the Little Ivies in rapid succession. I remember I was surprised because he was smart, a lot smarter than I was. It never occurred to me that he was anything other than he seemed, this devil-may-care guy who could do anything and liked a good time. I knew he had a temper, but I'd never seen him use it on anyone who didn't deserve it."

"I take it you reconnected after prep school?"

Dodger nodded. "We bumped into each other my senior year when he came back to the school to visit a cousin, and on impulse I invited him home with me for spring break. I knew my parents worried that I didn't have enough friends at school. I wanted to show off this paragon of all the virtues I thought boys should possess at the time."

He shook his head at the memory, and he needed a couple of minutes before his voice felt strong enough to continue.

"Anyway, that visit was the start of a lot of stuff between Joey and my sister Abby."

Again he hesitated, and she looked at him with concern in her eyes.

"The Thanksgiving that it happened, I was a senior at Brown and Abby was a freshman at Swarthmore. I didn't go home that term until Thanksgiving break. Abby and I arrived at the same time, and she was full of news about school and the people she'd met there. We had a nice Thanksgiving dinner, I remember, just the four of us. My parents and Abby went to visit family friends afterwards, but I stayed home. I remember the house was very quiet, but there wasn't anything odd about that. The lots were large, and there wasn't a lot of traffic on our road anyway. I was watching TV in the den when the doorbell rang. When I looked through the peephole, I saw it was Joey. If I'd had any sense, I'd have let him keep ringing, but I'd known the guy for years. Just because he'd had a dust up with my sister didn't do away with that. Anyway, Abby wasn't there. So I opened the door. I didn't even let him come in. We just talked for a minute, and he gave me a package of records he said Abby had lent him. There was kind of an awkward pause. Then he asked me if I wasn't going to have him in, and I told him that I couldn't, that I'd promised my parents not to have anyone over unless they were home, which was a lie and pretty stupid for a guy my age, but it was the first thing that popped into my head. I felt bad about it, but I knew they wouldn't want him in the house after everything that had gone on between him and Abby."

"What happened then?"

"I thought he'd get mad, but all he did was pull out a flask. 'At least, let's share a drink for old times,' he said, handing it over. 'It's one of your favorites.' I took a slug, and he said 'Can't hold your liquor anymore, huh?' And so I took another slug and handed back the flask and he took a slug — at least I thought he did. Then he said goodbye and left. I'll admit I was relieved; the guy still intimidated me. I watched TV for a little while after that, and then I got sleepy. I realized later that I must have been drugged, but at the time the thought didn't cross my mind. I dragged myself upstairs and fell on the bed, still dressed, and more or less passed out. I didn't even know when they got home."

His voice broke, and he stopped, unable to go on. Jess reached out and squeezed his hand.

He'd never know what might have happened next, for he heard the elevator door open in the main part of the studio and turned to see Barbara Archer entering the room.

Thirty-Five.

·..•●●◎●●●..·

Life's A Bitch

Dodger walked into the library to find Jess, drink in hand, standing before the section where he shelved books on local architecture.

"Looking for something?" He'd changed, and now wore a jacket and slacks that would be suitable for wherever she wanted to go to dinner. He felt he owed her that at least. She'd listened and been supportive, and he suspected it hadn't been easy so soon after her own revelations and the stress the telling had caused her.

She turned when he spoke, and smiled.

"I wanted to read something about the pink house where Barbara and I had dinner last night, but that can wait. You're looking good, Dodger."

"And you look beautiful," he murmured, trying not to stare too appreciatively at the fitted red dress that hugged her body. "I'd say we could go anywhere and not embarrass ourselves, so what are you in the mood for?"

"Would you think I was crazy if I said I'd like to go back to the same place you booked last night? The food was fine, the atmosphere lovely, and I think it'd be neat to walk."

"Let me call and make sure they've got availability," he told her, getting out his cell.

The maître 'd was willing but unable to give Mr. Dodger the room and table he'd requested the night before, beside the fireplace in the candlelit sitting room of the old part of the house. A couple celebrating their anniversary had booked it.

"I know," Dodger said after a moment's thought, "how about the vault? Great, we'll be there in a few minutes."

They walked hand in hand across the square, moving in and out of the light cast by street lamps filtered through tree canopies. Then there was a short walk to the next square, and there was the restaurant, its rose façade glowing in the purple night.

The maître 'd made a fuss over them as he escorted Dodger and his "beautiful lady" to the vault.

"I love it," Jess exclaimed, "and it's all ours. Look at that darling little table."

"One of the most romantic places in the city," Dodger assured her, "and the most private."

The table for two was already set with bottled water in a wine cooler and handsome tableware. The maître 'd pulled out a chair for Jess, who rewarded him with a dazzling smile, and said the waiter would be there presently with a complimentary treat for Mr. Dodger and his special guest.

As promised, the waiter arrived almost at once with menus, accompanied by a server holding aloft a large platter of fried green tomatoes, portabello mushrooms, and artichoke fritters.

"Our signature Tavern Platter, with the maître 'd's compliments, Mr. Dodger. And he asks me to tell you that tonight he particularly recommends the salmon if you wish fish, the New York Strip if you prefer steak, the braised shank if pork is preferred, or the caramelized Vidalia onion and sweet potato ravioli if pasta is more to your taste. I'll return to take your order after you've had time to study the menu."

"What do you suggest?" Jess asked Dodger.

"It's all good," he assured her. "And if it isn't, we'll order something else."

She laughed, and he felt inordinately pleased, lighter than in a long time.

Taking a fried green tomato onto her plate, Jess dissected it with a knife and fork and lifted a piece to her mouth as if not sure it was meant to be eaten. Then a beatific smile lit her face.

"I love this," she said. "Why hasn't anyone told me about green tomatoes?"

"It's a Southern thing," he told her, "but you can have them as often as you want, whenever you come down."

"That guest room makes it tempting," she assured him. "But why should I come to you?"

"Because I'm always in Boston, and it's associated with what we do for Mystery Mavens. Savannah is different. Savannah is a place we can have fun in without maybe thinking too much about all the bad stuff that's gone before."

"How'd you learn about the city?"

"One of my mother's aunts had a house here. She lived in New York most of the time, but she kept a place here for winter. She said Florida was too cliché and the South of France too precious."

Jess lifted an eyebrow.

"I know, I know," Dodger laughed. "She was a lady of definite opinions, most of them unique to her. But she was good to me when I needed it most."

"Do you mean after your parents…"

The waiter appeared. They gave him their orders, and then Jess turned back to Dodger and made an apologetic gesture.

"I'm sorry if that sounded as if I'm fishing. I'm not. I'm interested, obviously, but you need to say what you want to say when you want to say it."

"I think if Barbara hadn't come in earlier, I 'd have finished the story then," he assured her. "As it is…"

A server arrived with salads and poured wine. When they were again alone, Dodger ate a bite or two, and then put down the fork.

"I want to finish the story," he told her, "for you."

And so Dodger told her about how on the day after that Thanksgiving he'd been awakened by the police and dragged down the hallway to see the bodies of his parents and then his sister, how his parents had been shot, his sister raped and strangled, how the smell of the blood remained as clear now as then, blood on the bed, the headboard, the floor, even the walls, how the cops at first thought he'd done it until a lucky accident led them straight to the killer, who turned out to be Joey Farraday, misidentified by the newspapers as a friend of the family.

Before he could make up his mind about what to say next, she jumped ahead.

"Did they prosecute?" she asked, frowning, obviously thinking about this in relation to her sister's case.

Dodger nodded. "They were going for Murder One, but the turd pled out."

"So he confessed and they sent him away?"

Again Dodger nodded, again keeping quiet about what, precise-ly, that had meant and how minimal the justice meted out had been. After all, he couldn't go there without straying into dangerous territory that included the role that he himself had played, and he knew that he wasn't willing to risk seeing the sympathy in her face turn to hostility or, worse, contempt.

He gazed at her, aching to reach out and touch the faint line between her eyes, wanting to tell her that, between them, everything would be better, maybe never completely right, but better than it could ever be for them apart. He decided in that moment that, whatever hap-pened, he would never willingly let this lovely, intelligent, kind woman learn anything about him that made him seem as bad to her as he did to himself.

"How long did it take you . ." she began, then stopped, clearly concerned that this might be territory that was too sensitive.

"A long time," he admitted. "I went ballistic. By then I was go-ing off the rails anyway. I'd dropped out of Brown when it happened and was sitting around brooding. About all I dealt with was the estate stuff, you know, the lawyers, the document signing, all the bureaucratic crap that follows death. Other than that, I messed up — too much booze, too many drugs, too much everything that was bad for me. I was twenty-two, an adult in legal terms, so nobody could force me to do anything I didn't want to do. At the same time, I wasn't old enough or experienced enough to handle all that had happened. That was when Aunt Jane stepped in. She remembered I liked art and got me into Pratt. I fought the idea at first, but I found out I was good at it. By the time I graduated, I knew that if I could make anything of my life it would be as an artist. Creating was what saved me. Creating and Savannah. I first came here with Aunt Jane — her place was at Isle of Hope, to the east of town. I'd come down and we'd wander around and watch the progress of the renovations. Sometimes, we'd talk about what it would take to re-do one of the old places in the Historic District. When she died fifteen years ago, she left me the Isle of Hope house, and I sold it and bought my place downtown. I moved here full time, and I've been here since."

"Do you ever go home?" she asked. "Back to where you grew up?"

Dodger shook his head. "No way. It took me a while to decide what to do with the place. I knew I'd never set foot in it again, and I didn't want it turned into some kind of murder-house attraction. I told the lawyers handling the estate that I wanted the house demolished and that they were to hire a landscaping service to turn the land into a bird sanctuary in honor of my parents and then they were to give it to an environmental group my mother had supported. I understand it's beautiful."

"That was a nice thing to do. It has to be the sort of gesture your parents would appreciate. Still, it's sad."

Dodger nodded. "Life's a bitch, but you have to get on with it."

The candlelight danced in Jess's eyes, and his own were full of tears.

Thirty-Six.

. .₀₀●●❈❈₀₀. .

Heroic Outtakes

Back at his house, Dodger and Jess sat together on the sofa in the dark library, nursing drinks, while the gas fire on the hearth hissed and occasionally gave a slight pop. An ambience of easy tranquility pervaded the room. It had taken a while, but after the walk back from the restaurant, Dodger felt himself again, the old fury abated by the presence of the woman next to him.

"Thanks for lending me the architectural history," Jess said. "I'll enjoy reading about the Pink House and seeing what it looked like before it was a restaurant. I'll return it the next time you're in Boston."

"No problem," he told her. "I haven't looked at that book in years."

"So you think you're through in Whitman?" Jess asked.

"I'd say so," Dodger said. "I did my thing. Now it's up to the Mystery Mavens board to decide what they want to do next."

"What do you think happened, just between us?" Jess asked. "I know what the report said, but if you absolutely, positively had to say where Danielle is, what's your best guess?"

"I don't know," Dodger admitted. "I hope she's still around somewhere. She was quite a girl. Hey, you want to see her in action? I almost forgot that Whitman sent me home with the ***Before A Hero*** tape."

Jess looked at her watch. "I'm not sure the whole movie's a good idea, given that I've got that red eye in the morning, but I'm up for selected bits and pieces."

"Danielle isn't in much of it, just a part toward the end," Dodger promised, "and I'm good with *Fast Forward.*"

He pulled the presentation box from his kit, opened it and removed the tape. "The director of the movie sent this to Charlotte Whitman to thank her for her help. I watched most of it the other night." He got up and went to the VHS player that he'd kept in the armoire so that he could watch movies that hadn't been released as DVDs or Blu Rays. "The part Danielle appears doesn't show up until about ninety minutes into the tape," he explained as he fiddled with the controls.

After a few tries, he found the place he wanted. The valiant young hero was running across the beach where he'd be shot. "Okay, here it is," he said, hitting *Pause* and returning to his seat on the sofa next to Jess.

"He gets shot in a minute and as he's falling he has a memory of the majorette squad at his old high school back home."

He depressed *Play*, the music swelled, the hero began to fall, and images of girlish knees, dimples, smiling lips, and batons cycled through his consciousness. When the tape reached the few seconds where the full majorette squad was shown, Dodger hit *Pause* again and went over to the screen. He tapped the third girl from the left. "This is Danielle." Returning to the sofa, he hit *Play* and the majorettes did their routine. When they finished, he was about to turn off the tape, when Jess stopped him.

"Did you notice how vibrant the girl looks? Your eyes go straight to her."

Dodger nodded. "In just about every photo, it's the same."

"With those kind of looks, she must have attracted a lot of jealousy in a small town."

"I think so, but maybe not as much as we might think. As good looking as she was, that doesn't seem to be how she saw herself. She was more interested in learning and books. Odds are at least some people thought of her as a nerd."

"Maybe," Jess said as she examined the presentation box. She took out the letter and scanned it. "That's interesting. The director says something about special material. Ten to one, he means outtakes. Why don't we skip ahead to the end of the film and see what's there?"

They were rewarded by a section headed *Happy Days in Whitman, with Thanks to Charlotte Whitman.*

Dodger turned to Jess. "You were right."

The images were a mixture of behind-the-scenes footage and outtakes. For the most part, the behind-the-scenes stuff showed actors and townspeople waiting to be called or rehearsing or sometimes just standing around and talking. The outtakes featured scenes not used in the movie, most of them because they'd included mistakes and had to be reshot. From time to time, Dodger would recognize someone he'd met during his Whitman visit, and pause the video to tell Jess about the person.

This personalized section would have had more significance for someone who'd been involved with the movie, and it struck Dodger as mundane and more than a little boring. The most interesting clip showed the mill intact, its parking lot full, a train car at the loading dock, people going in and out of its employee entrance. The building was so large that the river was no more than a sliver beyond and to one side of it. He found himself yawning when a very different scene came on. It was footage taken at The Library Pavilion.

"This is the building I told you about, the one that burned," he explained. "It was evidently quite a place."

"It's pretty. Is this the one with the Chinoiserie-style interior?"

He nodded. "Maybe they got something inside too." He let the tape roll, and in a few seconds they were rewarded with a professional-quality scene in which Charlotte Whitman and Danielle Standridge took turns explaining features of the room, intercut with shots of Travis Whitman and Lisa North (or Lisa Ryan as she was then) watching them from opposite sides of the room. Dodger wasn't surprised at Danielle's beauty. He'd been staring at photographs of her for some time, even before he started the collage. Charlotte Whitman's cool perfection, on the other hand, surprised him in spite of what Deputy Sutton had told him and the few images he'd seen of her. She did look a little like Grace Kelly, more than a little, he decided. As for Lisa North, née Ryan, she was young, fresh, and giggly, her soft loveliness nothing like the polished crispness of her adult persona twenty years later. The only points of unchanging similarity were the lilac eyes and lush black hair.

Dodger paused the tape.

"Charlotte's the one in white, of course," he pointed out. "Danielle's in green. The girl in yellow is Lisa North, the librarian you looked up. She'd have still been Lisa Ryan at this point."

"Three very attractive women," Jess concluded, "and just one man. Interesting."

"Whitman is the kind who'd draw women to him, probably then

as well as now. He has that mysterious air all of you like so much."

"So that's Travis Whitman?" Jess said. "He's handsome. Still, talk about wired — is he as intense as he looks?"

"In a low-key sort of way," Dodger told her. "He hides it better now. The guy's hard to read, but, you know, I like him. I even feel a little sorry for him."

Jess laughed. "Only you could feel sorry for a billionaire who's thrown hundreds of people out of work, Dodger."

Dodger paused the tape to respond.

"Just because he's wealthy doesn't mean he doesn't miss his wife or wish he hadn't had to shift production to China. My personal theory after meeting him is that the reason he hangs around Whitman is because he's trying to come up with something to replace the mill."

"Maybe." Jess looked doubtful. "But I still go for the 'follow the money' theory. If you ever do learn why Whitman continues to roam the hunting grounds of his capitalist forefathers, dollars to doughnuts it's because there's some personal benefit to him."

"Cynic," he laughed, and hit *Play* again.

At the end of The Library Pavilion footage, Whitman, his wife, Lisa, and Danielle stood together before a dragon-wrapped bookcase when the director yelled out that they should all express what they really felt. Whitman shrugged and made a face. His wife looked with exaggerated adoration at, first, her husband and then at Lisa and Danielle, mouthing 'my co-stars', Lisa did an in-place jig, and Danielle mugged, eyes crossed, fingers pulling her lips into a rictus, sharp elbows jabbing at the air. Then all four of them collapsed in laughter, forming a loose circle of intertwined arms and touching heads similar to a football huddle. Then the scene went black and a big *Thank You, Charlotte!* filled the screen.

"Why did he thank her?" Jess asked. "I thought it was Whitman who owns everything in sight."

"She facilitated production in some way," Dodger explained. "Now that I've seen all of it, I think I should return this. I'd be willing to bet that Whitman doesn't know this end section is on here. He might enjoy seeing his wife again in a happy moment. There don't seem to have been too many of those, especially later."

"What do you think he expects, concerning the tape I mean?"

"Nothing," Dodger admitted. "He didn't care for the film. I'm not sure he was all that enthusiastic about the role that his wife played in helping the production company. I'm not sure it was even that meaningful to her. She hadn't bothered to open the presentation box. As for the director's note to Charlotte, I've already told him about it. He didn't care; he told me to put it back in the box. Then he gave the whole thing to me."

"Then I'd let it go. It may be painful for him if you return it or even bring it up again."

"In case he changes his mind, I'll have it duplicated next week and send the presentation box and its copy to you to give to the board if they decide to proceed. In fact, I think I'll get two duplicates."

"What's with the second duplicate — are you keeping it for your personal video-bests collection?" She laughed.

"You guessed my guilty secret," he grinned, then shook his head. "I know someone who'd liketo see Danielle again. I'll get it to him."

"You're a sentimentalist, Dodger," she told him, patting his arm.

He leaned over and kissed her on the cheek, or at least that was his intent. She moved just as he did and instead he found himself brushing her lips, and then seeking them in a soft, deep kiss. Putting his hands on her shoulders, he drew her to him, and affection became passion.

"Whoa," Jess said, pulling back. "I don't think this is a good idea."

"What makes you say that?" he asked, breath faster, heart pounding, every ounce of his body wanting to get as close to her as he could and stay that way.

"It's been an intense day, Dodger," she said. "Both of us did something very difficult and personally significant. It's wonderful that we trust and like each other enough to be able to say the things we did. I shared things with you I've never before told anyone, and I suspect you did the same with me. I want to think about whatever this is before we go further. The last thing either of us needs right now is a pity fuck."

For once, he had enough sense to keep his mouth shut.

Thirty-Seven.

. . ₀.₀₀●○◐◑○●₀₀. . .

Missing Something

Dodger stood in the first-floor stair hall as Jess's footsteps descended to the guest suite. He thought it was the most discouraging sound he'd ever heard, as if every few inches made it that much less likely he'd ever learn her true feelings. He could understand her caution. He was more than a little conflicted himself, but at least — after years of on-again, off-again relationships marked by superficiality — he was willing to try. Why wasn't she? Had last year's accidental straying into intimacy been such a mistake from her perspective that she'd be leery of him forever? That wasn't good. In fact, that was seriously bad, for he suspected that he was falling in love with this tall beauty whose sad eyes and dazzling smile dared him to leave the past behind.

He sighed, picked up his case, and headed upstairs. He hesitated before the door to his bedroom, then went back to the stairs and continued upwards to the studio, where the familiar sights and smells at once began their work of recalling him to what he did best, the one thing capable of giving him enough perspective on existence to make it not only bearable but sometimes even pleasurable. Going to the collage he'd begun Wednesday night, he at once saw what he needed to do to it. After working nonstop for half an hour, he placed it under the light he used for drying, and went into the tiny kitchenette to make a cup of coffee.

Carrying the mug and his kit into the sitting area, he plopped down on the sofa and thought about what had happened here just a few hours earlier. He was surprised at how close he'd come to admitting to Jess that he was responsible for the death of his family. He hadn't pulled the trigger of the gun pointed at his parents or yanked the scarf around his sister's neck, but he might as well have. If it hadn't been for him and his desire to impress Joey Farraday, they'd still be alive. That's what he'd thought at the time; that's what he still thought. That was, however, his private hell, a place of unending self-recriminations and personal doubt, and he couldn't believe he'd almost let someone else catch a glimpse of it. Maybe that was why Jess's pulling away at the last minute hurt so much. He'd let her see the real him, or at least a significant part of it. Now, he couldn't help wondering if he'd made a mistake. Could anyone who knew even as much as he'd told her come to care for him?

There was no point in going there, he told himself. Everybody had his or her demons; his were just more fearsome. His eyes fell on the case that he'd brought back from Whitman. Maybe it was because they'd just looked at the **Before A Hero** video that he found himself wondering if there were someone who felt the same way about whatever happened to Danielle as he did about his family. Was there an individual who, even now, woke at night reciting a litany of "what ifs" and regretting every one? But who would that person be — someone who'd helped her run away, someone who'd sheltered her, someone who'd introduced her to a person who'd proven untrustworthy, someone who'd had a reason to help the person who'd hurt her conceal the fact? The problem was that he still had no idea as to which scenario was more likely to be true: the girl leaving on her own; or the girl kidnapped and subsequently murdered or imprisoned.

But what if it wasn't either one? What if the truth lay somewhere in between? If that were the case, all bets were off. The thought floated through his consciousness and evaporated as he walked over to the collage incorporating Danielle's photograph. It was as dry as he wanted for the next step, so he removed it from the light and replaced it on the easel, where he considered it for some time. He had the oddest feeling, as if he were missing something that the photograph displayed for anyone with eyes to see. Frustrated, he went back to the sofa and got out his iPad. He'd put all the images he'd accumulated in Whitman in a folder, which he now opened to look at each in turn. What wasn't he seeing? He closed the folder and remembered he had unread emails related to the case.

The first one he came to was Jess's on the interlibrary loan requests that Danielle had made in the summer and early fall before her disappearance. He'd asked for information on titles that weren't textile related, not because he had anything specific in mind but because he thought it might be instructive to see what she'd been interested in during the months before her disappearance. The notes Jess had sent on the four non-textile titles were clear and concise. At the end, she'd added a summary of the topics represented: Shakespearean prose style; security enforcement in industrial workplaces; influence of social environment on personality development; and industrial diseases. The second and fourth titles she'd asterisked as probably related to Danielle's textile-industry research. He glanced over the other six titles Danielle had requested, all textile related, but nothing struck him as capable of being connected with the girl's disappearance.

The next email, he thought, might be more revealing, for it was from Jason Sutton.

Here's the scan of Danny's diary from the forensics lab.

The scan was attached. Dodger clicked onto it. In spite of the fact that the small page size had encouraged Danielle to make her entries proportionately small, the combination of printing, writing, and drawings was legible, and Dodger read the little book in no time. However smart and good-looking Danielle had been, much of her diary read like that of any other teenager, for the most part full of boys, school, and her relationship with her mother. Dodger couldn't help smiling as he re-read some of the entries.

I think J.S. likes me.

I saw J.S. with J.J. – she is such a slut, and he makes me so mad.

A.H. gave me cool new purse for my b'day – best friend ever.

We're going to be in a movie! Learning new routine for it.

Mrs. H. doesn't like me – called me to office for being late get-

ting back from rehearsal.

Mama's so mean — she won't buy me dress.

Mrs. K. keeps asking me questions — nosy lady!

There were, however, several entries that caught his eye as different from the others.

> *D.B. says I can't come to her birthday party. She says somebody told Mrs. B. I said a dirty word and I didn't! I don't care — didn't want to go anyway.*

> *S.F. says I'm the smartest girl ever.*

> *S.F. wants me to leave W-B and go to her school.*

> *I caught S.F. watching me — creepy.*

> *I saw what Daddy was doing to Debbie. Should I tell Mama?*

The date of the last entry — which was the final entry in the diary — corresponded with the time frame Debbie had mentioned for Danielle's walking in on her and their father as he was molesting her in the guest room. Dodger wondered if Danielle had told May Standridge what her husband was up to and, if so, what May had said in return?

> *You think I don't know? Get your head out of the clouds, Miss Priss. I look the other way about your sister to keep his hands off you.*

If confronted, she'd have said something along those lines, he thought, which was enough to make a smart, sensitive girl want to run away from home. Not only is her father abusing her sister, but her mother knows about it and condones it. Worst of all, self-serving as May Standridge was in her prime, she would have managed to make the situation somehow seem Danielle's fault because it supposedly existed to protect her.

Anything May might have said was pure conjecture, of course. For all he knew, Danielle had never said a word, which would have suited her parents and sister. Danielle discussing what went on at home was the last thing any of them would have wanted. Not only would it have made things even more complicated around the Standridge household, but if she'd kept talking on the outside it would have imperiled the high regard in which the oh-so-respectable family was held and perhaps put Andrew Standridge's job in jeopardy.

The identity of most of those represented by the initials was clear. *Dorothy B.* was obviously Dorothy Bowland, just as *Mrs. B.* was her mother. *J.S.* was Jason Sutton, *A.H.* was Andrea Hand. *Mrs. H?* What was said didn't make sense if the initial referred to Andrea's mother. He consulted the name list he'd kept, and found Mrs. Hufstutler, the school principal, which would fit with the entry. *Mrs. K?* He'd bet that was Mavis Karroll, as she'd been then.

He couldn't find anyone on his name list with the initials *J.J.* or *S.F.* Given the context, *J.J.* was a classmate. He could ask Sutton about a girl he'd known with those initials.

S.F., on the other hand, was probably from another school. The entry indicated she tried to get Danielle to leave Whitman-Brown and enroll at her school. It was logical that Danielle could know someone like that, he thought. Her activities could have brought her into contact with students from any school in the area, or even beyond. Sutton might or might not be able to identify her; and, if he couldn't, Dodger had no idea of how, from this distance in time, she might be found.

Danielle followed an identifiable pattern in her entries. Each name or initial was boxed with a shape or decoration. The most ornate was the heart around *J.S.*, the most ominous the skull-and-crossbones adorning one corner of the box around the word *Daddy*. The others had boxes with little curlicues on each corner, at least all save *S.F.* — its box was drawn in a zigzag shape with short lines angled through the basic outline. It seemed this person had special significance for Danielle. He thought it might be important to learn whose initials these were, and decided he'd call Deputy Sutton tomorrow on the off chance he knew. Then he remembered that Sutton was on vacation, as of end of work today. He thought about Sutton in Disney World and tried to envision the wound-up deputy on a ride with yelling kids and failed, but maybe he relaxed away from work. Anyway, he hoped all the Suttons, large and small, had a good time.

At last he came to the email from Enid Blythe, Whitman's assistant, to which was attached the scan of Charlotte Whitman's charge-card statements from August and September 1993. She'd circled the items from The Darling Shop. There were four all told, two from early August, one for $38.75 and the other for $22.15. Those weren't the dresses; the amounts weren't large enough. On September 9, there was a charge for $15.77, again not a big-enough charge for a dressy dress. On September 24, he found what he sought – a charge for $498.28. He thought that still sounded cheap for two "nice" dresses, but maybe it hadn't seemed that way twenty years ago. So, it was Charlotte Whitman who'd given Danielle the dresses. So much for his idea that maybe it was someone else and the someone else might have had motives that were not as altruistic as Charlotte's.

He looked back at the scan of the diary. To learn who *J.J.* and *S.F.* were, the logical thing was to call Sutton on his return from vacation.

Dodger began to yawn prodigiously and decided it was, at last, time for bed. Too bad he was going there alone.

Thirty-Eight.

. . ..

Glimpse of a Glimmer

Dodger slept restlessly, maybe because his mind was in overdrive. Breakfast was a hurried affair, and this morning it was so early that there was no sun to flood the breakfast room. Jess looked tired and out of sorts. Even Mrs. Lorenzo was glum.

The only bright spot was that Dodger had awakened with a glimmer of an idea about Danielle Standridge's disappearance. Well, maybe not even quite an idea as yet, but at least the glimpse of a glimmer. It was enough to make him eager to get back from the airport so he could call Harrison North and test one part of his theory.

He hummed on the way in spite of Jess's disapproving silence. At the airport, he carried her bag to the security checkpoint, and then leaned down to kiss her on the cheek.

"Have a good trip," he told her. "Don't do anything I wouldn't do."

"You're chipper today," Jess said, as if put off by the fact.

"Something came to me about the Standridge case," he explained, and realized he sounded almost apologetic. "Anyway, I expect you're already thinking about the Maxcliff thing tonight."

"If by that, you mean that I'm dreading it, then yes. But what can you do? These days, what you write doesn't matter as much as the fact that everyone knows you're writing it and, furthermore, that they have an opinion about you or your work strong enough that they can't wait to tweet it and post it on their Facebook page."

"Art's about the same," Dodger told her. "You think I'm going to San Francisco for the opening of the collage show in December because I can't wait for our friends the TSA agents to get personal with me again? The last time I flew, one of them grabbed my privates."

Jess grinned at that. "Can't blame him, can you?"

"It was a her," he protested. "As for the social-media thing, what the gallery owner hopes is that I'll go to the show, chat up some people, maybe a celebrity or two with a big following, who'll mention it online, with any luck linking to the gallery's website, and that they'll be flooded with queries, which will lead to checks. It sounds optimistic to me, but it can happen thanks to the power of the almighty tweet."

"But half of what gets tweeted or posted is wrong," Jess wailed.

"You know the old joke — 'I don't care what you say about me as long as you spell my name right.' Just look at it that way and wear something outrageous tonight. You always look as if you should be on a Red Carpet anyway. Work it."

She punched him in the arm and hoisted up the heavy bag.

"Jess?"

She turned, and he reached out and took her hand.

"I really appreciate this — your flying to Savannah. You'll never know what it means to me."

"Sure," she said, "anytime. Just whistle." Then she detached her hand from his and took off.

He stood and watched until she cleared the security gate and headed up the concourse, her long legs carrying her effortlessly through the throng. He watched until she was out of sight, but she didn't look back, not once. That bothered him, but not as much as it would have if an intriguing conjecture had not been circling in his mind.

Could that be what it was all about? Did it make sense? He'd check the list of books and do some research on his own. Jess had enough on her plate today without distractions.

Outside, the sun was up, but weak, and he made the return drive in a pale gray light that failed to dampen his excitement. Even the usual craziness where I-16 intersected with I-95 didn't bother him. Back in the Historic District, he was so distracted by what had occurred to him that he failed, for once, to savor the approach to his house from around the square. As a rule, he enjoyed glimpsing it through the trees, its windows sparkling, its brick a warm red. This morning, however, he didn't even look up as he drove around the corner, made the left through his gate, and put the Prius next to the ProMaster.

The house was quiet; Mrs. Lorenzo must be at the market. His feet sounded like thunder as he hurried up the stairs to retrieve his iPad

Mini. With it in hand, he went into the Standridge folder and consulted the original scan of the interlibrary-loan requests Danielle had made in the summer and early fall of 1993. He found the title he wanted, put it into the browser's search window, and waited, tapping his fingers. Maybe the book was too old. Nope, there it was. Both Alibris and Powell's Books had it, and the description, he thought, pretty much told the story.

To be sure, he went into White Pages and looked up the number in Whitman for Dwayne Simmons, who was home and, though surprised, cooperative. He listened as Dodger read him the titles of the interlibrary-loan books, thought for a moment and confirmed that, yes, the book on Shakespearean style could be for something Danny was writing for one of his honors group assignments, also that, to the best of his recollection, it was in the early '90s that the school had first offered a course in gender identity.

"It had something about societal expectations in the course title as I recall."

"You're sure?" Dodger asked. "That was a long time ago."

"It's been a long time," Simmons acknowledged, "but, yes, I'm sure. I was already thinking about whether or not I could come out here and still be allowed to teach, so I was very much attuned to anything that could be construed as a hint."

"Did you get the idea that any of the other teachers were in the same place as you?" Dodger asked. "About coming out, I mean?"

"Not really," Simmons told him. "Statistically, of course, given the number of teachers and the average incidence of gays in a general population, there were bound to be, but Whitman was a conservative place then and we didn't have a club where we all got together and talked about it." He laughed. "The only thing I remember like that was a rumor that was making the rounds. I always thought it was silly, but people talk in a small place, given the least provocation."

Dodger asked him for the name to which the rumor had been attached. Simmons hesitated, but then provided it with the caveat that he'd never believed the gossip and that Dodger should by no means repeat it, as it might still be a problem.

"Thanks for the help," Dodger told him, without committing, and rung off.

The next order of business was to locate the phone number he'd purloined from Sutton's office.

"Mr. North, my name is Art Dodger. I'm working with Jason Sutton, and I need to ask you a question about your divorce from Lisa Ryan North."

He waited with all the patience he could muster as Harrison North told him what he thought of that.

"I understand, Mr. North. Please don't hang up. I'm not asking you to break your agreement with Travis Whitman, and no one will know we spoke, including Deputy Sutton. All I want is for you to verify for me that it was not Mr. Whitman you could have named as the correspondent who broke up your marriage."

There was dead silence at the other end. When North spoke, he was both calmer and more cautious.

"How do you know that?"

"Does it matter?" Dodger asked. "Listen, it's very important. Whitman wasn't the 'other man' was he? I'm ninety-nine percent sure of that. What I don't understand is why he was so determined to keep it quiet."

Again, there was the dead silence.

"He was trying to protect her position," North said finally. "Now I have nothing else to say to you, so please don't call me again."

He hung up.

"Yes!" Dodger exclaimed, slapping his open palm against the desk.

Now, there was just one piece of the puzzle that was missing, and he thought he knew where to find it. Luckily, he still had the key to the mini-museum Charlotte Whitman had set up to memorialize Danielle Standridge. It was a bonus that Travis Whitman was still out of town and so no embarrassing explanations would be required for his host. All he had to do was to take advantage of Gladys's reminder that he had an open invitation to return at any time. He could check the mini-museum, spend the night, get up the next morning, say he needed to get going to take the photographs he'd come for, and take off, this time leaving the key to the little museum in the desk drawer of the guest room.

Looking at Delta's flight schedules, he was now glad for the earliness of Jess's departure. If he hurried he could catch a flight that would put him in Charlotte before three, where he could pick up a rental. Flying wouldn't save much time, but he could continue to work on his theory on the plane. Anyway, he wasn't in the mood to repeat the drive to Whitman.

After an experience filled with the pointless irritations and inconveniences that made him resist commercial flights nowadays, he was at last on the road, in an uncomfortable vehicle whose name escaped him and whose interior smelt of stale cigarette smoke, whatever the rental agency might claim. On the plus side, both Joe and Gladys greeted him with enthusiasm when he arrived at Mill House, and he was glad he'd thought to call from the Charlotte Airport and asked if he could crash for the night. Joe lifted an eyebrow but did not otherwise comment on the deficiencies of the rental as he took the keys, and Gladys had used the time it had taken for him to make the drive by preparing a fresh batch of the cranberry-and-nut muffins he liked.

As he ate, he trotted out for her the justification for the return visit so soon after his departure, but realized he needn't have bothered. Travis Whitman had blessed his presence on the premises, and he had made a good impression. That was all she needed to accept him as welcome. He could be there just to cadge free meals, and it would have made no difference to her.

When he'd finished enough of the muffins to repay her efforts, Dodger said he'd like to go upstairs and freshen up.

"Then let me help you with your bag," she said. "I'm sorry that Billy isn't here. When Mr. Travis is away, if there are no guests, we allow vacation days to be taken. Tonight, Joe and I are all the staff here."

Dodger waved her away from his case, which was all he carried. "I packed light," he grinned. "I'm planning to be here just the one night. I can see myself up, if that's all right. Is it the same room?"

"Yes sir. I checked it after you called. The room is ready."

"I don't doubt that for a minute," he grinned. "You run the most efficient household I've ever seen."

Leaving her beaming, he headed for the small elevator up the hall, thinking that Gladys's gratuity envelope would be gratifyingly full in the morning.

Thirty-Nine.

· · •••••••• · ·

Memento Mori Twice?

Dodger decided to wait until after dinner to return to Charlotte Whitman's private museum, reasoning that Joe would be off duty for the night and Gladys occupied with cleaning up after the meal. Not that it mattered. He had never stipulated to anyone that he would or would not examine it again. If someone did come, he could always say he was looking for photographs to scan to send along with his report to Mystery Mavens. Still, however good his excuse, he preferred not to be caught in the room. He wasn't sure why, but instinct told him it'd be simpler.

In the guest room, dressed and waiting for the proper time to go downstairs, he called Jess to wish her luck (and, also, truth be told to share his excitement at what he'd figured out), but she wasn't there. He hung up without leaving a message. Then he called Barbara Archer, told her he was working on something, but to continue with the collages and he'd meet her in the studio Monday morning. Before leaving Savannah, he'd written a note for Mrs. Lorenzo to say that he'd been called out of town, so there was no need to contact her.

At dinner, he wondered why women felt the need to stuff him. At 6'3" and 210 pounds, he wasn't a lightweight. Even so, Gladys, like Mrs. Lorenzo, seemed to be under the impression that he needed fattening, and she laid a table that would have done a small dinner party proud.

"I hope you don't mind eating in the kitchen, Mr. Dodger," she apologized. "The breakfast room is cold at night, and that big dining room is so empty with just one person, I thought you'd prefer this."

"I do," he assured her, taking another corn muffin. "This is much nicer. Why don't you join me?"

She allowed herself to sit, but had only an iced tea. "You see, I snick and snack while I'm cooking, so I'm not hungry."

"That's why you're such a good cook," he told her. "You cook from taste. Your palate must be superb. You have a wonderful touch with herbs and spices."

"Why, thank you, sir. I appreciate you noticing. So you're taking more pictures tomorrow?"

"Yes, I am. Let me tell you what I'm after and perhaps you can suggest something else." He recited the list of locations he'd prepared as cover.

When he finished, she thought about it and suggested he might wish to include Whitman Methodist, as that was the church Danielle attended.

"She sang in the choir sometimes. She had a pretty voice, I will say that."

"She sounds like an exceptional girl," Dodger agreed.

"Well, I don't know about that," Gladys sniffed. "Everybody always made over her, so she thought she was God's gift to the world."

"Oh, teenagers, you know," Dodger said, hoping the comment would divert Gladys. There was something he wanted to explore with her before she started on a rant about her niece.

It worked. After a brief digression about the general degeneracy of the young, Gladys began to clear the table, giving Dodger his opportunity.

"It's interesting what you said about Danielle having a pretty voice because I'll tell you somebody I met here a couple of weeks ago who has the prettiest speaking voice I've heard in a long time."

"And who is that, sir?"

"The woman who runs the library. Lisa something or other."

"Oh, that Lisa North who comes here every chance she gets," Gladys made a face. "Butter wouldn't melt in her mouth. It's my opinion that she fancies herself married to Mr. Travis, running this place, but I'll tell you the simple truth of it — the day that woman sets foot in the house to tell me what to do, I quit."

"I didn't get the impression that she and Mr. Whitman are that close," he reassured her, to see what she would say.

"Oh, she's been after him for years. Especially when Miss Charlotte was alive, she'd make excuses to hang around the house or take part in things, just to stay on her good side while she scoped out Mr. Travis. She's a sly one," Gladys frowned. "Still waters run deep, and that woman's a bottomless well."

Then she shut up, her lips in a thin line, and Dodger knew he'd probed all he could. The discreet housekeeper was through talking.

Upstairs after dinner, he listened to the stillness, wary of any sound that the elevator might make. Satisfied that there was no movement, he checked his pocket to make sure he had the key and went at once to the little memorial museum.

It didn't feel spooky tonight, he noticed as he flicked on the lights. He knew what he was after and went immediately to the correspondence folder he'd examined before. Flipping through its contents, he found what he wanted. He read it twice and saw that it was as he remembered. After scanning, he returned the half-finished letter to the folder, which he then replaced on the shelf where he'd found it. Afterwards, he stood for a moment in the middle of the space, looking around, certain that tonight would be his final time in this place held sacred to the memory of the girl who'd gone away. Then he opened the door, turned out the lights, closed the door, turned the key in the lock, and returned to the guest room that was as posh as the penthouse suite in a luxury hotel. He put the mini-museum key in one of the envelopes engraved with the image of Mill House, which he then dropped into the desk drawer.

The quietness of the house continued to surprise him. Now, with no servants on the premises to create a floor of noise, he swore he could almost hear the house breathe. It made him uncomfortable.

He retrieved a paper pad from the desk drawer (no one could say that Travis Whitman didn't provide his guests with creative necessities), and sat down to marshal his conclusions. He spent some time over each of the elements — who, what, where, how, and why, the last in particular, as it was the most puzzling. What he'd found in the binder in the mini-museum had fleshed out a half-formed idea that kept niggling at him. First, he conceded, reluctantly, that Danielle Standridge had been either kidnapped and/or murdered, probably the latter. He didn't think a fifteen-year-old, no matter how smart, was capable of disappearing forever on her own. So, for the sake of this train of thought, he dismissed the idea of voluntary disappearance. At the same time, for someone to have murdered Danielle Standridge, there was a reason. Without a reason, a very good reason, rational people didn't make the decision to murder, much less take the steps necessary to plan and execute murder and then to hide it for two decades. So who would have had a reason? It had to be someone with a lot to lose if Danielle remained around. That suggested someone with whom Danielle was close. He had an idea there'd been something in the correspondence binder in the mini-museum, and he was right. What he found this second time through was what he expected.

If he had this right — and he rather thought he did — this was about love, sex, position, jealousy, and loss of face. Had the affair gone beyond wistful/wishful thinking? Had Danielle's innocence and age prevented any further advance? He rather thought it had. Still, if there had been nothing physical, then there must have been some very specific communication that gave the show away. As 1993 was well before social media and instant communication, that suggested a letter. He hadn't found it, but he had found the correspondence addressed to "Special Friend," which corresponded with convenient symmetry to the *S.F.* of Danielle's diary. He'd also found other bits that, put together with what Gladys had said tonight, confirmed his growing suspicion. Gladys had it backwards, of course. It hadn't been Travis Whitman on whose account Lisa North hung around back in the old days, but his wife, which meant she was bound to have been jealous of anyone of whom Charlotte was fond. By all accounts, the wealthy young wife had made no secret of her affection for Danielle. That must have driven Lisa North crazy. So what had happened then? Had she seen the high-school girl as such a threat that she decided to get rid of her? Then another idea struck him. Lisa and Danielle had spent a lot of time together, thanks to Charlotte's insistence that the librarian help the girl with her textile-industry report. It was plain that many people felt an almost instantaneous attraction to the smart, pretty student. Had Lisa turned out to be one of them? Had proximity led to desire?

That would be ironic. Perhaps it was Danielle whose attention she had wanted all to herself, and when she proclaimed her feelings, the girl had rejected her in such a way that made it clear Lisa's position in Whitman would be threatened once word got out. How hard was it to get a job as librarian back in the early 1990s? Probably not hard enough to justify murder, he decided. So it must be the loss of pride that was the trigger. Remembering the hard certainty on the beautiful Lisa's face, he could buy that. She was not a woman who would want people snickering at such a story forever; and even if she'd left Whitman, the episode would have stuck to her like glue, wherever she went.

He re-read the notes he'd made and nodded. It looked clear to him. The question now was what to do next. He had no authority. He also had no proof, just a clear-cut theory buttressed by a certain internal logic. So, what next? First, he should take enough photographs tomorrow morning to reinforce his cover story and then return to Savannah at once. Back there, he could decide which interested party to call first — Josh Bedingfield of Mystery Mavens, Deputy Sheriff Sutton, or Travis Whitman himself. It would have to be someone who wouldn't give Lisa North a heads up.

He yawned. That could wait for tomorrow. The long day had caught up with him. Had it been just that morning that he took Jess to the Savannah Airport? He thought of her as he showered and dried, unable to stop yawning. He wished she were here now, so he could share with her the satisfaction he felt at having unraveled the first skeins of the deceit that had concealed Danielle's fate for so long.

When he'd showered, slipped between the silky sheets, and turned off the light, he expected to go to sleep at once. It didn't happen. Everything kept bugging him, especially the likelihood of surprising Lisa North into a confession (unlikely was the logical conclusion). Even an hour of **Midsomer Murders** didn't help. At last, feeling silly, he got up and propped one of the straight-backed chairs under the doorknob. He wondered who he thought might be coming in, Lisa North? That had to be wishful thinking on his part. Recognizing the threat he represented to her successful crime, would the gorgeous Lisa change her affiliation so to speak and attempt to bribe him with what appeared to be one of the best bodies he'd seen outside a magazine spread? Hah, that'd be the day. Blushing, he tried the door. He had no illusions that the dainty little piece of furniture would hold up against a determined onslaught, but at least he'd have some warning if anyone entered the room.

After that, he went to sleep and stayed asleep until his iPad alarm went off. It was still dark. His return flight left Charlotte at ten, so he had to get an early start. He put on fresh underwear and the one clean shirt he'd brought, and then put on the jeans and jacket he'd worn the day before. He clipped his phone onto the belt of the jeans and slipped the iPad into the inside pocket of his jacket, glad that he'd traded the larger screen size for the Mini's ability to fit in almost any pocket he possessed. He didn't have to worry about toiletries. Knowing how well stocked the bath here was, he hadn't packed any. After throwing dirty clothes into his case, he was done.

For a long moment, he stood, looking around the handsome room, and then closed the door behind him and headed up the hall. It was hard not to feel a little wistful. Not only did this trip promise to produce resolution, but he suspected he'd never again have accommodation so luxurious on a Mystery Mavens' scouting expedition. He was surprised at his good spirits. It was a sad thing he thought he was about to bring to a close. On the other hand, Jess had come to Savannah and, furthermore, had indicated she was not averse to coming back, and he thought there was a chance that next time she'd come up the stairs with him at the end of the day instead of descending to the guest suite.

In the kitchen he grabbed a couple of the muffins Gladys made the day before, ate one and put the other in his case. He knew she would be insulted that he'd skipped breakfast, but he thought the gratuity and note he was leaving on the kitchen table would salve her irritation. In the garage bay, he found the rental, keys in place, waiting humbly between the Beemer and a Corvette of collector-worthy vintage. He started its engine, which had the virtue of being quiet, and rolled from the courtyard into the drive in the direction of the road between Whitman and Blevins. By now, it had begun to grow light, and when he rounded the curve past the garage bay he was surprised to see a dark Lincoln blocking the road beside the purpose-built building that served as Travis Whitman's business headquarters. A tall, thin man stood next to the driver's window, gesturing, giving instructions. As Dodger's vehicle crept closer, the silhouette became flesh, and he saw that the instruction-giver was Travis Whitman. He'd recognized Dodger, for he mouthed his name and waved toward the parking area in front of the business building.

Fuck, Dodger thought, caught. Well at least he had his story ready, not that it mattered. Then it occurred to him that this was his chance to speak with Travis Whitman about Lisa North and clear up some of the points that dangled with irritating persistence. Maybe Whitman's appearance was for the best.

He returned the wave, parked as directed, and waited for Whitman, who made his way over to the rental, seeming to take forever.

Although he looked tired, the billionaire greeted him cordially enough.

"Didn't think I'd see you here again so soon, Dodger, but it's just as well. We need to talk."

Forty.

· · ·°•◉◉◉◉•°· · ·

Whitman Gets A Laugh

The desk in the entry area of the business building was manned by a different guard, who peered at Dodger and Whitman through the heavy glass before buzzing them inside.

Whitman nodded and continued through the entry, past Enid Blythe's glass-fronted office, around the corner and to another door, this one solid. Here, he repeated the palm-over-pad maneuver, and the door opened to reveal a large, traditional office of the type that proclaimed "I don't need to show off my grasp of the latest styles because I'm richer than Croesus and could care less what anyone thinks." The walls were paneled in black walnut with matching flitches. The Oriental-patterned carpet had been woven for the room, as the borders followed the shape of the bookcases that formed niches in the walls every three to four feet. The cases themselves held a mixture of antiquarian books and business binders. In a glass-shelved section on the far wall, a large assortment of glass and metal awards was ranged, their surfaces aglow in the soft light. In each corner of the big room sat a globe on an antique stand — the nearer was the biggest celestial globe Dodger had ever seen. To one side of the room was a comfortable sitting area with sofa and two armchairs angled toward a large cabinet painted in the Chinese style. Above the cabinet was a large flatscreen TV set into the paneling.

"Nice office," Dodger said.

"It's comfortable," Whitman agreed.

In this better light, Dodger could see that the man was not his usual dapper self. The clothes were all right — the gray slacks, the camelhair jacket, the crisp white shirt — but his personal grooming was not as meticulous as usual. His eyes were bloodshot, and there seemed to be new wrinkles across his brow. He'd missed a spot when he shaved, and a small cowlick sprung from the back of his head. Had he been on a bender? Most obvious, though, was the change in his movements. When Dodger had first met him a couple of months earlier in Boston, he'd been lithe and jaunty as a man in his twenties. Even a couple of weeks before, when he'd explained a slight limp as a tennis sprain, he'd seemed almost the same. Now, Dodger saw that he moved with difficulty, and his color wasn't good.

Seemingly oblivious to this surreptitious examination, Whitman walked at a slow pace to the other side of the room, and went behind an antique rosewood desk that measured at least six by four feet. Taking the swivel chair behind it, he waved Dodger to the facing rosewood-and-leather armchair. Unlike many of the type, it was, he discovered, both handsome and comfortable. Dodger wondered where Whitman had found it, but decided against distracting the man from whatever it was that he had on his mind. In spite of the coolness of the office, Whitman wiped his forehead with a white handkerchief square. It was very quiet here, and Dodger used the moment to fine tune his own agenda. Would it be possible to get the proof he needed from Whitman himself? Maybe, he thought, with the right approach. If he tried and failed, would there be consequences that could affect any subsequent investigation by Mystery Mavens or anyone else? He weighed the options as Whitman patted his brow. A faint throat clearing made him look up to see that his host now watched him, as if able to read his mind. Then Whitman smiled faintly, resuming the role of perfect host.

"Can I offer you something to eat or drink? There's a 24/7 canteen at the other end of the building. It isn't haute cuisine, but they're not bad with ham and eggs."

"I'm fine, thanks," Dodger said, glad that he'd eaten one of Gladys's muffins on the way out the kitchen door. The last thing he wanted to do was eat, not when he was on the verge of assembling what he now viewed as an almost complete chain of clues.

"So, what brings you back to our neck of the woods?" Whitman asked, the attempt at jocularity falling somewhat short as he peered at Dodger, who noticed again his gray gauntness.

"I like to send photos to accompany my Mystery Mavens' report, and I realized that I'd left in such a hurry, I'd skimped that part of the process." He pulled the list he'd prepared from his pocket.

Whitman listened to the explanation, but not as if he cared.

"That's as may be," he said, dismissing the subject with a wave of his hand. "What I want to know is how to go about withdrawing my request to Mystery Mavens."

"I'm not sure I understand," Dodger temporized. "What do you mean by withdraw?"

"I'd like to make a formal request that your organization's involvement be ended and that all material developed to this point as part of it be returned to me. I'd pay whatever compensation the board thinks fair."

"I'm not sure I know the answer," Dodger admitted. "It hasn't come up before. I'll have to check with Josh Bedingfield, our projects director. Can I ask why the sudden change of heart?"

Whitman shrugged. "The more I think about it, the more pointless it seems. It's been so long."

"Would you feel any different if I tell you that I think I know who was responsible for Danielle's disappearance?"

Whitman's gaze intensified, and Dodger felt as if a laser were focused on him. The man had presence, no doubt about it.

"Are you sure?" Whitman asked.

"I'd be surer if you'd answer a question for me."

"And that is?"

There was an expectant stillness about Whitman that reminded Dodger of a predator waiting for prey, and he hesitated, but not for long. The worst that could happen was that Whitman would get mad and throw him out.

"Why are you protecting Lisa North?"

Whitman's expression was incredulous. "What makes you say that I am?"

"The way her divorce decree is worded and the fact that we've discovered Harrison North was influenced to file in that way by you."

Whitman grimaced. "Be careful in what you say, Dodger." He thought for a moment and then made a connection that jumped the conversation ahead considerably. "Are you claiming that Lisa North was responsible for whatever happened to Danny and that I've helped cover it up?"

Surprised at the speed with which the point had been reached, Dodger hesitated, but then decided to go for it.

"It seems logical," he said. "Given what I've learned, my guess is that Danielle discovered something about Lisa that would have made it impossible for her to continue working in Whitman, and let Lisa know she knew, maybe something to do with the fact that Lisa swung both ways. What I don't understand is why you're protecting her. You weren't the 'other man', were you? Was he someone you wanted to protect, or had you become attracted to Lisa by then and wanted to make sure she could stay around?"

Whitman listened with growing astonishment. When Dodger paused for breath, he began to laugh, at first in an abrupt, irregular "I can't believe I'm hearing this" pattern, then in a guffaw that rose from his stomach and shook him so that the swivel chair in which he sat began to move, and he almost slid out of it. Even after he managed to stop guffawing, the effort turned into hiccups, and his eyes streamed with tears that rolled unchecked down hollow cheeks. He began to cough, so hard that his chest heaved with the effort and he held the handkerchief to his face, as if to hide it.

"Are you all right? Can I get you anything?"

"Whitman shook his head and gradually regained control.

"You think that Lisa North…" Whitman spluttered, then began to laugh again, this time hitting the leather-lined top of the big desk with his closed fists.

"What's so funny?"

Dodger was becoming borderline angry when Whitman grew calm and looked at him with an appraising expression.

"You've asked me a very leading question. Are you sure you want to know the answer? Think carefully. Answers sometimes cause other things to happen."

Dodger nodded.

"Then give me your phone."

Puzzled, Dodger unclipped the iPhone and handed it over.

Whitman put a hand under his desk and made a motion, and Dodger heard a decisive thunk. It seemed to come from the direction of the door into the hall.

"We don't want to be interrupted, trust me," Whitman told him.

"You might as well get comfortable. This will take a while."

Dodger nodded.

Whitman leaned back in his chair, tapping his fingertips together. "Let me say up front that in no way have I ever been interested in protecting Lisa North."

He paused, gathering his breath, when there was the sound of a faint beep.

"Excuse me," Whitman said, pulling a bottle from his pocket. "Got to take a pill."

Dodger watched the careful way he poured water into a glass from the carafe on his desk, took a drink, put the tiny white tablet on his tongue, and washed it down with a gulp of water. It was clear that pill taking did not come easily to him.

Whitman patted his lips, and then directed a too-bright stare at his guest.

"I suppose I should start with the fact that I loved my wife and I believe that, to the degree that she was able, she loved me. Also, it helped that she was crazy about my mother and my mother about her. The signs that we'd be happy were good. She was from another old textile family. She knew what was involved in coming to live in a company town."

"I'm sure," Dodger said, wondering where this was going. "It must be a big responsibility, becoming part of the first family in a place like this."

He knew the comment sounded sarcastic. That wasn't what he intended, but it was done.

Whitman grimaced and fixed Dodger with what amounted to a glare. "I recognize you, or at least your type. You probably have no idea of what I mean by that. My guess is that you come from money, but what I think of as telescope money. You observe the source from a great distance, and put the telescope down when you no longer want to be bothered. Also, it's money without any particular footprint — it's made by the second-hand movement of assets. When the money comes from a physical asset with which your family has kept up a close connection, like Whitman-Brown Mills, there's nothing second-hand. You know the processes, you know the men and women who manage and operate them, you know the bricks of the buildings that house them. To some extent, the people who work for your family are part of your life from the time you're born, and you quickly learn that you are a very large part of theirs."

He lifted his eyebrows. "Do you understand what I mean?"

Dodger nodded. "I think so."

"As I indicated, Charlotte was born into the same world that she knew she'd inhabit with me. When we married in 1985, I was twenty-seven and Charlotte was twenty-five. My mother gave us this house as a wedding gift — she was a Brown and it was her family home. Charlotte was delighted. There was nothing she liked better than renovation and decoration, and she at once set about finishing the interior streamlining that my mother had begun before she and my father built their new house in Rington."

He took a careful sip of water as Dodger waited.

"I was already active in the management of the mills. Charlotte was comfortable being the lady of the mills. I think she even liked giving out the prizes and making the speeches and doing civic good works, just as my mother had. She was very good at knowing the right thing to say and do, whatever the circumstances. When we'd been married three years, my father had a heart attack, and my parents decided to retire to the South of France. He retained the chairmanship, and I was named CEO. I was swamped for several months during the transition period; and when I resurfaced, Charlotte had changed, become quieter, more distant. In some ways she was a stranger. I took her on a long cruise, and she seemed to have recovered. We enjoyed ourselves for a couple of years, and then there was a regression. I realized she'd begun to drink more than was good for her and insisted she do a stint in rehab. It was a hard time."

He stopped and took another sip of water.

"When she returned, she threw herself into what she always called 'my good works'. She began to take a lot of interest in Whitman-Brown High School. That was when she became friends with the Standridge girl. She'd encountered her off and on over the years, even made her into something of a protégé, but this new stage of the relationship was different, more intense. When they were together, they acted more like sisters than mentor-protégé. They even had pet nicknames for each other — Special Friend #1 and Special Friend #2."

"*Charlotte* was Special Friend?" Dodger was surprised. He'd assumed it was either Lisa Ryan (as she was then) or another schoolgirl. Where did this new bit of knowledge fit with that assumption, with his tidy scenario?

"Yes," Whitman answered. "As I told you before, I didn't think it was healthy, but Charlotte brushed me off. I'll admit I let it ride because Charlotte was trying to get pregnant, and the doctors seemed to think this time it would be possible. I assumed that, once she was about to have a child of her own, this willingness to take on other people's children as special projects would pass. Nothing happened on that front, however, and Charlotte revved up her involvement with the girl even more. That was the point at which she became obsessed with the idea of getting Danny into the best possible school, and put her to work doing the textile history. Lisa Ryan was the assistant librarian, and from what Charlotte said, I knew she was involved in a lot of what they were doing. While all that was going on, the movie people contacted the local government and wanted permission to film at certain places around town. Also, they'd heard about Whitman-Brown's champion majorettes and wanted to incorporate them into the film. Charlotte was enthusiastic, to say the least. My guess is she was responsible for their decision to film more here than they'd intended."

Dodger interrupted. "Speaking of which, the tape in that **Before A Hero** presentation box you gave me has footage at the end that is specific to that copy. You may want it. It shows you, your wife, Danny and Lisa in The Library Pavilion."

Whitman shrugged, not bothering to answer before continuing his story.

"So, at the end of that summer twenty years ago, that was how everything stood when Charlotte and I left on a business trip. She caught a cold and came home a couple of days early. I didn't think anything of it. The trip was important, and I was focused on what was going on there, not here. As it turned out, I finished a few hours earlier than I intended, and Charlotte had sounded depressed when we spoke on the phone at lunch. I suspected she was about to go on one of her drinking binges, which infuriated me. The corporate jet was on standby, and I decided to return home then rather than waiting for the next morning."

Wanted to catch her out, Dodger thought, but said nothing.

Whitman coughed, and then took another drink of water.

"I got here late Friday night. Charlotte was in the bedroom, almost catatonic. When I finally got her to talk, all she'd say was something about The Library Pavilion and Danny being dead. It made no sense, but there was something wrong or at least she thought there was. I'll admit at first I thought it was just the drink talking, because I could smell booze. To be on the safe side, I decided I'd better take a look. When she grew sleepy, I gave her a mild sedative, tucked her in, and went out to the Pavilion on foot.

"It was hard to move fast — you've seen the woods, so you know what the walk would be like on a dark night. As I approached, I could see interior lights, but apart from that nothing seemed out of the ordinary. In fact, everything appeared normal until I unlocked the door and went inside. Then I could hear a faint knocking from the direction of a storage room that was hidden behind one of the panels. You opened it by pressing against a gilded dragon tail that was applied to the wall. When I pulled the panel back, Danny literally fell into my arms. She was a mess. She was barefoot, and all she had on were a half-slip, a very tiny bra, and a long scarf around her neck. Her hair was matted with blood, there was dried blood covering one side of her face, and one of her arms was so badly scratched that it had bled not only at the wound itself but onto her side. She was hysterical, crying. I remember I got her water from the bathroom. When that didn't help, I poured a tumbler of brandy and had her drink it.

"When I got her calm enough to make sense, she told me an outlandish story about how she'd been trying on dresses and Charlotte was photographing her and then Charlotte had, as she put it 'made a pass'. Danny said in defense she grabbed up the first thing at hand and lashed out, and that was all she could remember until she woke in the dark, alone. She went on to say that I had to get her to the sheriff, that she had to tell the sheriff, that people shouldn't be allowed to do things like that and get away with it."

He took another sip of water. Dodger noticed that his hand trembled, and there was a long pause, as if he'd rather not say what came next.

"That was when I strangled her," he said matter of factly.

"My God, Whitman, why?" Dodger couldn't believe what he was hearing.

"I didn't plan it," Whitman shrugged. "It was pure impulse. That damned long scarf was wrapped around her neck, and she was screaming about making sure Charlotte got what she deserved. One second I was standing there horrified, propping the girl against the wall to keep her from falling, and the next thing I knew I was pulling on the scarf, to stop the screaming and all of a sudden she was making a gurgling noise. I swear, she was dead before I realized what I was doing. I'm not excusing what I did, simply stating a fact."

Whitman stared at Dodger, as if wanting to make sure he understood there was total acceptance of what had happened.

"What'd you do then?" Dodger asked.

"We kept large contractor-type trash bags in the kitchen for clean-up after parties. I got one and stuffed her body into it, and then tied and taped the bag. I put that bag into a second and repeated the tying and taping. There was a low trolley in the pantry area for moving supplies and books. I rolled it out and put the bag on it, then trundled the whole thing out to the left-hand side of the lodge."

"The one with the damaged books piled up in it now?"

"Yes," Whitman answered. "There's a hatch inside — it was covered by a heavy rug then — that opens onto steps that go down into an area that my grandmother had begun to turn into a shell grotto before she died. It was never finished, and nobody knew about it outside the family and the old gardener who worked with her. I remember it was hard to hang onto the flashlight and pull the bag at the same time and by the time I got it down into the grotto, the bag was damaged, so I came back up here and got two more bags for good measure and put them over the other bags. There were several large piles of stones and shells in the grotto, so I put the bag in a corner and covered it several feet deep with them. Upstairs, in the gate building, I pulled the rug back over the hatch and locked the door that led into the area. Back inside the Pavilion, I cleaned up every trace of the girl and put it in a contractor bag that I carried back with me to the house."

"You put Danielle's body in trash bags?" Dodger was shocked at his casual logistical efficiency in the face of such horror.

"I intended it to be a temporary solution," Whitman defended his decision. "I couldn't wait any longer to get back to Charlotte to hear her take on what had happened. When I rushed back to the house, she was still out of it. I stayed awake all night, watching for the first sign of life, and then I pumped her full of coffee and tried to get a coherent account of what had gone on. It was the same story the girl had told, but with important modifications. According to Charlotte, when she returned from the trip, she found a message from The Darling Shop saying that the two dresses she'd ordered for Danielle were in and she could collect them anytime. She said she'd planned to wait until the following week to collect them; but when she saw Danny at the mall, sitting on the car hood, she had the urge to pick her up and go and get the dresses that afternoon. She said she thought they'd both enjoy choosing which one Danny should wear to the dance.

"She said Danny went with her to get the dresses but waited in the car because she was embarrassed to be seen walking around town in the old-fashioned majorette outfit. After that, they drove back to The Library Pavilion and Danny tried on first one dress and then the other — I recall Charlotte saying she lent her jewelry to wear with one of them — while Charlotte took photographs so Danny would have a record of how she looked in both. Then, as Danny was removing the second dress, she tripped and when Charlotte went to help her up, Danny misunderstood and went crazy. She grabbed a pair of paper shears from the table behind her and lashed out at Charlotte. Charlotte said that all she did was put up her arms and try to push the girl away. That was when Danny fell and hit her head against one of the gilt fire-dogs shaped like dragons that you see in the photographs. Charlotte thought she'd killed her and dragged her body into the hidden storage area. She'd hidden in the house ever since, trying to decide what to do, and drinking, of course." The last was said contemptuously.

"Did you tell her she hadn't killed the girl?"

"Not then," Whitman said. "I didn't think she could handle what had happened, and I had no intention of telling her what Danny had said. My first thought was that I had to get her focused enough so we could decide what to do together. Then, I thought, I'd choose the right moment to tell her." Whitman shook his head and frowned. "In the end, once she was sober enough to understand what was at stake, we realized the only thing that made sense was to hide what had happened. It wasn't hard. Everybody was so focused on the movie people that no one seemed to have noticed Charlotte and Danny together that afternoon. What made it easier was that the Standridges took the attitude she'd run away. Nobody was pressing for anything to be done. We could just let the girl stay where she was, and nobody would be any the wiser."

"And you got away with it."

Whitman shook his head and laughed with bitter awareness. "We didn't have a decent day after that. Charlotte drank more and more; and even though I never admitted to her what I'd done, I think she might have suspected, or maybe she just resented that I knew what she thought she'd done. Either way, she set up that damned museum to taunt me. She even used my charge card to order the mannequins that looked like Danny. Things went on that way for a while, and then I discovered she was having an affair with Lisa North. I knew she'd never been that much into sex with me, but I thought she was just cold. As it turned out, according to the detective I hired, sex with Lisa was anything but. Once I discovered that, it crossed my mind that it was Danny who'd been telling the truth and that Charlotte had made a pass at her. I was angry and without thinking, I accused her of it, and that was when she had to know the girl was alive when I found her. She never referred to it, but she never spoke to me again unless she had to when others were present. Then Harrison North realized what was going on and became so angry that he let me know he was divorcing Lisa and naming Charlotte as correspondent. I couldn't have that. Charlotte had responsibilities here, and I still had hopes we might work things out. I paid off North on condition that he leave the correspondent unnamed and get out of town. So you see, I wasn't protecting Lisa."

"You were protecting Charlotte," Dodger finished.

Whitman nodded.

"After Lisa's divorce, when I told her to leave Charlotte alone or I'd have her fired, Charlotte's drinking got worse. Then those boys torched The Library Pavilion. I held my breath for weeks while the police and state arson investigators poked around. I was positive the hatch to the grotto would be discovered in spite of the way I'd covered it up. It wasn't, but I couldn't risk new construction that might breach the grotto. I didn't rebuild; I didn't even file an insurance claim. Instead, I had the site cleaned up and announced my intention of leaving it as it was — the remnant of a foundation and the surviving gate. I even thought that perhaps the destruction of the place would improve Charlotte's state of mind. I was wrong. She reached a point where she stayed more or less drunk all the time. I had no idea where it would all end, then a few months later she ran that damned little sports car off the road at Ceil Gap and halfway down the mountain, and it was over."

He shook his head. "I thought that finished it. Then that hack writer called Jase Sutton, who told me, and I realized I needed to do something to put him off. After everything else, I wasn't going to let the whole thing be dragged up again."

"Which was when you applied to Mystery Mavens for help."

Whitman nodded. "Call it a clumsy attempt at information discovery. I wanted to see if a casual investigation would turn up anything that could be a problem after all this time. I didn't think so, but I wanted to be sure."

"And if it had?"

"I'd have offered the writer a job so good he'd forget about magazine articles and missing girls. "

"What about Mystery Mavens?"

"I'd have done whatever was necessary to divert or end the investigation. Covering things up seems to have become a habit. That's all. I've never hurt anyone except Danny. I never would."

Dodger stood up and started to reach for his phone, which lay on the edge of Whitman's desk. Whitman's hand went to the open desk drawer and a gun appeared, pointed straight at Dodger.

"Please sit down."

Dodger sat down. Whitman's voice was mild, but his manner was sure, and it was a very businesslike gun.

"See," he said, "here's the deal, Dodger. Since I came to Mystery Mavens, circumstances have changed. I learned I'm sick, more than sick. I'm dying. Advanced colon cancer."

"I'm sorry," Dodger said, and — in spite of everything he'd just heard — he was.

Whitman nodded in acknowledgment.

"I've been at Duke this week for tests, to see if there's anything else that can be done. There isn't, not anything with any likelihood of success at any rate. They give me three to six months, and I don't intend to spend them in a jail cell or under house arrest or in a hospital bed besieged by the media. After I'm gone, I don't care what happens, but for now this remains our little secret."

Dodger wondered where this was leading. "So what now?"

"Don't worry, I have no intention of killing you. I will admit that the possibility of a providential accident did cross my mind after Billy let it slip he'd shown you the mannequins. I assumed the majorette outfit would give it away. It was, after all, the outfit the girl was wearing when she disappeared. Then there was the matter of the prom dress — it was one of those Charlotte had picked up that last afternoon. I realized those damned mannequins were practically a diagram for what had happened."

"That's why you moved them."

Whitman nodded. "For a while, given that you hadn't recognized their significance, I thought the danger point had passed until Enid told me about The Darling Shop receipts you asked for and Joe mentioned that you and Jase had gone for a long walk in the direction of The Library Pavilion ruins. I knew you'd figure it out sooner or later, if you hadn't already, and I've laid my plans."

"And they are?" Dodger asked, playing for time, trying to keep his voice as calm as possible in spite of the fact that his face felt hot and his palms sweaty. However civilized the man opposite him might appear, he'd just confessed to murder, and common sense suggested he wasn't about to take the consequences.

"Let's just say they're made, and leave it at that," Whitman told him. "All I need is a head start, which your absence is going to give me." His free hand went under the desk, and there was a whirring noise. Dodger looked around to see that part of one of the black-walnut wall panels was moving to reveal a room beyond.

"That's the panic room the security people insisted on building into the place. What I want you to do is to get up and walk inside."

Dodger hesitated and looked back, a question in his eyes.

"It isn't a trick," Whitman assured him. "The room has an adequate oxygen supply. There's nothing in there to harm anyone in any way. It's just an empty room with some interesting features, among which is my ability to lock it down from here so it can't be opened from the inside or outside. When I leave I'll tell the guard that you're working in my office and aren't to be disturbed for any reason or by anyone unless you call. Sooner or later someone will miss you and you'll be released. All that will have happened is that you'll get hungry and thirsty. Think of it as a free spa cure."

Whitman waved the gun, and Dodger stood up again.

"Wait," Whitman said. "I've told you all this. Now, there's something I'd like you to tell me."

"What's that?" Dodger sat again.

"While you've been out sniffing around, did you come across anything that would explain the way Danny acted if Charlotte told me the truth? They'd known each other for a long time, and I'm convinced Charlotte cared for the girl as she would a younger sister or even a child. Why would Danny think Charlotte was making a pass at her?"

He looked not only curious but also perturbed, and Dodger decided to tell him.

"A few days earlier, Danielle had walked in on her father raping her sister, and my guess is she thought she might be next. Also, from some research on lesbians she was doing that summer, it's likely that Lisa had made a move on her while she was working at the library on the textile-history paper. Also, she was thinking about taking a course in gender studies at school. The topic of sexual identity and behavior was definitely on her mind. All of her antennae would be alert to the possibility of inappropriate sexual contact."

Whitman considered that and shook his head, a sad expression on his face. "Poor kid. Poor girl. Poor, poor girl."

Dodger bought his sincerity, but noticed the gun did not waver.

The room was so quiet it was as if it were wrapped in cotton wool, and Dodger realized it must be soundproofed. Whatever happened here, even a gunshot, would not be heard.

"It's an odd thing," Whitman continued after a long silence, "all my life I was schooled to believe that you did what you had to do and were man enough to live with the consequences. In the natural course of things, people in my position have to make choices that can be too hard if you allow yourself the luxury of regret and self-recrimination.

When I panicked and did what I did to Danny, I defaulted to damage control because it seemed to me that it was necessary. Even after I'd had time to reflect, I could justify my decision. The girl was dead; destroying everything wouldn't bring her back. Damage control was the only thing that made sense. I thought, over time, I'd reconcile myself to that necessity. I thought I could learn to live with it as I had with so many other things."

All this time, he'd been staring into space. Now he shifted his gaze so that his eyes locked into Dodger's. He looked impossibly exhausted, and his voice cracked when he finally spoke. "But when I wake at night, I see her face. I hear her voice. I remember how the stones slid over the bag when I covered it up. I remember having trouble breathing as I climbed the steps and left her body there, all alone. I haven't been in the grotto since. Even thinking of the place fills me with dread, but I can't forget a single detail. Every day I hear myself as I was before that night telling me how I should have handled what happened, appalled at what I actually did. That's the worst thing of all, Dodger. I can't stop the voices, hers or mine."

Whitman's voice had grown louder, and his eyes had a not-quite-focused look that Dodger didn't like. He was debating whether to risk a lunge across the huge desk to grab the gun when Whitman regained his composure.

"But that's enough about me," he said in more or less his normal voice. "I apologize for treating a guest in so arbitrary a manner, but there's a schedule to be followed."

He gestured with the gun, and Dodger rose even as he calculated his odds if he made a play for the gun. With Whitman close behind, holding the weapon at his back, he edged toward the open door of the panic room. Almost there, he heard a faint noise behind him and turned to see Whitman lifting up a metal statuette. He tried to reach out, to grab the gun, but the statuette reached him first. The next minute his head exploded and he was falling.

It was the last thing Dodger remembered.

Forty-One.

· · ·●●●●●●· · ·

Dodger Whistles

It was dark and noiseless in the panic room, and when a very groggy Dodger began to wake up and tried to move he couldn't. A few minutes and several degrees of consciousness later, he realized his hands and feet were tied, albeit not very well. He managed to use his teeth to undo the fastenings around his hands in a few minutes.

He remembered that Whitman had kept his phone. The question was, had he found the iPad Mini? Dodger wrestled to sit up and grappled in his inside jacket pocket. The device was still there! At first he couldn't believe it, thinking its continued presence a trick of some kind. Then he remembered what Sutton had said about Whitman's dislike of and unfamiliarity with what he considered "gadgets." He hadn't thought to look for anything other than a phone! For once, a useful Luddite, Dodger thought, pulling out the Mini. He opened the SmartCover, rotated the device, and was rewarded by a steady glow that revealed the room was indeed empty. Fortunately, he'd recharged the night before. Heart thudding, he clicked onto Skype and found Sutton's number. No answer. Damn, he'd still be on vacation. But why wasn't anyone else answering? Because it's Sutton's cell, dummy, which is probably turned off and sitting on a charger in his house. He found the number for the police station, where the phone was answered at once by Roberta's familiar drawl. He tried to tell her where he was and that he needed help, but she misunderstood the nature of the situation and said she'd give the temporary deputy the message when he arrived and hung up. When he hit re-dial, she repeated what she'd said earlier and hung up again.

More because he wanted to hear her voice than from any conviction she could offer assistance from Boston, Dodger clicked the number for Jess Hannah and waited impatiently while the rings began. He knew her pattern. If she hadn't answered by the fifth ring, it'd go to the message box. What kind of message did you leave for this kind of situation he found himself wondering, and giggled. The sound surprised him. He was wondering if he might have a concussion when Jess's voice came on.

"This isn't a good time, Dodger."

"I need help, Jess."

"Don't we all, Dodger. Listen, I don't know what you're up to, but this isn't…"

Taking a deep breath, he puckered his lips and tried to whistle.

"Damn it, Dodger, don't play games. Are you whistling?"

"You said if I needed you, I should whistle. I need help. I'm hurt and I'm trapped. I'm not kidding, Jess." His voice sounded funny, and hers seemed to be coming from very far away.

"Where are you?" she asked, suddenly businesslike.

"Whitman. Mill House, Travis Whitman's place. Business building out back. First floor. Whitman's office. Hidden panic room."

"Hidden where?"

He could hear her moving, as if she were already on her way to the door and he felt better if somewhat sleepy.

"Behind wood paneling. Use button under desk. God, Jess, I don't feel so good."

Everything went black in spite of the fact that the Mini maintained its steady glow.

Forty-Two.

· · ·●●●●●●● · · ·

In the End

This time when Dodger woke, there was a bright light. Wasn't there something about dying being like going toward a bright light? He began to struggle. He didn't want to die, not with Jess sitting there, not with Sutton standing behind her watching with great interest.

When she realized he was struggling to sit up, Jess let go his hand.

"Damn, Dodger, scare a girl. You've been out so long I thought you were about to do the death thing."

He rubbed his head and touched a sore spot that throbbed like blazes. "Where am I?"

"Carolinas Medical Center in Charlotte," Sutton told him.

"What day is it?"

"Monday afternoon."

There was something he had to tell Sutton, something he had to do. Dodger tried to clear his mind, but whatever it was hovered on the edge of his consciousness.

He settled for a question. "What happened to me?"

"My guess is you were brained with the brass statuette that was lying by the door," Sutton said.

"What door?"

"To the panic room in Travis Whitman's office."

As soon as he heard the name, Dodger began to remember.

"Whitman? Where…"

Sutton shrugged. "Your guess is as good as mine. Did he do this?"

Dodger nodded and immediately regretted the movement.

"He's dying. He wants to die where he won't be bothered."

It made perfect sense to him when he said it, and he couldn't understand the lack of comprehension on their faces.

"He's the one who killed Danielle Standridge. It was an accident, sort of. I remember now. He thought it was Charlotte, but the girl wasn't really dead and then Whitman..."

"Slow down," Sutton said. "There's no hurry. Mr. Whitman is long gone." He got out his notebook. "Start at the beginning."

And so, with an audience of two following every word, Dodger told his story, at least as well as he could, for some parts remained fuzzy.

"So you didn't go there to confront him?" Sutton asked when he'd finished.

Dodger shook his head. "I thought I had it figured out, but I needed confirmation on something from him to be sure. The next thing I knew he was spilling his guts."

"He was tired of running away from it," Jess said quietly. "Tired of the accusations in his head. He wants to die in peace."

There was a funny look on her face.

A nurse came in and gave Dodger a shot, and within minutes he was asleep again.

In the days that followed, Jess hung around, reading funny things to him to keep his spirits up, kissing him on the cheek when she thought the pills or shot had taken effect and he was asleep. Better than anything she did was the simple fact that she was the first thing he saw whenever he opened his eyes.

Several times Sutton showed up to report what was going on. It was he who told Dodger that Whitman had sent his private jet on a flight to northern Canada, where a horde of policeman descended when it landed, only to find it devoid of any passenger save for a confused Mill House yardman wearing some of Whitman's clothes. It seemed that no one who'd come forward had laid eyes on Whitman since he left an unconscious Dodger on the floor of the panic room. Another time he announced that they had found the mannequins that were clones of Danny, hidden in a disused upstairs laundry room at Mill House. Finally, and with some reluctance, he told Dodger that the forensics people had gone to the Gothic gatehouse beside the ruins of The Library Pavilion, lifted the hatch, descended into the grotto fragment, and dug through a sizable pile of stones and shells to find Danny's body where Whitman said he'd left it twenty years before. The garments he'd described — and the scarf with which he'd killed her

—remained bagged with the bones. As soon as they finished with the necessary testing, the remains would be released to her sister.

"I've talked to Debbie and my mom," Sutton said, his expression solemn, "and we've agreed she'll be buried in my family's plot."

"That's good," Dodger got out before he drifted off to sleep again.

Two or three days in, listening to Sutton, Dodger remembered what it was he wanted to ask. "Why aren't you at Disney World?"

"Boy came down with infected tonsils. We didn't go. So when Jess here called from the airport in Boston and convinced Roberta that it was urgent she speak with me, I was there to take the call."

"But your cell wasn't answering," Dodger protested. "I'd just tried it."

Sutton was sheepish. "I forgot to charge it and I disabled the message box a long time ago. Didn't want people to think they'd reached me when they hadn't. Roberta put the call through on my home landline."

Two days later, Dodger was released and on a flight to Savannah, with Jess next to him.

"Are you sure you've got time to do this?" he asked. "What about Maxcliff?"

"Maxcliff can wait," she grinned. "That's one thing about being his creator. I can make that suave sucker do anything I want — and love it."

Dodger laughed so hard that others turned to look. The more he tried to stop, the more he laughed until, finally, he just wound down. He knew it was release of tension, no more, no less, but it made him think of Travis Whitman and that last day in his office and the way he'd laughed so hard he'd almost slid from the big swivel chair. The man was a monster, albeit of a very human variety. Dodger was still trying to wrap his head around the fact that Whitman had sat not five feet away from him and admitted that he was the one who'd extinguished that bright young life, who'd done it moreover more or less by mistake and then covered it up as a matter of expedience. It was horrible, unthinkable, unforgivable.

At the same time, in spite of himself, as he wondered where Whitman was, he hoped that the voices were still, at last.

The End

Titles by Linda Hewitt

Nonfiction

Afternoon Tea: A Contemporary Guide

Another Look at Chippendale and All the Rest

Christmas and the Other Grandmother

English Teatime: Historical Survey

50 Top-Paying Jobs: Rewards and Requirements

From Book to Audiobook: An Author's Guide To ACX

Georgia's Great Undertaking: The Beginnings of the Western & Atlantic Railroad

How and Why Darwin Killed Rationalism

Maggie and Me: A Granddaughter's Memoir

Movie Star Hopscotch and the In Memoriam List

Networking for the Career-Minded Student

Risk and Realization: American Investment in Germany in the 1920s

The Student's Guide to the Job Market of Tomorrow

Tea: The Muse's Nectar

The Japanese Tea Ceremony and the Shoguns

Workplace Violence: Definitions and Examples

Fiction

Antiques Are Us Series

Christmas Dress

The Day I Died: A Novel of Fantasy, Redemption, Friendship, and Romance

The Mystery of the Missing Majorette: Art Dodger File #1

Upcoming Titles in the "Mosteller Family" Series

For Journey We Must: A German Comes to Colonial America

American Journey: From Pennsylvania to Alabama in the Eighteenth and Nineteenth Centuries

Maggie and Dennis: From Farm to Mine Town

Book Notes

Colophon

The cover design for *Art Dodger Case File #1: The Mystery of the Missing Majorette* is by Robert Hewitt. The book is laid out in Adobe InDesign CC. The body is set in Adobe Garamond Pro, the chapter names in Chalkduster, and the chapter numbers in Brinar Bold. The page numbers are set in Hoefler Numbers: Indicia. The chapter ornaments are Ann Dividers.

Issue and Edition Notes

Art Dodger Case File #1: The Mystery of the Missing Majorette is available as a Kindle edition and trade paperback.

Rights Contact Information

Art Dodger Case File #1: The Mystery of the Missing Majorette is copyrighted, with all rights reserved to the author. For rights information, contact:

rights_info☉arbeitenzeit.com

www.ingramcontent.com/pod-product-compliance
Lightning Source LLC
Chambersburg PA
CBHW070059030726
47506CB00002B/518